A VISIT TO

CHILE

AND THE

NITRATE FIELDS OF TARAPACÁ

ETC

BY

WILLIAM HOWARD RUSSELL, LL.D.

With Illustrations

BY MR MELTON PRIOR

LONDON
J. S. VIRTUE & CO., Limited, 26, IVY LANE
PATERNOSTER ROW
1890

LONDON
PRINTED BY J S VIRTUE AND CO , LIMITED,
CITY ROAD

TO THE READER.

For the views expressed in this book I alone am responsible. In the introductory remarks I state "How and Why" I went to Chile. Whatever I say of that country or of its people, is the outcome of personal opinion and observation.

WILLIAM HOWARD RUSSELL.

LONDON, *May*, 1890

CONTENTS.

INTRODUCTORY.

CHILE AND THE NITRATE FIELDS OF TARAPACÁ—WHY AND HOW I WENT THERE 1

CHAPTER I.

THE VOYAGE.—LISBON TO CORONEL.

Our Fellow Travellers—The *Galicia*—Pastimes at Sea—St Vincent—Cape Frio—Sharks and Sharpshooters—Rio de Janeiro—Yellow Fever—A Church Service at Sea—Tijuca—Whyte's Hotel—Difficult Banking Operations—A "Pampero"—The La Plata—Flores—Inland Quarantine—Monte Video—Cape Virgins—Patagonia—Straits of Magellan—Tierra del Fuego—Sandy Point or Punta Arenas—Ancient Mariners and Explorers—The Straits—The Scenery—The Fuegians—Cape Pillar—Entrance into the Pacific Ocean—Its Bad Behaviours   5

CHAPTER II.

CORONEL.

Arrival at Coronel—The Town—The Arauco Railway Station—The Port of Coronel—Excursion to San Pedro—The Posada—The Bio Bio Bridge—Concepcion—Messrs. Hicks, Manby, and Bidder—The Present—The Future—The Coal Fields—Lota—Lota Parque—Departure from Coronel . . 33

CHAPTER III.

THE ARAUCO RAILWAY . . 46

CHAPTER IV

FROM CORONEL TO VALPARAISO.

The Coast Steamers—The *Chiloe*—The Pacotilleros—The Scenery—Tomé—Sensitive Oysters—Talacuhano—Concepcion—The Tidal Wave—The *Huascar* and the *Shah* and *Amethyst*—Pierola's Prestige—British Complaints of the Foreign Office . . . 59

CHAPTER V.

VALPARAISO.

The Harbour and City—The Scenery—The Hotel de France—The "English Corsair," Francis Drake—The City as it is—European Influence—Foreigners and their Work—French, German, American, and British Clubs—The Chilian Press—The Suburbs . 67

CHAPTER VI.

PRESIDENT BALMACEDA.

Visit to Viña del Mar—An Interview—The President's Policy—Exchange—The Dollar—Early Intelligence from Europe—The Cable—The Copper Syndicate 81

CHAPTER VII.

VALPARAISO TO SANTIAGO.

The Railroad to Santiago—The City—The Streets—The Hotel Oddo—Santa Lucia—Colonel North's Reception by the President—The Cousiño Parque—The O'Higgins Statue—Gubler and Cousiño's Brewery—Macul—A Picnic—The Vineyards—Macul Wine—The Club—Señor Maciver—The Cauquenes Station—The Drive to the Baths—Giant Cactus—Cauquenes Baths—The Establishment . . 87

CHAPTER VIII.

BATHS OF CAUQUENES.

A Chilian Carlsbad—Señor Soto—Mr. Reed—The Corral—The Vaquero—Lassoing—The Samacuecca—Chilian Horsemen—An Equestrian People—Humming Birds—The Valley of the Cachapoal—A Picnic of Two—Farewell to Cauquenes 107

CHAPTER IX

SANTIAGO ONCE MORE

Return to Santiago—President Balmaceda—St. Dominic—The Cemetery—The Holocaust of the Campaña—Banquet at Valparaiso—Mr Woodsend—The *Cotopaxi*—Hotel Colon—A Manta Difficulty—Don Luis Zegers—St Vincent da Paula—The University—The Esmeralda Shield . . 114

CONTENTS. ix

CHAPTER X
VALPARAISO—VIÑA DEL MAR

Viña del Mar—Petitions and Petitioners—A Scholar in Distress—Excellent Askers, Givers, and Takers—Drink for the Church—A Herald of Winter—Farewell Festivities—How Small the World is !—The Great Ball—Captain Simpson—Departure from Viña del Mar . 121

CHAPTER XI.
VALPARAISO TO IQUIQUE

Departure from Valparaiso—The *Serena*—Aconcagua—The Coast of Chile—Birds and Fishes—Coquimbo—A Cosmopolitan City—The Copper Crash—Drive to Serena—" English Corsairs "—Early Visits to Serena—Huasco—Its Grapes—Carrizal—A Visit to a Workshop—Caldera—Spoils of War—Pacific Rollers—Antofagasta—Mr Hicks' Anchor—Candidissima Causa Belli . 128

CHAPTER XII.
IQUIQUE

Iquique—Friends in Waiting—The Nitrate Railway Station—The Water Boats—Festivities on the Coast—Mr. Rowland—Our Quarters—Anglo-Chilian Cuisine—Chilian Diet—Steamboat Fare—A Chilian "Crewe"—The City of Iquique—Its Wonders—The Fire Brigade—Living on Nitrate of Soda—Iquique in 1835—Iquique in 1885—Visitors from Above—Projectors—Mining Speculations—A Bird's-eye View from my Balcony—The March of the Trains—Up and Down the Andes . . 138

CHAPTER XIII
IQUIQUE TO THE PAMPAS.

The Ascent to the Pampas—The Moving Mountain—Mollé—A Silver Mine—The Pampas—Darwin's Description—The Central Station—A Nitrate Clapham Junction—The Nitrate Kingdom—Pozo Almonte—The Resources of Civilisation—Saturnalia of the Salitreros—The Scenery—Maquinas—Buen Retiro—San Donato—Ramirez—The Liverpool Nitrate Company . . . 160

CHAPTER XIV
PRIMITIVA.

Primitiva—Our Quarters—Mr Humberstone—The Staff—The Workmen—The Pulperia—The Early Morning—Quo quousque ?—A Look Round—Drive to the Calicheras—The Operations on the Calichera . . . 175

CHAPTER XV.

Various Oficinas—Agua Santa—The War on the Pampas—Caleta Buena—Rosario di Huara—San Juan—Argentina—Ramirez—La Paccha—Jaz Pampa—Chilian Oficinas—Las Lagunas 195

CHAPTER XVI

THE NITRATE RAILWAY.

Ignorance and Bliss—*Raison d'être* of the Railway—Early Concessions and Forfeitures—Monopolies—New Companies and Loans—Lawsuits—Mortgages—The War—The Nitrate Railway Company of 1882—The New Loan—"Ikiki"—The Termini—The Decree against the Railway—The Appeal—The Decision of the Law Court—The President's Action—Diplomatic Interference 218

CHAPTER XVII.

VISIT TO PISAGUA—RETURN TO IQUIQUE.

Seals, Sea Lions, Pelicans, Sharks, and Swordfish—The Capture of Pisagua—The Railway Station—A Train for the Pampas—An Englishman's Experience of Peru—The Bolsa Men—Shipping the Nitrate—The Mussel Divers—The Nitrate Scales—The Bodega—Return to Iquique 227

CHAPTER XVIII

EARTHQUAKES.

Shocks at Iquique, on the Pampas, at Santiago—Effects of the Temblor—The Noise—The Effect—The Giant's Kick—The Tidal Wave—Make for the Open—The Mountains of Refuge—The Indian Woman and Child—H.M.S. *Caroline*—Pisagua—An Earthquake Register—Darwin's Remarks—The Moral Effects 240

CHAPTER XIX

OUR LAST DAYS IN CHILE.

The Intendente—The Power of the Intendente—The Press—Gonzalo Bulnes—General Baquedano—Colonel Bulnes—Law and Lawyers—The Chilians—The Immigrants from Europe—Chile for the Chilians—"Viva Chile"—Preparations for the Voyage Home—Last Night in Iquique—"Adelante"—Our Last Day—Adieux 250

CHAPTER XX.

FROM IQUIQUE TO PANAMA, ETC.

Homeward Bound—The *Cachapoal*—Stowaways—The Paris Exhibition—Arica—Sad Anniversary—The Last of Chile *pro tem.*—Mollendo—Chala—Cruelty to Animals—Millions of Pelicans—Pisco—Callao—Lima—The War—Guayaquil—Panama—The Canal—Special to Colon and New York—Fever—Departure for Europe . . 258

CHAPTER XXI.

THE GENESIS OF THE SALINAS.

The Rainless Region—Darwin's Theory—Inland Arm of the Sea—Captain Castle—Inland Seas—Mr David Forbes—The "Salinas" of Marine Origin—Recent Elevation of Coast—Salinas slowly formed—The Lagoon Hypothesis—Tropical Swamps—Vegetable Decomposition—Volcanic Exhalations not necessary—Doubts and Difficulties—The Chilian Commission—The Local Experts—Camanchaca—General Conclusions 280

CHAPTER XXII.

CHILE AND HER NEIGHBOURS

The Pacific Coast—The South American Republics—Peru and Chile—Bolivia—Santa Cruz—The Confederation of Peru and Bolivia—The Liberating Army—Invasion of Peru by Chile—General Manuel Bulnes—Battle of Yungai—The Frontier Question—Bolivia and Chile—Melgarejo—The Desert of Atacama—The Secret Treaty—Mr Hicks—*Causa belli*—Antofagasta—The Corruption of Riches—Mr. Rumbold's Warnings—Temptations—Crime and Violence—The Feudal System—Law and Order in Chile—The Republic—An Oligarchy with a Chief—The Constitution—The Suffrage—The Council of State—The President's Messages 299

CHAPTER XXIII

NITRATE OF SODA LEGISLATION

The Government of Peru—Attempts to Expropriate the Salinas—Compulsory Sales—Peruvian Certificates—The Export Duties—The War—Chilian Occupation—The Reaction—The Classification of Oficinas and Certificates, 1882—Foreigners and Natives—Iquique—Initial Difficulties—Overproduction—Restrictive Combinations—The Comité Salitrero—Comision de Peritos—Their Duties and Attributions—Their Measures—Their General Character—The Comite Salitrero Expires—Attempts to Combine to Regulate Production—The Government and the Nitrate Makers—Expediency of a Policy of Give and Take 323

CHAPTER XXIV.

THE USES OF NITRATE OF SODA

Guano—The Buccaneers—Known to Indians—Old Nitrate Works—Paradas—Fossilized Forests—The British Farmer—The Comité Salitrero—Prize Essays—Dr Stutzer—Professor Damseaux—Professor Wagner—Lawes and Gilbert—Experiments—Results—The Imports of Nitrate of Soda to Europe—Statistics . . . 338

APPENDIX 355

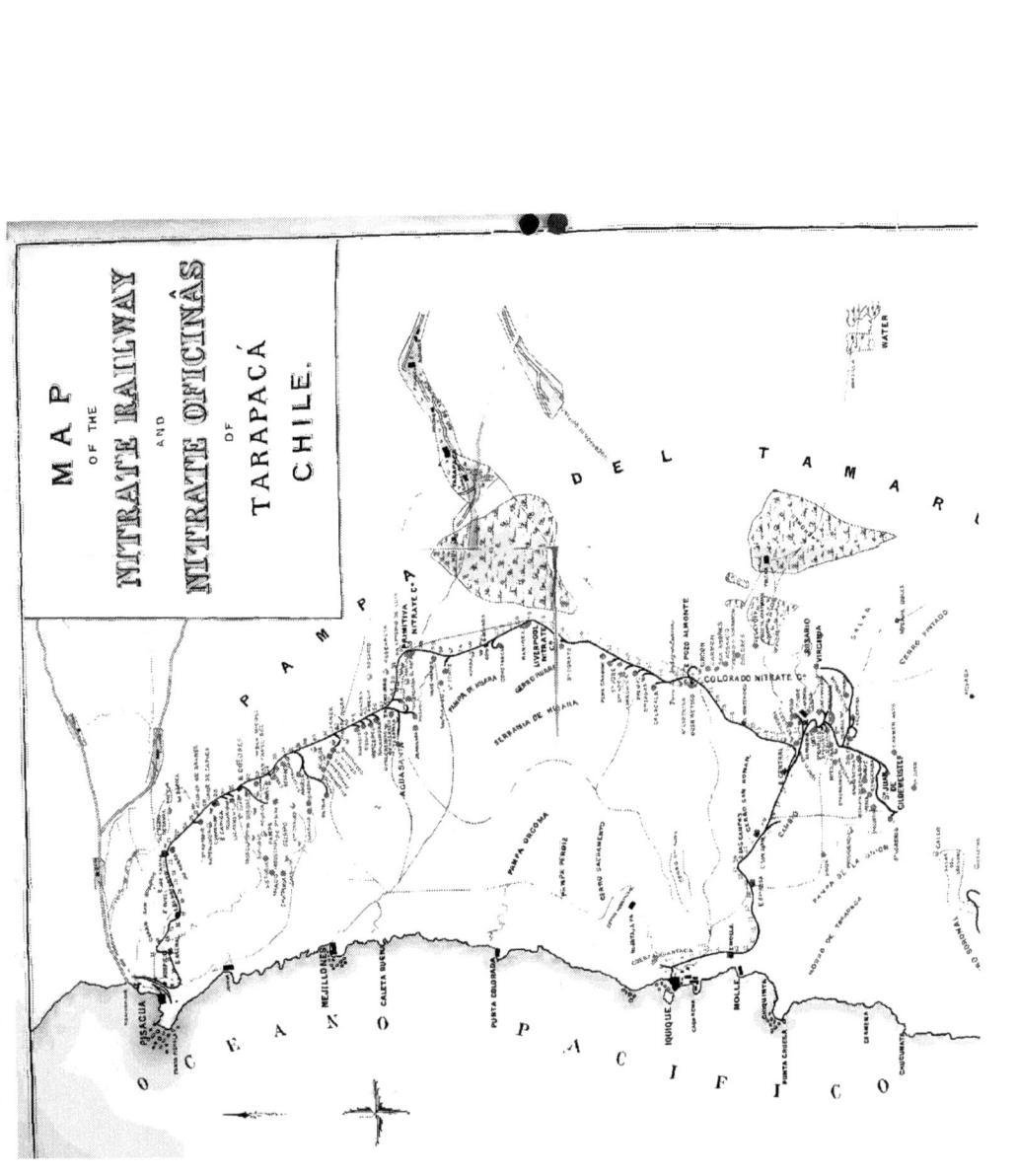

CHILE AND THE NITRATE FIELDS, &c.

INTRODUCTORY.

WHY AND HOW I WENT THERE.

On 13th February, 1889, my wife and I embarked at Lisbon on board the Royal Pacific Steam Navigation Company's steamer *Galicia*, Captain Adey, for Valparaiso.

But a few days previously, intending to spend a couple of months in Egypt, I ordered an outfit at Silver's, engaged apartments at Shepheard's Hotel, Cairo, and retained places to Ismailia in the Peninsular and Oriental *Mirzapore* for 7th February. We were leaving England that we might escape the remaining severities of a winter which had tried us both, and that I might visit friends I much valued, in a land which has always had for me great attractions. An accidental meeting and a few minutes' conversation with Colonel North at a luncheon party on 28th January, changed our destination from Cairo to Chile.

Crippled by the results of a crush under my horse in my last campaign, in the Transvaal, unable to ride, obliged to walk with a stick, I have in my old age a lingering love of travel, a desire like that which animated Lord Lovel "strange countries for to see." I had never been farther south on the western coast of the American continent than

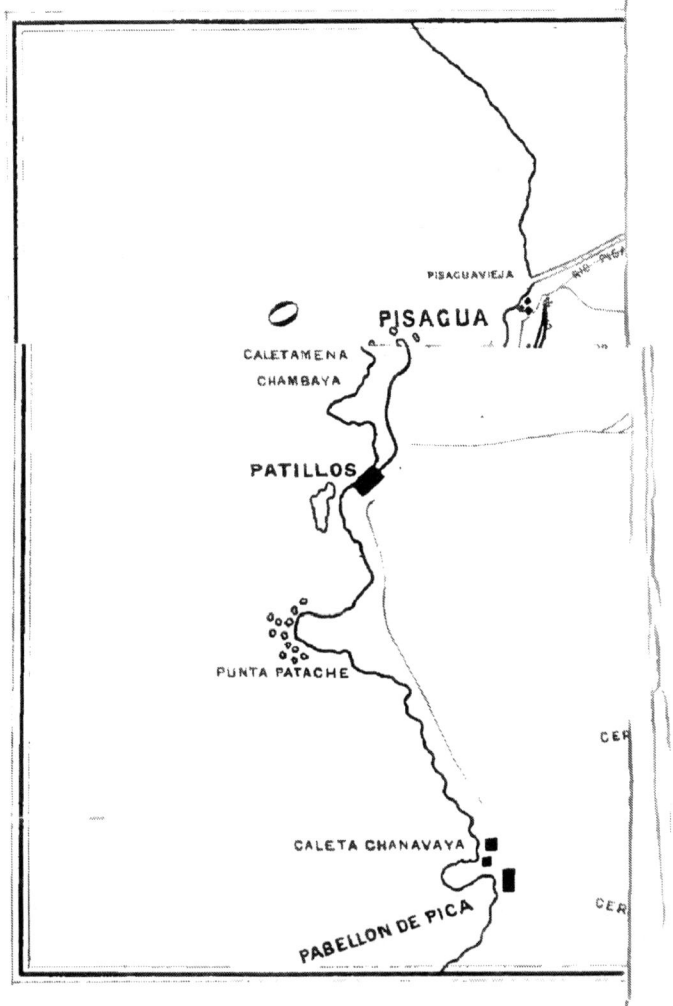

CHILE AND THE NITRATE FIELDS, &c.

INTRODUCTORY.

WHY AND HOW I WENT THERE.

On 13th February, 1889, my wife and I embarked at Lisbon on board the Royal Pacific Steam Navigation Company's steamer *Galicia*, Captain Adey, for Valparaiso.

But a few days previously, intending to spend a couple of months in Egypt, I ordered an outfit at Silver's, engaged apartments at Shepheard's Hotel, Cairo, and retained places to Ismailia in the Peninsular and Oriental *Mirzapore* for 7th February. We were leaving England that we might escape the remaining severities of a winter which had tried us both, and that I might visit friends I much valued, in a land which has always had for me great attractions. An accidental meeting and a few minutes' conversation with Colonel North at a luncheon party on 28th January, changed our destination from Cairo to Chile.

Crippled by the results of a crush under my horse in my last campaign, in the Transvaal, unable to ride, obliged to walk with a stick, I have in my old age a lingering love of travel, a desire like that which animated Lord Lovel " strange countries for to see." I had never been farther south on the western coast of the American continent than

Panama. The Straits of Magellan exercised a strange influence over my imagination, or what was left of it. And so my compass began to turn from east to west, and the direction which at first I regarded as impossible, presently became obviously easy and desirable.

I was invited to go out that I might see and report what had been done and what was being done, and to examine the works which had transformed the desert of Tarapacá — wastes without a sign of life or vegetation—into a centre of commercial enterprise, and which had covered it with animated industry and prosperous life. It had been asserted in certain journals that commercial enterprises in that region were shams—"swindles," indeed, would be the word to use if they were what those organs described them to be—and that a railway, in which the public had invested largely, was "a tramway ending in a marsh." Although I cannot say I was a very Gallio in respect to these things, I certainly knew nothing of them. I told my friends that I was perfectly and altogether ignorant "in that connection" "So much the better!" All I would have to do was to judge for myself and relate what I saw. There was no mystery to penetrate, no theory to demolish or sustain, no complex problems to study.

There was only one objection—the voyage—there was the rub! By the exercise of dialectic skill, when we were settling the details of our Egyptian expedition, I had overcome my wife's preference for Venice or Brindisi, as points of departure, to Tilbury. I had persuaded her that where time was of no consequence, it was much better to take ship in the Thames and to proceed direct to the Suez Canal, improving her mind by the inspection of Gibraltar and Naples, or Malta, rejoicing on the way in the genial airs and bounding over the azure waters of the Mediterranean, than to endure the long and tedious railway journey to an Italian port. (I must admit the *Mirzapore* had by no means a cheerful experience of the Bay of Biscay, and had we been on board I should perhaps have been exposed to some just reproaches on the ground of misrepresentation.) But when I told my wife, in speaking of the proposal so suddenly laid before me, that the main impediment I saw to the acceptance of it was the fear of her suffering from the attacks of an enemy, much dreaded and hitherto always invincible, she at once declared that she was ready to encounter the miseries of the *mal de mer*, in the hope that she would not suffer more than the young ladies who were to be her companions. I had my doubts, for I knew what she endured when crossing over to Ireland or France.

But I hit upon an expedient which satisfied my conscience, and which had a comforting effect on both of us. It was not possible to join the party which was to sail from Liverpool on 6th of February. I had to make arrangements for an absence of six months instead of one of as many weeks—to provide for contingencies which might arise when I was thousands of miles away. I could come back from Egypt in six or seven days. I could not reach London from Santiago in less than six or seven weeks.

It was arranged, therefore, that I should complete my preparations and take the "*train de luxe*" from Victoria to Lisbon, where we were to embark on board the *Galicia*, which was to arrive in the Tagus on the 13th. Thus the dreaded Bay of Biscay and the tumultuous rollers off the Spanish coast would be evaded. If—judging from our five or six days' experience of it between the Tagus and St. Vincent—there was no prospect of my wife becoming accustomed to the sea, I resolved to abandon the prosecution of our voyage, to land on the island and take the first ship back to England. It so chanced that had it been expedient to act on that idea we should have had the quarantine to face and to suffer at St. Vincent. But it was not necessary.

After three or four days of *malaise* in her berth, my wife, fortified by "Pope Roach's Specific," defeated the enemy, got what sailors call her "sea-legs," and appeared upon deck triumphant. Although she sought retirement and disappeared when "the fiddles" were on the table, she eventually became a very fair, if fair-weather, sailor, quite ready for a voyage round the world. There was indeed seldom occasion for the application of these same fiddles—the stormy petrels of the festive board at sea—at our banquets.

CHAPTER I.

THE VOYAGE.—LISBON TO CORONEL.

Our Fellow Travellers—The *Galicia*—Pastimes at Sea—St Vincent—Cape Fio—Sharks and Sharpshooters—Rio de Janeiro—Yellow Fever—A Church Service at Sea—Tapoca—White's Hotel—Difficult Banking Operations—A "Pampero"—The La Plata Flores—Inland Quarantine—Monte Video—Cape Virgins—Patagonia—Straits of Magellan—Tierra del Fuego—Sandy Point or Punta Arenas—Ancient Mariners and Explorers—The Straits—The Scenery—The Fuegians—Cape Pillar—Entrance into the Pacific Ocean—Its Bad Behaviours

COLONEL NORTH's party consisted of his daughter and her friend, Miss Wentworth Smith, Mr. Beauclerk, Mr. J. M. Power, C.E., Mr. Melton Prior, the artist of the *Illustrated London News*, and Captain Brough, a mariner of long experience in the merchant service in the Pacific and Atlantic seas, coasts and in all parts of the world, and our two selves. Mr. and Miss Gilling, who came on board the *Galicia* at Lisbon, were added to the members of the expedition, which was further augmented by Mr Cook and Mr. Blain, two young gentlemen who were travelling for pleasure and improvement to the American continent. Mr. E. Spencer, M.P., and Mrs. Spencer, who made Colonel North's acquaintance at Liverpool, and who were going to Valparaiso and New York, in the same vessel, accompanied the party So we were a goodly company of fifteen, to which, later on, was added " a private secretary."

The *Galicia*, an easy, comfortable old ship, built by the Napiers, with engines by the same firm working as well as the day they were born—eleven years back—had little adverse sea or winds to test her seagoing qualities, and ran westward day after day, with an average run of over 300 miles, from the time we left the Tagus till we sighted the highlands of Brazil on Tuesday, 26th of February.

Resources which lie dormant on shore are developed on board ship; many remember the experiences of long voyages and revive them for the benefit of their fellow passengers. The ample flush-deck of the *Galicia* was a capital playground for the usual sports of the younger passengers, and if such things as Ethiopian minstrelsy, poker, marine roulette, &c, were interpolated, it was rather as ornamental and occasional diversions than as settled pursuits. We had many foreigners and several hundred emigrants on board, and they were amused and astonished at the energy with which, as soon as the lotteries on the day's run and the pool auction were over, the English men and women, led by the Colonel, applied themselves to races, deck-tennis, cricket, running and jumping, and other amusements, which, culminating in dance and song in the eventide, lasted till it was time to put the lights out.

There were not many external attractions. There were of course flying-fish and porpoises which never come amiss, and there was one little excitement as we approached St. Vincent. A suspicious case of illness between decks was reported, and if the *Galicia* had come to anchor and if the health officers had come down upon that "case," we should not have been allowed to start with a clean bill of health for Rio, and our one passenger, an English *employé* at the telegraph station, who was to land at St. Vincent, would have been clapped into quarantine. So Captain Adey kept the screw gently moving and the *Galicia* slowly turning, in the harbour of St. Vincent under very easy steam, with all kinds of officials holding on to us alongside, until at last our passenger was got rid of and restored to his wife and family, and we continued on our way over sunny seas.

Each day passed exceedingly like the other. Sometimes there was "*una calma furiosa,*" and presently we were "in

Native Divers. St. Vincent.

the doldrums." Then, after a while, came puffs of muggy wind, and we were in the tropics; anon we had crossed the line, and "no one ever felt it"—and the Pole-star dropped astern. Every day there were lotteries, auctions, games, and capers. Signor Bottoni blew his cornet, and other performers produced guitars and banjos to vary our entertainments. But it was an effort, and a sea change was needed. After a week or so even the sea-gulls got tired of us and at last dropped behind the ship; and there was no outside sensation worth mentioning till, on the 26th of February, we were off Cape Frio.

"It was there," said one of the passengers, pointing to a rocky bay, "that Her Majesty's ship *Thetis* tried to batter the Cape down but went down herself with all her treasure on board." While we were looking at the fine bold coast rapidly rising to view on our starboard bow, as the ship was screwing her course through a mirror-like sea, there appeared above the surface, within easy shot, the back-fin of an enormous shark, which gave at once an impetus to the owner of every rifle in the ship. Attracted probably by fish upon which island-like clouds of "molly-hawks," boobies and noddies, blackening the ocean, were feasting near at hand, shark-fins enough to satiate a colony of Chinamen rose above the glassy surface of the easy-rolling sea, and became speedily the objects of indiscriminate practice, and when Captain Adey made a very palpable hit, and the owner of a floating bull's-eye churned the water in an angry circle, there was widespread and loudly-expressed satisfaction at the feat. But the sea did not give up its dead. The shark did not float as we expected and hoped it would, and presently, as if the news of danger had been made known down below, the sharks' fins disappeared altogether.

In accordance with the custom which prevails in the ships of the great English companies at sea, there was divine service on board the *Galicia* every Sunday. The foreigners regarded the religious ceremony in the saloon through the gratings, or when service was on deck, looked on with something like amusement in their faces. One of my fellow-passengers observed that "he did not think

Englishmen were a bit better for all their Sunday praying and singing! They came out to make money, and they drank and swore, gambled and quarrelled, and cheated just like other people!"

On the 27th February the *Galicia*, saluting the Imperial Standard as she passed the fortress of Santa Cruz, anchored in the harbour of Rio de Janeiro. The day was intensely hot. The glorious landscape of this most beautiful bay was seen through a quivering wall of air waves which, if it imparted a grace to the town which close inspection completely dissipated, concealed the details of the scenery. There were, however, plainly visible the well-named Organ Mountains (Orgãos) with pipes and barrels towering aloft as the background to the sharp outlines of the lower ranges, the peaks of La Gabia, and of the Sugar Loaf, and the gigantic outline of a face variously called Lord Hood's, Bonaparte's, &c.

The Health Officers came off at their leisure an hour or so after we anchored, but they made a close investigation into our sanitary condition, "jalousing," as a gillie would say, the arrival of a fresh supply of Yellow Fever, of which there was already more than enough on shore. "What on earth," exclaimed one of our British brethren, "are those absurd coffee-coloured chaps doing now? Why do we put up with such confounded nonsense?" The Brazilian Health Officers and the authorities thus slightingly designated had, in fact, turned out the whole of the passengers, first, second, and third class, the ship's company, officers, and all, and accompanied by the doctor of the *Galicia*, were proceeding to a strict examination before they would admit us to free pratique. They were exceedingly suspicious, indeed, though we had not communicated with land since we left Lisbon. The first-class passengers were passed *nominatim* rapidly enough, but as there were between four hundred and five hundred emigrants, chiefly Italians, on board, considerable delay occurred before the scrutiny was complete, and we were free to land

Of all nations, those of Portuguese descent are the most exact and strict in their observance of quarantine regulations, and certainly they have good cause—these Brazilians—to watch narrowly any possible importation of the scourge which has so afflicted their country. Notwithstanding the enlightened opinion of experts, the confirmed prejudices of mariners and the incredulity of English authorities regarding the value of seclusion, I must express my own strong conviction that it is almost possible to entirely shut out cholera and Yellow Jack by quarantine regulation. If there be any truth in the doctrine of the propagation of disease by microbes and bacilli, it surely stands to reason that, although these germs cannot be quite excluded from the air, the diffusion of them from personal centres can be nearly stopped if all the latter be shut up in isolated places.

The news brought by the consular officers and the Company's agents when they were allowed on board was not cheering. "Twenty funerals a day," some said—"Twice as many," according to others—mostly of victims to *vomito*. But that was nothing to speak of compared with the usual mortality of a bad epidemy at Rio. The ravages of Yellow Jack in the city were unusually widespread, and we were by no means encouraged to spend a night in one of the hotels in the town. But the coaling of the ship, inevitable and imminent, ports closed, doors shut, heat, dust, and smother, were evils to be shunned, even at considerable risk, so it was with much content we heard that we could make an expedition to the hill of Tijuca—I am not certain

The Harbour of Rio de Janeiro.

[To face page 13.

of the spelling—a few miles outside Rio, where a hotel, several hundred feet above the bay, would afford us delightful shelter for the night.

Presently our party were collected on deck, handed over the side, and rowed off to the Quay, where brightly painted wooden stalls were laid out with fruit, vegetables, sweetmeats, and bottled abominations to tempt the unwary stranger.

The pleasant impression of the place produced from the deck of the ship was shattered when we landed. The bright colouring of the buildings gave to Rio a bright and cheerful aspect from outside, but it was "distance" that "lent enchantment to the view." The crowd that looked so picturesque through the glass was resolved into unseemly elements, men and women of every shade and colour from the deepest black (a great many of them) to the milkiest, sickliest white, in garments of many colours, their heads covered with eccentric structures of straw and coloured stuff, many ragged, some, if, indeed, it were not excessive jollity and merriment which made them caper and shout as they reeled along holding each other's hands, not quite sober. Close to the landing place there was a market, and the quay near it was ankle deep in abominable vegetable refuse, rotten cocoanuts, pumpkins, gourds, oranges, covered with swarms of flies. The smells were very offensive. I could not help thinking that the sanitary officers might begin their labours on shore before they went off to sea to visit the shipping.

Whilst our baggage was being landed, we strolled about the streets. Savage and civilised life rub elbows together in Rio. The lately-emancipated slave miserable in his freedom—"lord of himself, that heritage of woe,"—the creature whose ideal of life is animal enjoyment, clad in tattered clothes, idle, ill-fed, and helpless, jostles the dandy, dressed as if he were going to the Grand Prix, and negro "mammies" shamble alongside the dainty dames in Paris costumes, emerging from the Rua Ouvidor to look for their carriages. Rude carts drawn by oxen rumble over the execrable pavement, and tramcars filled with a very motley democracy warn off well-appointed carriages with finely-accoutred servants and horses. Electric lighting, the telegraph, the telephone, the tramway are, nevertheless, in full activity in a city, the mass of the dwellers in which are lodged in habitations destitute of due provision for decency and comfort. We heard many things in relation to cleanliness and morality in Rio which, if true, leave much to be done by the sanitary science man and the Christian missionary But reflecting on the likelihood that a foreigner would, if he were not an emancipated negro, see many things to shock him in the east end of cities nearer home, I thought it would be well, perhaps, not to be too severe on Rio, where the book-shop windows were placarded with terrible prints illustrative of the life and times of "Jack the Ripper," sent, probably, from Lisbon, where coloured representations of the deeds of that monster were to be seen on every wall. The sight of the appliances of civilised life in the midst of a population which seemed to have so little need of them, gave rise to a feeling of dissatisfaction with the work of civilisation by no means reasonable. The people would not be less wretched were there no tramcars or railways. The patronage bestowed on the former by the very poorest proved that they were a valued boon Probably the indolence of the natives, who never walk if they can help it, swells the dividends of the companies, which are said to be very flourishing indeed.

The introduction of electric telegraphs and lighting, the development of railways, and the improvement, including the suppression of mendicancy, such as it is, of Rio, are mainly due, it is said, to the Emperor's initiative and enlightened encouragement; but I could not find from residents that there was any great regard or attachment exhibited by his people to Dom Pedro, whose ill-health and seclusion in his highland residence outside the capital have led to the creation of the dangerous breach, between sovereigns and their subjects, which may be filled up by indifference—if not something more aggressive at last—when the former are not visible to their people.

As for the decoration of the city, "Nature," says a recent visitor, "has undertaken it, and amid the palms, and under the shade of large-leaved tropical trees in the public gardens and walks, the absence of sightly buildings is not felt." But there are some fairly luxurious *maisons de campagne* at Botofago, a charming suburb on an indent of the sea, which makes many incursions along the line of beach. The rocky shore encloses many pretty wooded headlands in its languid arms, and up above in the Seira de Los Orgaõs, nearly 3,000 feet above the sea level, lies Petropolis, where the Emperor and the Court reside in the long-lasting unhealthy season, and where the foreign residents and native gentry seek shelter from the heat and sickness of the plain. It is selfish, but it is natural.

From the end of the Plaza, or Alameda, or whatever it may be termed, off which the market is situated, we started, fifteen souls and bodies—some of the latter considerable—in a tram-car, through a long straight street of one-storeyed houses, diminishing in respectability of appearance till the road ceased at the commencement of the ascent to Tijuca, which is on one of the chainlets of hills of varying height in which the matchless Bay of Rio is enclosed. It was growing dark There was some delay at the posting establishment ere the hostlers brought out a lofty *char-à-banc*, harnessed to four mules, to essay the steep to Whyte's Hotel Nor could we start till order was evoked from chaos in the telephone room, where there was a confused jangling of Portuguese, English, and French, between the operators in the hotel aloft and our amateur interpreters in the coach office, who were bent on ascertaining what accommodation and what provision for their creature comforts they had to expect when they reached their goal.

It was pitch dark when the journey began, but the night concealed the dangers we were tempting on our way, and it also enabled us to enjoy the brilliant spectacle of the lights in the city and in the ships clustered in the bay. It was as though we were looking down on constellations from some prodigious height to which we had soared in an impossible balloon. Though the road was excellent and was admirably engineered up the sides of the hill, the curves were sharp and the boundary at the edge of the precipice low and slim, and as the mules were whipped full tilt round the corners, the *char-à-banc* swaying under the top weight came at times within a scarcely measurable distance of the margin. The lights below blinked in our faces. Once or twice an involuntary "Oh!" followed by an exclamation, "That was a near thing!" gave evidence that some of us were not quite indifferent to fate.

For four-fifths of the journey there were gas lamps along the road. Then came black night. It was some comfort, when we came to a steep bit, that the mules could no longer be lashed into a gallop Presently we had achieved the mountain top, and then came a short descent into a

THE VOYAGE—LISBON TO CORONEL.   15

valley, on the other side of which gleamed the illuminated windows of the hostelry to which we were bound. There was still not indeed "a river," but a streamlet, "to cross" with an uncommonly acute twist over a little bridge. We mounted up once more for a few yards and pulled up in the

Whyte's Hotel, Tijuca.

courtyard in front of Whyte's Hotel, where a welcome from the proprietor, a good supper and clean beds awaited us.

Next morning we were early on foot, some wandering up the hillsides, others wandering in the charming garden adjoining the buildings of the hotel, which is on a small platform in a cup, between high and steep mountain sides, clothed with tropical forest and vegetation, through which winding paths have been cleared to the summits. The height and beauty of the palms and of the other trees around us, especially of the *ipu*, were phenomenal, the blaze of colour of the flowers and buds dazzling—an infinite variety of vegetation, climbing plants, creepers, tree ferns, in riotous excess, revelling in strength in a land where man, sunned down so much that he loses fibre and energy, is often dwarfed. Brilliantly-coloured butterflies, "as large as thrushes," some of my friends said, "bigger than crows," said others, fluttered along the alleys in the garden. Humming-birds hung like brighter flowers from the petals of the plants, where they were seeking their insect food, or flashed like jewels from shrub to shrub along the borders of the paths. A streamlet waters the garden of the hotel and feeds in tiny cascades two open-air swimming baths cut in the living rock shaded by bamboo, plantains and mangoes, where we had a swim before breakfast. One—the higher of the two—is reserved for ladies.

Tijuca is indeed a delicious retreat, and it is not to be wondered at that the merchants of Rio seek its pleasant shelter from the fervid heat of the city below. We left Whyte's Hotel with regret. The road downwards to the sea level is bordered by villas—many of considerable size—in detached gardens full of orange-trees, palms, bamboo clumps and plantains, with elaborately-worked, gaily-painted or richly gilt, iron gateways.

We were whirled at a breakneck pace down towards the town and were fully able to appreciate in the garish light of day the dangers we had escaped in our ascent at night.

It was only after we had got on board we ascertained why so many of the villas we had been admiring on our way were closed, and with blinds down. Our lovely Brazilian Pæstum, Tijuca, was the headquarters of Yellow Fever, which was inflicting more fatal ravages there than in the city below!

The interval between our arrival in Rio and the departure of the *Galicia* at 6 o'clock in the afternoon was spent in visits to the market, to curio shops and to the select establishments in the Rua Ouvidor, through which no vehicle is allowed to pass. Visitors who had to make necessary purchases of clothing were loud in lamentation over the prices. In these I shared, for my wife had to pay £12 for a common cotton morning gown.

It was only by the exercise of patience, the services of a friend in the Consulate, and the use of many words in three languages, I came to obtain change for a circular note at the Bank. The bankers admitted that they were the correspondents of Coutts, Messrs. Coutts were good for the money, but they wanted some proof that I was the man who had signed "W. H. Russell" to the note, for I might have copied it from a "letter of indication";—finally, after forty-five minutes' delay, a gentleman in his shirt sleeves, smoking very bad tobacco, proceeded to give me piles of dirty paper—Brazilian notes. But I was going to Chile, and the notes of the Bank would be of no use "Senhor! They are as good as the notes of your Bank of England. And you can change them outside! Our gold clerk has gone out with the key and won't be back till 4 o'clock." The *Galicia* was off at 6 o'clock, probably before the "gold clerk" returned.

At noon next day (March 1st) we were two hundred and thirty-four miles from Rio, and were gradually drawing away from the coast of Brazil, the bold ranges of which offered picturesque views for many miles after we had passed out of the Bay, by the southern channel, to sea

A "pampero," a wind off the pampas, sprung up on 3rd

March, and a sea which would have been heavy had the ship been farther from the coast, rose and somewhat interfered with the usual sports of the passengers on deck. In the evening heavy squalls and torrents of rain came off shore, and soon the awnings were flecked with dragon-flies, moths, and various insects sheltering from the storm on the under surface of the canvas. A humming-bird fluttered into the rigging—a Mother-Carey's chicken, dazed and storm-battered, flopped over the stern railing and was caught by one of the sailors, who handed it about for inspection When it was liberated by a popular vote it came on board, and could not be induced to take to its seafaring life again. Whilst we were still four hundred miles from the mouth of the La Plata, the colour of the sea showed the influence of the great river.

At eight P.M. on March 4th we anchored off the quarantine station at Flores Island, in the sea-like expanse of the muddy La Plata. It was too late for the health officers to visit us of course. Those officials do not stir out after dark, and the passengers who had to land there next morning contemplated with rueful countenances the whitewashed barrack, built on a rocky ledge of the desolate island, which was to be their residence for an uncertain number of days. As many of our friends were bound for Buenos Ayres and for the Argentine cities, there was a farewell party or rather there were many such parties on board the *Galicia* that night.

Next morning the port and sanitary officers came off from Flores Island The *Galicia*, having touched at Rio, which was an infected port, had exposed her passengers to the pains and penalties of quarantine. The Uruguayans are not, it is said, at all over-courteous to their Brazilian neighbours. Quarantine, if there be any pretext for it, is certain to be obligatory and rigorous for all who land, and if there was a solitary suspicious case on board, the *Galicia* would not be allowed to go up to Monte Video The passengers of the *Potosi*, which had left Liverpool a fortnight before the *Galicia*, were still on Flores Island. Our friends surveyed them, dotting the rocks or walking on the gravel path down to the little quay, with rueful countenances. One small vestige of green on the island was examined with wonder and satisfaction—a little field of half-an-acre in which goats, sheep, and cows were laboriously feeding on the scanty herbage.

The medical examination was not, I am bound to say, very strict. The emigrants for the Argentine Republic, of whom there were some three hundred men, Italians, Spaniards, &c., women, and children, many pale, city bred, and half starved, were mustered and passed after a brief inspection on deck. I believe the cost of their maintenance is borne by Government, but the charge for board and lodging in quarantine at Flores Island, for ordinary passengers, is about one pound a day. A young Irish gentleman named Manders, our champion runner, intent on horse farming in Patagonia; Mr. Beit, an Englishman, and his Spanish wife, who had sung her native songs for us delightfully; Senhor Vian de Lima, Brazilian special envoy, on his way to Lima to settle certain boundary questions with Peru; M. Bottoni, cornet player and poet, skilful in the dance, and other companions of our pleasant journey, were passed over the side and taken off to their imprisonment on the quarantine island amidst much cheering and waving of handkerchiefs from their friends on board

Then the *Galicia* weighed, and breasting the great river full speed, came to anchor outside the tiers of shipping at Monte Video at 2.30 P M There was little of interest to note on our way. The river rolls its mud-coloured waters between low banks, of which the southern is barely visible and the northern is low and uninteresting. Many very dark-coloured fish, apparently mullet of six or seven pounds in weight, were floating dead in the ochre-hued stream, and a gentleman on board asserted that at times poisonous gases issue from the bed of the river which kill millions of fish; but we only saw one kind of dead fish, and there must be many species in the La Plata.

We could not land at Monte Video. Our acquaintance with the capital was made through telescopes and opera glasses, and we only saw straight streets running up from the river intersected by parallel lines of other streets, slaughter-houses and provision-curing establishments down by the water's edge, ships of many nations, British predominating, along the shore, and inland the conical hill overlooking the town, from which it takes its name, "The Mountain of the Vine." The port authorities were kind enough to let us send letters for Europe on shore, but the correspondence was subjected to a preliminary drenching of some fluid out of watering pots and big bottles to disinfect them, which must have had a damaging effect on some of the addresses. To make amends for the disappointment about landing, there was a ball on board, inaugurated by Colonel North, which was declared by the passengers to be a great success, and which was given in an installation creditable to the taste and ingenuity of the officers of the ship, who converted the deck, by walls and ceilings of the flags of all nations, into a capital dancing saloon, with a buffet, drawing-room, and boudoir, complete.

We left Monte Video early on the morning of March 6th, passed Flores Island at 7.30 A.M. to the sound of M Bottoni's cornet and the farewell cheers of our quondam fellow passengers, and steered south for the Straits of Magellan. For the next three days the wind was adverse, and the *Galicia* was retarded by the sea, which for the first time came in on the deck over the bulwarks. The temperature fell sensibly.

From Saturday to Sunday we only made 260 miles, but at 6 30 P M. on the latter day (March 10th) we anchored north of the Point of (Patagonian) Dungeness, under the lee of Cape Virgins (a barren and lightless bluff 135 feet high) for the night, and awaited the coming of daylight for the run up the Straits of Magellan to Punta Arenas, or Sandy Point. The shore of Patagonia on our right offered nothing to attract or fix the eye. Through the glass the land, dotted with nubbly hillocks, looked bare and brown with patches of dark vegetation, treeless and waterless. The Eleven Thousand Virgins in whose honour Magalhaen* named the Straits, because he discovered it on their day on the calendar, would not like the situation as well as Cologne.

With daylight the ship weighed, and entered the Straits of Magellan. Tierra del Fuego was indistinct in the mist. The shore of Patagonia near the eastern end, at Dungeness, is, as I have said, quite destitute of interest When I looked out in the morning we were passing through the "First Narrows"—two miles broad—shores dreary and lifeless, a great current running, in which swarms of puffin and shag were fishing. Then the steamer, passing out of Phillip Bay, some fifteen miles broad, entered the Second Narrows, which seem to be closed in at the west end by Elizabeth Island, named after Queen Bess by Sir Francis Drake.

* Variously spelt Magellan, Magallanes, Magellanes, Magalianes, Magalhães, which last is the orthodox Portuguese. Our Admiralty chart gives the preference to Magalhaen.

The outlines of the Brecknock Hills, near Punta Arenas, from 1,400 feet to 2,000 feet high, were visible presently, but the land on the left was a dead, sandy, or marshy level, with faint indication of hill ranges in the distance. There was a sharp wind, the sea was black looking and sullen, and the general effect of our surroundings was depressing, as the *Galicia* made her way through the Straits. But we were not at the mercy of winds, waves, or currents; we were in a great vessel impelled by irresistible force. There was an assured ascendency for us over the ocean—rocks apart—as long as the machinery worked. There was board and lodging of the best—fresh milk, butter, bread, meat, poultry and vegetables—ice to cool our drinks, a doctor and medicines for the sick, skilled seamen to guide us in the familiar course, of which they knew every day's journey as if it were marked by milestones; no superstitious terrors, no fear of unknown dangers, no ignorance of what there was in store for us beyond this point or that; means of escape if the ship was on fire or became unsafe. Contrast our condition with that of mariners three or four hundred years ago, in vessels of a couple of hundred tons,[*] their provisions salt meat and fish, bad biscuit and water, beating about month after month in these strident seas in fear and trembling, burthened with armour if they went on shore, ever vexed with anxieties and cares, and harassed by fears of the unknown. How worthy of admiration and honour were the men who braved such dangers, whether they were impelled by thirst of gold or by the love of discovery! The sailors who gathered the early laurels of these watery

---

[*] M Frezier records how, on May 25, 1713, an entrance to the South Sea from the Straits of Magellan was accidentally discovered by the "tartane St. Barbe," a tartane being a one-masted vessel with a lateen sail, something like a fishing-smack of to-day.

plains belonged to countries which have now receded from the front rank of the nations, but they must ever be famous for the deeds of their sons, and the Englishman who now sees his flag predominant east and west and north and south, should remember what he owes to the daring of the Portuguese, Spaniards, and Dutchmen, who led the way from the shores of Europe to the mysterious *terræ incognitæ* filled " with Gorgons, hydras and chimæras dire," now peopled with prosaic plodding communities. Our narratives say that the first steamer to pass the Straits was H.M.S. *Virago*, Captain Houston Stewart. Sailing ships rarely tempt the Straits—there are currents, and violent squalls, changes of weather, and reefs, very dangerous—but brave the passage round Cape Horn.

I do not intend to write an account of very well-known routes, nor to indulge in travel talk. Thousands of people of all nations pass through the Straits of Magellan every year in the steamers of the Pacific Steam Navigation Company and of the French and German Companies, and in the trading ships which ply between the Pacific ports of South America and Europe. One of our party, an ex-captain of one of the British liners, had been through the Straits no less than ninety-seven times! But to me, as I think to most people, the coasts of countries seen for the first time are full of interest Patagonia lay on our right, and far away (twenty-two miles) on the left were visible Cabo Espiritu Santo and the low, dreary, rugged outlines of Tierra del Fuego.

We looked in vain for giants on the rocks or for savages in their canoes, but if the tales we heard of the increasing find of gold on the mainland and in the island be true, there may soon be busy communities on these desolate shores. Gold there is, no doubt. Its existence was known many years ago, and native gold was frequently found in the sand of the sea at certain places near Cape Virgins. There is now talk of a company on a large scale for the scientific exploitation of the mines. Great expectations were entertained of much good arising from the discovery of lignite some years ago, but labour and other difficulties prevented the extension of the output There was, indeed, some disputation lately between Chile and the Argentine Republic concerning the boundaries of territories which would be of little consequence but for the possible value of the mines which are supposed to exist in them.

It was nearly dark when the *Galicia* anchored off the wooden shanties on the beach, which were all I was destined to see of the town of Punta Arenas, except the details I could make out through my telescope—a background of wooded hills, two wooden hotels and a Custom House, a large building — the Governor's house, or a barrack, or a goal—*les trois se disaient*—a *debris* of trunks of trees on the edge of the water — the remains of a forest consumed by fire, a tumbledown-looking wooden jetty for landing and embarking—a small Chilian Government steamer, showing the national flag—white star on blue fly and white ground—near at hand, and some small trading vessels riding uneasily to their anchors The bones of one large steamer lay on the rocks west.

The Chilians call the place Colonia de Magellanes. It was established in 1851 by emigrants, who had grants of land from Government, and it was selected as the site of a convict settlement, with great want of forethought as to the possible evil consequences of such a location. As soon as the port authorities would permit them the American and Chilian fur traders came off and spread out their merchandise of seal, vicuna, guanaco, and fox-skins on deck, and there was a lively market for some time, but the prices asked were generally deterrent to intending purchasers. More interesting to me was the arrival of a young gentleman who had charge of a large sheep farm in Tierra del Fuego opposite, and who gave some interesting particulars of the work he was doing. According to him there are large districts in the island suitable for sheep-farming, and the land taken in is increasing every year. The natives are troublesome; so are their dogs. I suspect they are both dealt with in the same way. Seeing the "joggle" of the sea and the ricketty pier, I declined an invitation to land, for which I had every reason to be grateful to myself when our party returned, full of wrath, having had their legs wet in a leaky boat, and having tumbled about in the lampless "streets" without seeing as much as they would have had brought to their feet, had they remained on board.

The mails for Punta Arenas were duly landed from the *Galicia* and deposited in the Post Office, but the master thereof, being an official of routine and of staid habits of business, declared it was too late to open the bags; whereupon a mass meeting of twenty or thirty citizens resolved to storm the Post Office, and were about to do so when the Postmaster capitulated. The traditions of the town favour overt acts, and *voies de fait*. I met an old Chilian officer who was in garrison here, in 1877, when the *detenus* in the then convict establishment, who were joined by some, if not all, of the troops, rose, and committed horrible outrages; an outbreak which caused the Chilian Government to abandon the place as the site of their penal settlement.

There is a very obliging British Consular Officer, who is Lloyds' Agent as well, and as all steamers through the Straits touch at Punta Arenas, he might be very useful to the commerce of the world but for one obstacle. There is no telegraphic communication with the outer world from the Straits! Therefore there can be no announcements of the passage, arrival, or departure of vessels—a very serious and lamentable want. Punta Arenasians, however, believe that with certain gold, mutton, and bread, probable water, wood, and coal, the town has a promising future.

Next morning early the ship forged ahead from her moorings and showed her stern to the Sandy Pointers who were up. To the contentment of those who had been told that there was little likelihood of its being clear enough to enable them to see the magnificent scenery of the Straits, the sun shone brightly in a blue sky. Men may pass twenty times through the Straits of Magellan and not have one fine day. Fogs, mist, rain, prevail the greater part of the year. We were most fortunate indeed on this 11th March. I have no hesitation in saying that it would be quite worth while to undertake the journey from Europe, in order to behold the glorious panorama of forest, mountain, and glacier which we saw unrolled in the full blaze of day with rapture—not always silent—on either side of us, till as night fell we passed Cape Pillar on our left and breasted the roll of the miscalled Pacific. It was our good luck to see the beautiful combination of mighty alp; of glaciers, fringed by moraines, moving with slow "resistless mass" as they have done for countless ages, fed by icy mountain-breasts thousands of feet above, melting in the waters of innumerable creeks; of primæval forest clothing the sides of lake-like inlets, up to the verge of the eternal snow-fields—which has no rival in the world. We could look into the blue crevasses up awful valleys lost in recesses of rock and ice, and watch the cataracts that fell into unknown gulfs hidden in clouds of mist, mile after mile, from early morn till night fell.

As the straits narrowed and the eye rested on the wooded shores of the Tierra del Fuego on one side and of Patagonia on the other, it seemed at times as if the ship were embayed or hemmed in by the coasts of a *fjord* from which

Straits of Magellan.

there was no exit. The shore of the mainland is formed by a bank of shingle or a line of rocks covered with drift timber, and at the base of the rising ground begins thick vegetation, brushwood, berberries, myrtles, calceolaria, &c., up to the edge of the forest. The sea was calm, but squalls from the high land blew at times with startling suddenness. There was a strong current from the west, and the presence of shoals of fish was indicated by the flocks of gulls, dusky petrels and the many kinds of divers, busy around us. Once a great whale heaved its black bulk, spouted up a column of steam-like spray, and dived deep in front of our bows. Seals, nearer shore, popped their bullet heads above the water or splashed off the rocks to join their busy fellows.

There is a wide opening west of Cape Froward, which is the most southern point of the American continent, where we were warned to look out for the Fuegian savages. And we were not disappointed. As the ship turned a point and gave a clear view of the straits in front, three canoes, pulling hard to cross our course, were visible. It was rather rough in the reach, and though the sun was bright the air was sharp, and as the *Galicia* slowed for the first canoe to come alongside there was an exclamation of pity and wonder from the passengers as they looked down on its occupants.

A woman with straight black hair, white teeth, and dancing black eyes, quite naked to the loins, sat in the stern of the frail craft of plank and bark, with a child in her lap, handling a clumsy, ill-shaped paddle; at her feet there crouched a child of some three years old, naked and apparently quite contented, close to the faggots and burning embers placed on the stones which served as ballast. Another woman sat on a thwart, and plied her oar with one hand, while she held out the other toward the ship, holding up a couple of otter skins, and asking for largesse, and her appeals were enforced by shrill screams for "Bacca! bacca!" from her companions. A man in a white hat, ragged blue frock coat and trousers, supplied the falsetto to the chorus of the women. But I could not recognise the "Yamaschoona! yamaschoona!" which Darwin speaks of as Fuegian for "Give me! give me!" The man was of a sickly yellow, the skin of his face puckered and withered like that of a monkey, his arms were thin and muscleless, his eyes dull and unintelligent; the women were darker hued and far more pleasant to look upon. Their arms and limbs were round and well shaped, their shoulders were plump and full. One of our party, an old Straits traveller, was shocked at their degenerate assumption of clothing, scant as it was. "In my time they had not a stitch on them!" Certainly they had but little now! In a cutting wind, which made us glad of our warm coats, they sat with their naked children, almost naked themselves, smiling and happy—at least they looked so when the ship opened a fire of biscuits, bread, fruit, old clothes, and some small missiles of tobacco, on them. The little ones set to work at once on bananas, and the mother clapped a fancy smoking-cap, which was flung to her, on the head of the elder. The old garments which were thrown over to them were carefully put away, and were not used, for the moment at all events.

For some reason or other, neither they nor the Fuegians in the other canoes, three in number, which were waylaying the *Galicia* and dropped alongside, would come on board, though the port-ladder was lowered. The savages in the canoes were all much alike, with little variety save in age, all the women with dazzling teeth, straight hair, and black eyes, rather prominent cheekbones and square jaws; the younger lusty enough, and better and stronger looking than the men. They seemed to be aware of the fact that they showed to more advantage than the males, for they put on far less covering of skin than their husbands or brothers. As long as there were hopes of offers for the poor seal and otter skins and bunches of red berries they held up, or of any gifts of bread or other edibles, they hung to the ship, never ceasing to scream "bacca," "I say! bacca," and "galieta" or "biscuito."

When the screw began to churn up the foam and the ship gathered way the Fuegians cast off with their spoils—pumpkins, bananas, a cask of biscuit, probably not the best, hats, coats, and the like. Those which left us made off towards the land as fast as they could paddle, the men standing upright with outstretched arms, the women pulling, and all no doubt yelling "Bacca!

Fuegians alongside.

bacca!" in the distance. In Crooked Reach, other canoes were seen pulling out from the shores—too late. In one there were four women and one man, in another two women and two men and a boy, in another five men and women, two children, and two dogs. "They are not Christians," said one of the Chilian passengers, "nor are they likely to become civilised, less so than ever now since the sheep-farmers shoot them. The latter say they must shoot Fuegians to prevent them stealing their sheep." The Fuegians may—or might—say, "We did not ask you to come to our country with your sheep, and we can't help stealing sheep when we are hungry." No estimate has ever been made of the number of these wretched creatures, and they will probably die out rapidly now that sheep farming has come into vogue, just as the Australians and their dingoes did. They have more to fear from civilisation

Straits of Magellan.

as it is presented to them than from their cruel natural foes, cold and starvation. Altogether, our acquaintance with these specimens of our fellow-man, such as it was, did not last over half-an-hour.

The scenery from Cape Froward to Cape Pillar at the southern extremity of the Channel, which we passed well to our left, as I have said, just at dusk, never loses its interest till the shores recede from sight. As we passed the southern extremity of Smythe's Channel, those who had heard of the beauty and grandeur of the scenery along its shores inside the Strait, regretted that Captain Adey did not take this inland canal, which would have brought the ship out into the Atlantic several hundred miles north of the Straits of Magellan, but the sagacious, careful and urbane captain explained that he would then have had to anchor every night, as it would not be safe to proceed through the Channel in the dark. The steamers of the Kosmos line take Smythe's Channel, and passengers who desire to see the beauties of this wonderful canal should take the coasting German steamers, which are in no hurry and draw comparatively little water.

The *Galicia*, giving a wide berth to Evangelistas or Direction Island, stood out well to westward. There are currents off the Chilian archipelago but little known, much as the channels have been explored, which play strange tricks with sailors' reckonings.

When the ship was out of the Straits the long roll from the south-west created an unfavourable impression of the Pacific, which was enforced by its behaviour in a gale next day. The Atlantic in "the roaring forties" could not have been worse with the same force of wind.

"The rolling of the Pacific and the waves thereof are like those of any other sea, only more so," as a philosophic voyager remarked while we were holding on by the weather railing.

> "The passage yet was good—the wind, 'tis true,
> Was somewhat high, but that was nothing new."

No land in sight, and frequent fogs, to perplex the mariner, who was, however, tolerably secure against the dangers of collision.

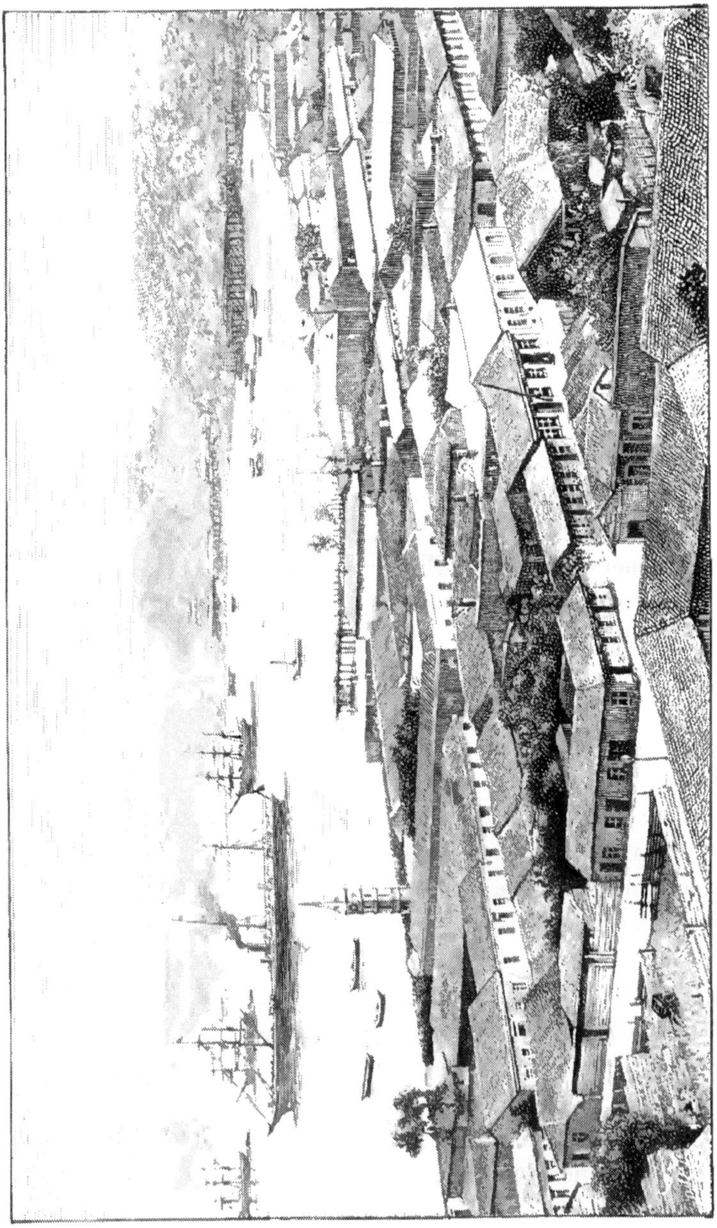

CHAPTER II.

CORONEL.

Arrival at Coronel—The Town—The Arauco Railway Station Friends in waiting—The Port of Coronel—Excursion to San Pedro—The Posada—The Bio Bio Bridge, Concepcion—Messrs. Hicks, Manby, and Bulder The Present—The Future—The Coal Fields—Lota—Lota Parque—Departure from Coronel

ON the morning of March 16th, four days after our exit from the Straits of Magellan, the *Galicia*, blowing her foghorn and firing signal guns, crept cautiously towards Coronel, the port at which we were to make acquaintance with Chilian soil.

The coast was shrouded by the white mist with which subsequent experience made me familiar as the usual covering of the Andes—at least at this time of the year—but above it rose a range of reddish grey highland—the range of the Cordilleras, which leaves but a strip of land, a mile or so in breadth, between the base of the mountains, which come abruptly down to the plain, and the sea. Presently the mist mounted upwards from the coast and gathered in a bank on the hillside. By the time the *Galicia* was moored, the sun shone out brightly, and there, about a mile off, was Coronel and its chimneys, showing a fair array of ships at anchor, with a pier or jetty, a Custom House, a clock tower, &c., to the best advantage, to the inquiring eyes of the strangers.

The town lies in a pretty bay well sheltered from the south winds, which in this part of the world are accompanied by bad weather, and are cold and rainy. The chimneys which meet the eye on shore belong to coal mines, brick kilns, and foundries, of which our excellent vice-consul, Mr. Schwäger, owns two. He certainly could not very well exercise his hospitable disposition without adjuncts to the modest consular pay he receives from the Foreign Office, even though it be augmented by his fee of fifteen shillings for signing the papers of the British ships which visit the port.

There was a great crowd of friends, many of whom had come from Valparaiso, awaiting the arrival of the steamer to welcome Colonel North and his party, and a fleet of shore boats put off to the *Galicia* with strangers, among whom I subsequently made acquaintances whose kindness I shall ever remember. But it is always a little disconcerting to find oneself in a company of old intimates and associates, of which you form no part. However, the courtesy and cordiality of those who later on became our friends soon made us forget that we had never seen them before.

Landing at the Custom House quay when the little *levée* on board ship was over, we walked along the promenade by a neatly kept Plaza with gravel walks, in the centre of which was a pretty clock tower, decorated with a bust of Arturo Prat, to the spacious Station of the Arauco Railway, where we were to have quarters, displacing, I fear, Mr Hicks, Mr. Manby, and others during our stay. The offices of the Staff and waiting-rooms, &c., are large, airy, and well-appointed, and the residence of the officials is exceedingly comfortable.

I was not prepared for the tokens of prosperity which the little town afforded us. Factory chimneys smoked, horsemen in ponchoes and broad sombreroes, carts laden with sacks drawn by oxen or mules, toiled along the street, enveloped in clouds of dust, and the names over the shops — German, Italian, Spanish, and English — indicated a cosmopolitan population. Altogether, Coronel was a place beyond my expectations. When I looked around me and saw the life, the good regulations of the port, the comparative comfort of the people, I could not help thinking of squalid towns on the coast of an island nearer to England. There were, to be sure, drinking-shops, pawnbroker establishments, cafés, and possibly the town had its other defects, but they did not rise to the eye.

The town of Coronel, called after a missionary who was killed here in 1592 by the Indians in one of their many desperate struggles to drive out the Spanish conquerors, is seldom named in early books of travel, and is not to be found on most maps. It has a population of about seven thousand people. It was not till 1851 that Coronel was elevated to the dignity of a port, and now it has its civil governor, and its maritime sub-delegate, a hospital and a lazarette, consular representatives of the great Powers, telegraphic communication, not merely with Chile and Peru, but with Europe and the world; and many other amenities, such as a charming climate and cheap and abundant supplies of most of the necessities of life. It was pleasant to find oneself within touch of Europe again. I could send a message to Buenos Ayres or Rio for the outer bound steamer with the latest news or a message direct to London, but the luxury was rather expensive. The markets are well supported with fresh fish, vegetables and meat. Every fifteen days a Pacific mail steamer from Europe drops into the bay, and another looks in for letters and passengers home; the coasting steamers of the same company arrive and depart twice a week, and the Chilian or South American Company's steamers communicate between Coronel and Valparaiso, and the ports on the coast twice a week also.

The bay of Coronel, between the points of Puchoco and Playa Negra, is a mile and a half wide. There is excellent anchorage, and with the daily increasing importance of the commerce, and the facilities for traffic afforded by the railway, there should be a future for the little town. There is coal, which is pursued down below the sea, at Boca de Maule and Rojas, notwithstanding some heavy blows and great discouragements, involving loss of life, by the incursion of the waters. There is also abundance of excellent earth for brick-making, and Coronel brick is sought for as a building material all over a country where stone abounds. Unfortunately, rushes, reeds, plaster and mud are more easy to use than brick or stone; they are also cheaper, and although they are surrounded with patches of cultivated land and by fruit-bearing trees, the dwellings in the outskirts of the town in which the poorer sort of people take shelter, are of squalid and wretched appearance.

The sea swarms with fish. Some time ago the bay was visited by shoals of smelts, or herrings, driven in flight by enemies or tired of a sea life and desirous of change, in such prodigious quantities that they formed a continuous bank on the beach. With the object of converting this extraordinary supply into oil, some enterprising gentleman erected boilers and furnaces, and prepared sheds for the casks which were to contain the expected produce. They waited for the fish when all was ready, but up to this time they have waited in vain; the fish have never since appeared, or if they have done so have kept well out at sea.

Messrs. Hicks, Manby, Bidder, and the Arauco Railway

authorities generally, were naturally anxious to show Colonel North the works for the construction of the great bridge over the Bio-Bio, which is to connect their line with the State railway at Concepçion, and so in an hour after our arrival at Coronel we were transferred to a special train which was in waiting at the station, and set out for the river.

The country through which the railway northwards is laid to San Pedro is not interesting. Seawards there are wastes covered with tall reeds and coarse rush-like vegetation ; here and there patches of cultivation, maize, potatoes, melons, vines, and fruit-trees Towards the hill ranges iced and plaster cottages, and strips of garden, and a background of wood. Farther on we came to coverts of the boldu-tree, of which the berries are coming into repute in Europe as specific in ailments of the liver. I would have called the tree a *peumo*, on the authority of Molina, but Mr Ball calls the unfortunate Jesuit "one of the most pernicious blunderers who have ever brought confusion into natural history," and I refrain.

Half-way from San Pedro the engine and carriage stopped near a half-way house, the Posada, where in old days (not long ago) the Concepçion diligence was wont to halt. We got out and walked through deep sand a couple of hundred yards under the trees, to the inn, a very primitive establishment, which had seen better days that were not to come again It is a large barn-like building, with poultry yard and stables wattled in, situated close to a bed of reeds, screening from sight a large lake embedded in forest trees, till you come, by a walk through a garden full of roses, dahlias, and sun-flowers, to the edge of the water. There is a general store and bar for the district and chance customers, and our German host, who has a fine family of rosy-cheeked children to attest the healthiness of the uninviting locality, had plenty of brown bread, fresh butter, ham, and Santiago ale to offer us.

I was struck as we passed through the brush and covert by the absence of life; not a twitter of a bird to be heard, nor any sound to break the silence, and I made a note respecting the fact which I would have applied to the whole country, arguing from a particular to a universal, had I not soon had occasion to come to a different conclusion.

Continuing the journey northward for five or six miles more, the locomotive came to a standstill near a row of sheds, and we alighted amid masses of machinery heaped in front of wooden workshops, large piles of rails and girders, and the huts of the railway staff. The high bank hid the Bio-Bio from us till we mounted to the verandah of the superintendent's residence, and looked down on the stream. It was a busy and animated scene which lay spread out below us.

The "ribs and trucks" of the grand Viaduct, were stretching from their firm foundation on the bank, out towards the other side of a great river, which now, at its lowest, ran in several channels between banks of sand out to the sea near Talacuhano on our left. On the shore opposite, perhaps a couple of miles higher up, the white houses and coloured *miradores*, cupolas and spires of Concepçion, looked so bright and graceful that it put one in mind of Venice. I am told it was distance lent enchantment to the view, for though the city is perhaps the best laid out and ordered in Chile, it has nothing of interest in churches or palaces to show. I say I am told, because I was fated not to see it. The bridge which will connect the Arauco Railway with the State line at Concepçion to

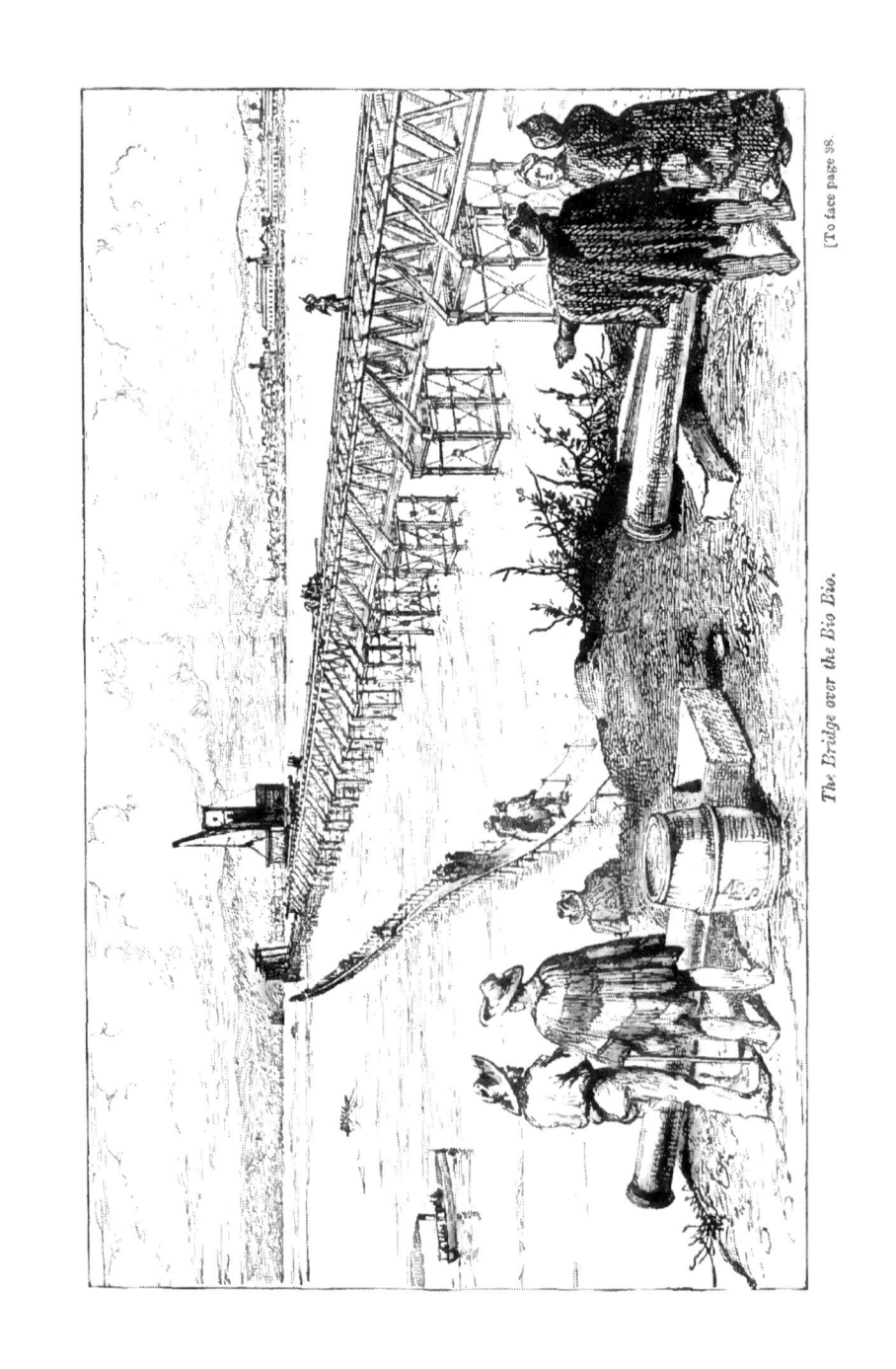

The Bridge over the Bio Bio.

Santiago this year* is 1,889 metres long from shore to shore, and is one of the finest engineering works of the kind in the world.

Two or three hours were spent in examining the works and inspecting the machinery and workshops at San Pedro. Foot races were organized for the amusement and profit of the boys of the village settlement, and the special returned, and brought us back to Coronel, in time to dress for dinner.

Mr. Hicks's banquet, which taxed the resources of the town and gave due warning of what was in store for the visitors to Chile, brought the first day to a close, lasted through the night—nay, invaded the morning. It was wonderful how mind triumphed over matter, and how many people managed to find places and to enjoy themselves at the feast. The morning and part of next day were devoted to a farewell visit to the *Galicia*, to bid adieu to her excellent captain, Adey, and to the officers, who had done their best to render the voyage agreeable, and then to make the final secession of the passengers and their baggage from shipboard to shore. On our return to land some of the more active of the party started in a launch from Coronel to Laraquete. They were rewarded by views of charming scenery, passing the bay of Coloura, where a pier will be constructed presently to connect the port, as the anchorage is well protected, with the railway.

Landing at Laraquete, where there is a pretty station laid out with flower beds, and a small settlement of workmen, the party proceeded by rail southward to the coalfields. The country improved. The alternating patches of sand and scrub gave way to broad stretches of pasture lands in which cattle and horses were feeding, fields of beans and potatoes, gardens of fruit-trees. Streams with

* 1889 It is now actually complete and working.

well-timbered banks enriched the plains, and the landscape gradually assumed an aspect so rich and joyous that one of the party exclaimed, "Why, we are in Normandy!"

The engine presently stopped at a station on the line, above which the residence of Mr. Bidder was perched like

The Arauco Railway.

an eyrie high on the wooded hill, to which the visitors made a laborious visit, for which they were well repaid.

Railway engineers have an especial knack in combining, in their official residences, the comforts of civilised life with whatever is characteristic of the country in which they are working. Mr. Bidder, a man of culture, of varied reading, and of high attainments in his profession, has obtained in Chile the regard of those around him, as he has done in countries nearer home, where his name is well known.

In the short chapter concerning the Arauco Railway there is some account of what some of the visitors saw in their scamper over thirty miles of coal-fields. Others made an excursion to the show-place of the coast, the gardens of Lota—I was about to say far-famed, but that I am reminded of the ignorance of all the party respecting them—which invited inspection. An extensive and well-arranged park and gardens, laid out with pleasure-grounds and hothouses, marvellous tropical vegetation, amid which humming-birds were flitting, clumps of unknown shrubs and laurels, &c.,—there was not a botanist among us—charming parterres, bosquets, through which the eye caught sight of the sea, the beach lined with foam, masses of beautiful ferns, seemed out of place in surroundings where one came upon sham stalactite caves, with glass balls swinging from the roof, giving the impression that the place was a Cockney tea-garden.

These and artificial "rockeries" were sad eyesores, but the house itself, bastard Renaissance, "*l'apothéose du Stuc*," as one of the party termed it, was the greatest of all. The interior contained some fine rooms, of which the decorations corresponded with the general style of the building. There was a Japanese ball-room, and there were stucco columns painted to imitate marble, ceilings panelled in blue with the ciphers of the name of the owner blazoned in gold. The lady, whose wealth places her high on the short list of the richest people in the world, rarely visits the beautiful spot on which she has had this residence erected at great expense. The climate is delightful, the views attractive, there is no deficiency of comfortable accommodation in the house for all the purposes of living. But Lota is a long way from Paris, and the stewards and the gardeners have certainly the greater part of the enjoyment which the property can yield out of it. The lady is perhaps justified in preferring Paris to Lota, and at all events it is very kind of her to keep up the park as well as her splendid palazza at Santiago for the delectation of others, but then Madame Cousiño, who is reputed to have an income of more than a quarter of a million pounds sterling per annum, can afford a little expenditure on places outside the sphere of her actual existence. The visitor can put up with the menagerie stocked with llamas, guanacos, &c., although the former show their bad manners by spitting, as is their wont, at strangers, but, provided that the beautiful park were spared, the rockeries, the statuary, and the grottoes might, even if the house went with them, be most advantageously removed by one of the tidal waves.

Whilst we were on our way between Europe and South America, the President of Chile, Señor Balmaceda, had been making a tour through the principal districts of the Republic. On various occasions, particularly at Iquique, he had made declarations in reference to the policy of the government in domestic matters, and to its intentions with respect to the great industries of Chile, which indicated the possibility of important changes, affecting materially the great interests of the strangers within her gates, being at hand, and the mining and nitrate houses, and the railway companies based on concessions, which were chiefly owned by foreigners, were very much exercised by these pronunciamientos, which were regarded by native politicians as mere diplomatic expressions. These discourses, and the anxiety aroused by them, of course, were made known to Colonel North on his arrival by his agents, and by the gentlemen in charge of the enterprises with which he was connected on the coast. It was desirable to understand what was really meant by speeches which were not, perhaps, quite accurately reported, as soon as possible. Of course, Coronel was but a landing-place—the first stage in our journey.

And so Colonel North, having visited the bridge at San Pedro, inspected the Arauco Railway and examined the coal-fields, left Coronel with his party the third day after our arrival, by special train for San Pedro, where they took boat and were ferried across the Bio Bio to Concepçion. They started late in the day. It was dark when they reached the banks of the river, and they had a very long, cold, and unpleasant passage across, sticking on sandbanks and losing their way in the mazes of the stream. Finally they were carried on men's backs to shore, and arriving very much tired at Concepçion, had to make a start by the early morning train for a dusty and hot journey to Santiago. When I heard of the *peripéties* of the journey, and that they would be leaving Santiago almost immediately for Valparaiso, where the President was expected presently, I was consoled for the loss of the company I would so soon rejoin, and I was very glad we had not undergone an ordeal which I, at any rate, could not very well have borne. For I was unfortunate in my early acquaintance with Chile. Whilst the *Galicia* was off Coronel I managed to catch a cold which took possession of body, bones, and brains, and kept me a prisoner in Mr. Hicks's pleasant quarters, enveloped in porous plaster, full of coughs, pains, and indignation, "cribb'd, cabined, and confined." I was reminded of a remonstrance addressed to me by my dear friend Richard Quain, M.D., for a sight of whose face I would have given many monkeys—if I had them—when once I said "It's only a cold," "Don't say *only*, as if it was of no consequence! A cold may mean a fever, and a fever may mean death; a cold is a door through which many enemies may enter." It was fortunate, indeed, that I was able to get to the famous bridge of San Pedro, the day after our arrival. This is a detail—an unpleasant one for me

I had to content myself with what I could see of the New World out of the windows of my room, which opened on the balcony, and it was thus I formed my first impressions of Chile, physically as a country "to look at," at Coronel. I am obliged to confess that they were not favourable. There was no "atmosphere," no limpid light on the mountain front, no play of shade and colour on the plain. The ocean rolled solidly in heavy folds on the beach, sent up invading columns of surf and spray against rock and bluff, and absorbed them back in foam. On the rocks and beach a uniform reddish-brown spread like a coat of paint; beyond, the strip of land extending to the base of the Andes, appeared, now, at all events, little gifted with green. On the face of the wall-like barrier of the Cordilleras rising inland to the height, apparently, of a couple of thousand feet, there floated a mist I was destined to see for many a long day, "the Camanchaca," which, varying in density and in depth, but never absent altogether, persistently shrouded the mountains.

I watched one morning the operations of a curious branch of industry which has been found out by the Chilian boatmen. The men in some half-dozen boats, which at first I thought were engaged in fishing, were hauling up dredges as longshore men do nearer home. No one could have guessed what they were doing. They were fishing indeed, but it was for coal! It appears that the colliers are loaded in the roadstead, where there is generally a considerable swell, from barges. The consequence is that coal is dropped in considerable quantities overboard, and it is suspected that the process is facilitated by the lightermen, who, when a collier has cleared out, know pretty well where to find a good haul of coal near her moorings.

In a few days, thanks to good nursing, I was well enough to think of continuing my journey, and Mr. Milne, of Callao, who had kindly remained behind to look after us, recommended that we should proceed northwards by sea instead of going by rail to Santiago, and thence by the continuation of the same line to Valparaiso, on the coast. A good steamer was expected soon, and I gladly availed myself of the chance of seeing the coast afforded by her.

CHAPTER III.

THE ARAUCO RAILWAY.

Now let any of my readers who do not care much for an account of the coal-fields of Lota and of the Arauco Railway, be pleased to skip over this short chapter and "go on to the next." I shall not be at all hurt if they do. But I can assure them that the statements in it may be relied on, for although I was unable, as I shall explain presently, to accompany Colonel North, I had the advantage of hearing the reports of two of my friends, very exact, disinterested, and competent observers, who were good enough to place the results of their visit to Lota and to the neighbouring mining districts at my disposal

When the great coal-field on the shore of the Pacific and the narrow strip of land, between the Andes and the sea, from Penco on the north to Tirna to the south, was discovered, the value and importance of such an immense aid to the resources of the State stimulated the mining and commercial classes of Chile to turn it to profitable account; but there was a want of capital and of experience in the country which prevented the Chilians being able to give full development to the mines. The coal-field, which has been even yet but imperfectly explored and only partially examined, runs from Penco, in the vicinity of Concepçion, to Coronel, where it is worked by Messrs. Schwager and Messrs. Rojas, and so on through Lota, southwards to Lebu,

ARAUCO COAL AND RAILWAY COMPANY.
COAL ESTATES.

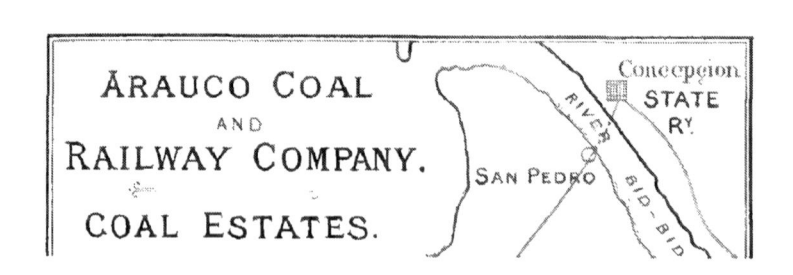

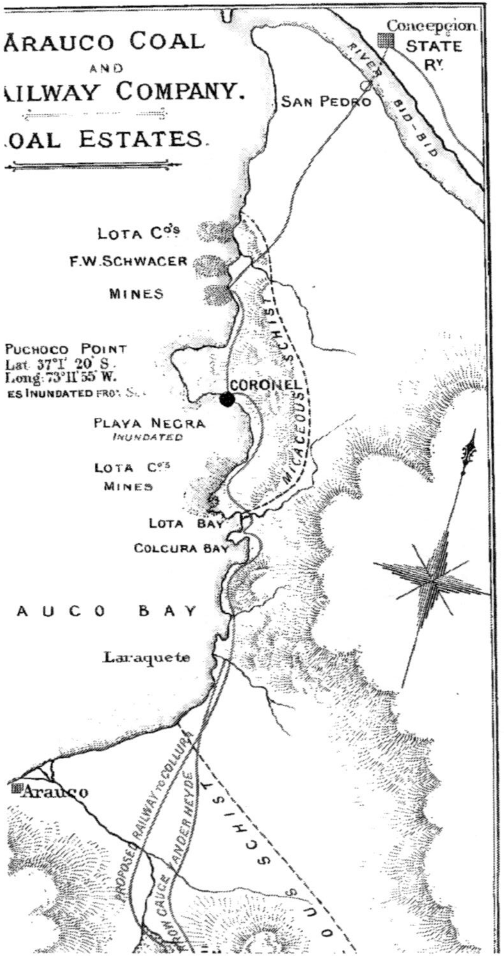

ARAUCO COAL
AND
ILWAY COMPANY.
OAL ESTATES.
Concepcion
STATE
RY.
RIVER BID-BID
SAN PEDRO
LOTA Co's
F.W. SCHWACER
MINES
PUCHOCO POINT
Lat. 37°1' 20" S.
Long. 73°11' 55" W.
ES INUNDATED FROM SEA
CORONEL
MICACEOUS SCHIST
PLAYA NEGRA
INUNDATED
LOTA Co's
MINES
LOTA BAY
COLCURA BAY
AUCO BAY
Laraquete
Arauco
PROPOSED RAILWAY TO COLLURA
ANDER HEYDE
ROW GAUGE
SCHIST
OUS

where the seams are worked by local companies, at Lota by the Lota Company of Messrs. Cousiño, and at Lebu by Messrs. Errazuriz, to the hills beyond Curanhilahue, and extends from the Nahuelbuta (or tiger) range of the Andes to the coast, striking down westward, farther than can be determined, beneath the sea.

The pioneer of the Chilian capitalists who began to work the various seams for which they had powers—naturally devoting their energies to the beds near the sea, originally commencing at Lota, as carriage from the interior was very difficult and costly—was Don Matias Cousiño. They burrowed under the ocean, following the seams westward from the shore, and in 1880 the coal-owners were turning out about 150,000 tons a year at Puchoco, near Coronel, when the sea broke through the roof and drowned the mine, and with it the miners. A similar disaster occurred at the colliery of Playa Negra, and these disasters intimidated the people and effectually arrested for the time the submarine coal-mining operations, but I believe that it is in contemplation to re-work the Coronel seams by an ingenious attack upon the sea-water in the pits, which is to be cut off, section after section, from the rift which lets in the enemy, and is then to be pumped out—the seams being worked laterally so as to turn his flank also. It remains to be seen whether miners and machinery will prevail in the combat with a terrible and persistent foe.

The Chilian Government granted a concession for a railway to carry the coal of the various companies and individuals who were at work, to a gentleman (Mr. Lenz), who sold it to the Arauco (or the Concepçion, Lota and Arauco) Railway Company, which was established by Mr. Edward Edmondson, Colonel, then Mr., North and others, about four years ago, and Messrs. Hicks and Abbott,

where the seams are worked by local companies, at Lota by the Lota Company of Messrs. Cousiño, and at Lebu by Messrs. Errazuriz, to the hills beyond Curanhilahue, and extends from the Nahuelbuta (or tiger) range of the Andes to the coast, striking down westward, farther than can be determined, beneath the sea.

The pioneer of the Chilian capitalists who began to work the various seams for which they had powers—naturally devoting their energies to the beds near the sea, originally commencing at Lota, as carriage from the interior was very difficult and costly—was Don Matias Cousiño. They burrowed under the ocean, following the seams westward from the shore, and in 1880 the coal-owners were turning out about 150,000 tons a year at Puchoco, near Coronel, when the sea broke through the roof and drowned the mine, and with it the miners. A similar disaster occurred at the colliery of Playa Negra, and these disasters intimidated the people and effectually arrested for the time the submarine coal-mining operations, but I believe that it is in contemplation to re-work the Coronel seams by an ingenious attack upon the sea-water in the pits, which is to be cut off, section after section, from the rift which lets in the enemy, and is then to be pumped out—the seams being worked laterally so as to turn his flank also. It remains to be seen whether miners and machinery will prevail in the combat with a terrible and persistent foe.

The Chilian Government granted a concession for a railway to carry the coal of the various companies and individuals who were at work, to a gentleman (Mr Lenz), who sold it to the Arauco (or the Concepçion, Lota and Arauco) Railway Company, which was established by Mr. Edward Edmondson, Colonel, then Mr., North and others, about four years ago, and Messrs. Hicks and Abbott, who had been early in the field and had secured concessions and contracts in the district, amalgamated their interests with those of the new Company. The Government, being naturally desirous of obtaining coal for shipping and lighting, and for the supply of Concepçion and Santiago, gave a guarantee of 5 per cent. for twenty years on £4,500 for each kilometre on the line, as it was approved of for public traffic.

The line beginning from the intended junction with the State Railway outside the city of Concepçion, was encountered at the outset by the Bio Bio, the largest river in Chile, which presented to the engineers the delightful difficulty of constructing one of the greatest bridges in the world before the railway could be continued southwards to Coronel and on to Lota, where there were collieries and mines, &c., in working order, and the engineers are busy in completing the sections between Lota and Laraquete. Here, at Lota, there is, within the measurable distance of half-a-mile of the line, the bay of Colcura, which nature, not prodigal in her gifts in that way along the coast, has endowed with great advantages as a port and harbour. It is in fact marked for the purpose of providing an outlet and inlet for the Arauco region, its products and its requirements. From Colcura, proceeding south by the rugged coast, the rail will run to Laraquete, where, in effect, it is now working through the Carampangue coal district to Peumo and Colico.* From Coronel to Lota the permanent way is made, completed, and open, between Lota and Laraquete it is in progress, and from Laraquete to Carampangue it is working, so that about 49 kilometres, including the line from Coronel to San Pedro, are open for traffic. The

* The reader must be pleased to remember that this description of the line applies to it as it was last year.

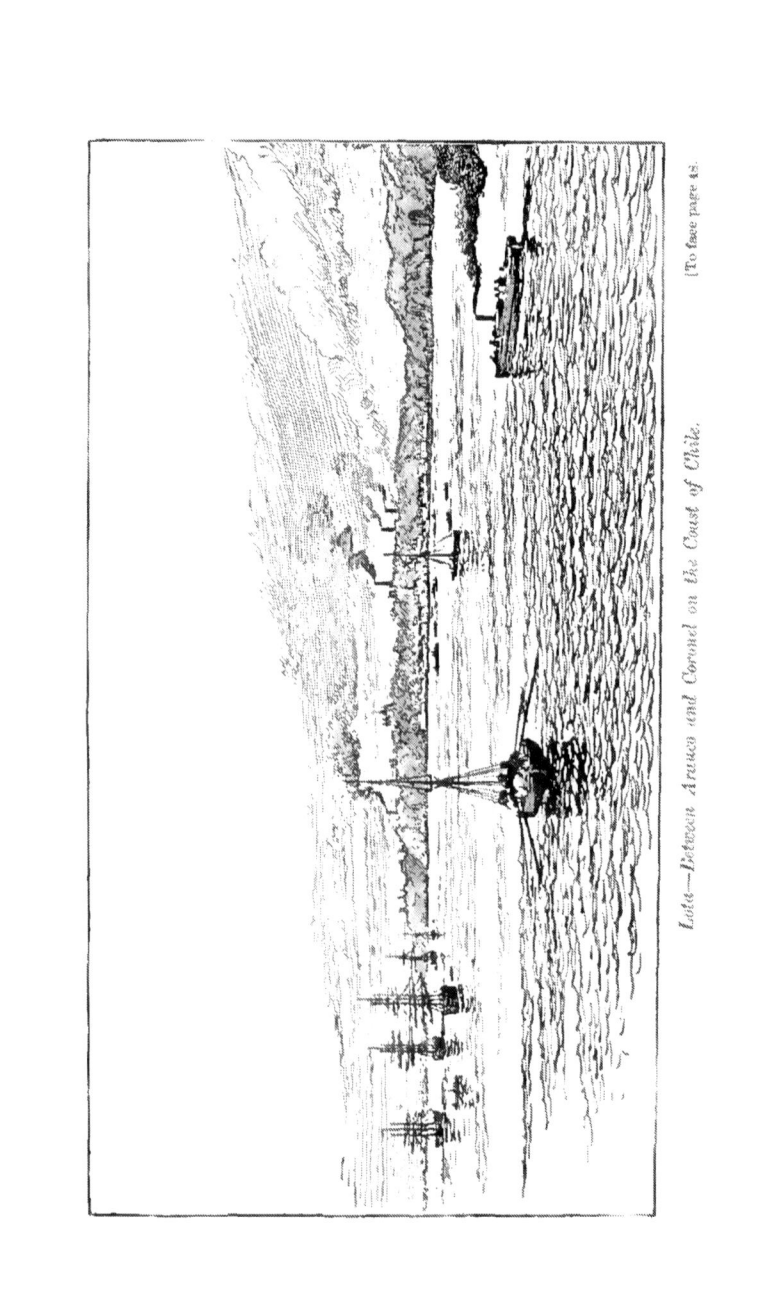

Lota.—Between Arauca and Coronel on the Coast of Chile.

[To face page 48.

rail between Coronel and Lota was not quite complete at the time of our visit, but it was supposed it would be open in a few weeks. The coast southwards from Coronel is bold and rocky and the line winds along the shore (in one place, Playa Negra, carried through rather a formidable tunnel), several smaller works of the same kind being

Arauco Railway Tunnel.

necessary, all now completed except two, before the railway reaches Laraquete.

The collieries near the Carampangue and at Maquegua had been worked for eight years before the Coronel catastrophe. Señor Van der Heyde sank a shaft in 1872, and worked the Morro (also called Mora) seam at a profit till 1875, when the price of coal fell so low that he could no longer cart it from the pit to the narrow gauge railway connected with Laraquete. The Morro mines were consequently abandoned till the Arauco Company renewed the working of the beds, which are of vast extent, and of the finest quality, and in places more than four feet thick, the working having been further developed, so that 1,000,000 tons are available, and the manager estimates that in March, 1890, there will be an output of 300 tons a day of coal in quality equal to the best West Hartley. The Maquegua and Quilachanquin fields, the estates and properties of the Carampangue Company, consisting of 31,000 acres freehold and 23,000 acres under coal lease, were purchased by the company for £175,000, including the narrow gauge railway rollings, &c., to Laraquete.

For a good many years a narrow gauge mineral line had been employed for the conveyance from the Carampangue properties of coal to Laraquete, where there is a good pier, and here the Arauco railway line, which has been carried southwards, as we have seen, in sections, starting once more on its course, crosses one or two streams to the valley in which the river Carampangue runs, to be crossed presently by a fine viaduct, thirty miles from Laraquete, and thence it is continued through the coal estates of the Company till it attains its terminus, Curanhilahue, sixty-two miles south of Concepçion. The line is 5 feet 6 inches gauge, and is laid with 50 lb. rails. The minimum curve radius is two hundred metres, and the gradients are not severe. The locomotives are furnished by Fowler & Co., of Leeds, R. Stephenson & Co., Newcastle-on-Tyne, and Manning, Wardle & Co., Leeds; the carriages are on the American principle, and were made by the Lancaster Wagon Company. These lines are in some places but the development of the old mineral tracks, such as that close to Coronel, where there is a branch line from the colliery of Buen-Retiro which is worked under water, and

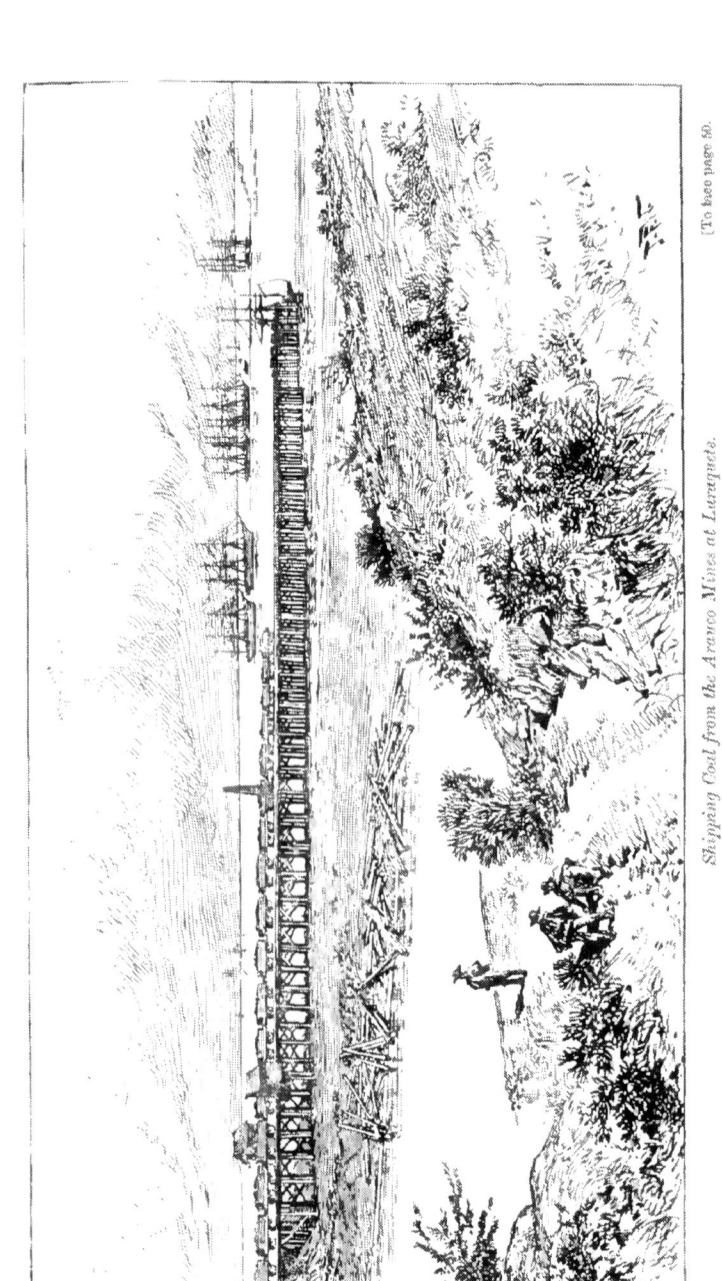

Shipping Coal from the Arauco Mines at Lurquete. [To face page 80.

as those at Laraquete, which were worked seventeen years back.

The Carampangue properties are covered with most valuable forest, and the seam yields $2\frac{1}{2}$ feet of clean coal, 33 yds. below it there is another giving $5\frac{1}{2}$ feet with shale

The Arauco Coal-Field.

strata. The mineral rights are vested in the company. Here there are numerous pits and drifts in full activity. When we were at Coronel it was calculated that the two estates could turn out 250 to 300 tons of coal a day, giving a shipment of 6,000 tons a month at Laraquete. The coal sells there for 7 to 8 Chilian dollars per ton.

Opposite Maquegua, on the opposite bank of the Carampangue, is an estate of 9,000 acres, called Peumo, abounding in coal, worked by the company on a royalty of less than sixpence a ton. The coal seams on this property are not yet developed; the railway runs through the estate from end to end.

Next to this estate, that of Colico, extending over 60,000 or 70,000 acres, the coal rights of which belong to the company, is traversed by the railway. It is in a beautiful park-like, undulating country, *accidenté* and covered with forest, which furnishes excellent timber for the shafts and galleries, and a boundless provision of planks beams, sleepers, rafters, &c., for the works, towns, and cities in the treeless region north of Valparaiso. There are no timber rights, I believe, attached to Peumo and Colico, but there are full rights to timber at Abellos, and other places where it can be bought for about $5 an acre. Then there is the Abellos or Descabezados field, 29,000 acres. Coal everywhere! Drifts and shafts find it omnipresent, the strata running 10° to 12° W., the level being E.E.N E. 12° in the belt of land, about 22 miles long, through which the railway runs The coal seams *sautent aux yeux* on every side. The railway is carried to the door of the workings along these mining properties, and thence it follows the valley of the Nahuellan from its junction with the Carampangue to the Porvenir field, at the southern boundary of which the Curanhilahue line is available for transport.

No wonder that after a gallop of thirty miles over the country the engineers and mineralogists of the party were astonished at the potentiality of the region. It is calculated that by the beginning of 1891 the yield of coal will be at the rate of 300,000 tons a year. The Chilian State railways take 100,000 tons for their own use, and the extension of the railway system before 1894 is over will lead to a largely increased demand. There seems, indeed, no possible limit to the future of the coal out-put and traffic of the Arauco Railway if hands can be got to work the collieries.

Coal Shaft, Arauco Railway Coal-Field.

As yet the coal market is unsteady. But British coal-owners are apt to make the same complaint. The price of coal at Valparaiso is from $8 to $12. Nevertheless, foreign coal has been sometimes brought in at such low rates that the native product was unsaleable at a profit, and in 1876

Maquegua coal was beaten down from $15 to $4 a ton. Mr. Bidder told Mr. Vizetelly that he could put the coal from these collieries on the railway at an average cost of $1 80, the Chilian dollar being 2s. 3d. Add to that the cost of transport, shipping, &c., and Colico coal should command $10 in the market, yielding a profit of $6, as it would not cost more than $4 a ton.

The properties of the coal are stated to be excellent. It has a high thermal value. It burns quickly and freely, furnishes a dense coke after a large production of gas of which the illuminating power is seventeen candles, it is remarkably "clean," and the clinker can be readily detached from furnaces, boilers, &c.

When the lines from the southern terminus are complete and an unbroken communication is established with Coronel, and thence on to the State railway at Concepçion, a great future looms on the Arauco country, which was but fifty years ago very debateable land between the Indians and the whites. The progress already made south of Coronel is remarkable. The engineers expected to have the line completed to Colico by the 15th January, 1890, and to Curanhilahue by 28th February, but they have been much impeded by the want of hands, and the Company had to trust to the consideration of Congress should the line be not opened at the fixed day, January 3rd, for an extension of time for three months more.* For which they applied and which they have since obtained.

The Chilians will not admit Chinese labour. Chilians are given to migration and emigration, and they are found, not only on both sides of the South American con-

---

* By the latest account the line was complete, with trains running, though the Chilian Government had not formally approved certain sections of it, Bio Bio, Lota to Laraquete, Carampangue to Colico. From the last place to Curanhilahue the line was just finished.

tinent, but high up on the Pacific coast of North America. The mortality among children—much of it preventable—is very great, and the general result is to be traced in the difficulty of obtaining labour, owing to the deficiency of population. The men are robust and enduring, and Mr. Abbott told me he preferred Chilians to Europeans, but he cannot get enough of them.

Mr. Bidder, who is the chief engineer in charge of the railway and of colliery operations necessary for the development of the coal-fields, has equal difficulty in procuring labour—the *manque de bras* is felt everywhere in Chile,—not only in procuring but in utilising it. The Chilian is strong, and when he must work, he is hard-working. But he does not love labour, as some people are supposed to do, and he does like drink, gambling, and pleasure. He is a devout observer of the feasts of the Church, and his week contains as many days of idleness for religious purposes as, having regard to the obligation to obtain money necessary for enjoyment, can be contrived for it. The managers of industrial enterprises assert that the truck system is indispensable. If the workmen were paid their full wages they would drink and gamble every penny away, and leave themselves without the means of obtaining food or clothing. They, therefore, have at every establishment a truck shop (*pulperia*), where the miner can obtain what he wants, the amount being deducted from his wages. It is not denied that there are handsome profits made out of the miners' wants in these stores. The principle is not defended, but the outcome.

Leaving the sections of the line through the coal regions along the sea shore south of Coronel, which are being energetically pushed forward—let us turn to the short line to the north.

The country between San Pedro and Coronel presents no difficulties, and there cannot be found a smoother or a straighter track anywhere than that over which our little train ran between the two points. At both stations the extensive workshops, stores, and offices, in what to us were out-of-the-way places, naturally attracted attention, and wherever we looked we saw English names stamped on machinery and implements, and cases which had contained them

Mr Manby, a very expert and accomplished member of the Institute of Civil Engineers, of which his uncle was an eminent official—*bon chien chasse de race*—the chief engineer of the Company, had to deal with a very difficult question. It was to find in a deep bed of river sand a $\pi o \upsilon$ $\sigma \tau \omega$ for a bridge across the river. He designed a bridge of lattice girders, each girder 83 ft. 8 in. long, and weighing 10 tons and tested to bear 120 tons, to stretch from piers, the emplacement of which was the crux of his problem. The wrought iron superstructure, amounting to about 2,500 tons, was supplied by John Butler & Co., Stanningley, and the cast iron columns forming the piers, amounting to about 1,800 tons, were supplied by Messrs. Fawcett, Preston & Co., of Liverpool, who are also manufacturing the powerful winding engines for the coal pits at Peumo and Colico. These piers are composed of six cast-iron pillars of from 15 to 12 in., sunk about 30 ft. into the bed of the river 81 ft. apart To Sir J. Brunlees is assigned the credit of devising the means of penetrating beds of sand by such hollow columns A Tangye pump connected with a tube carried down the hollow below its base drives a column of water with such force into the sand that the latter is quite broken up, and it makes way easily for the iron tube as it is screwed round by an endless rope worked by a steam capstan till it has settled to its appointed rest.

If the Arauco Railway does not advance by leaps and bounds, it "moves onward day by day." The bridge over the Bio Bio, at which we were looking in a state of transition, will be an accomplished work—1,889 metres of iron way—before the year 1889 is over. Then will come its time of trial. The Bio Bio, now striving laboriously for its exits to the sea through many channels scooped in the sand, will be a bankful river one mile and a quarter broad, rushing in one great volume from ten to fifteen feet deep to the bay of Concepçion. The engineers are preparing for the onslaught, and they entertain no apprehension whatever that the Bio Bio can prevail against them.

The engineers and chiefs of the works are English, and so are the contractors (Abbott & Co); the overseers are Europeans, the workmen Chilians. At the banquet given at the house of Mr. Hicks, who has from the very commencement been the able and energetic general manager of the Company, that night, after our return from San Pedro, Colonel North mentioned the fact that he and Mr. Abbott were fellow workmen on the coast at $4 a day six-and-twenty years ago, and they were both proud of the reminiscence.

All the machinery comes from England—whenever possible, from Leeds—the engineers and chiefs are English—the workmen Chilians. The rate of progress satisfied the contractors. A pier was completed every seven or eight days. When the bridge has reached the right bank of the Bio Bio, the line will be carried, through a tunnel 200 metres long in the bluff named Chepé Point, to the point of junction with the State Railway a mile and a half from the bank. How far south the railway will extend hereafter will no doubt be determined by the growth of traffic.

It is believed that the Arauco railway which opens up the Lebu, Carampangue, and Lota iron and coal districts and connects them with Coronel and the State Railway of Chile, must, when complete, pay very handsome dividends

CHAPTER IV.

FROM CORONEL TO VALPARAISO.

The Coast Steamers—The *Chiloe*—The Pacotilleros—The Scenery—Tome—Sensitive Oysters—Talcahuano—Concepçion—The Tidal Wave—The *Huascar* and the *Shah* and *Amethyst*—Pierola's Prestige—British Complaints of the Foreign Office

By the time the *Chiloe*, one of the Chilian line, arrived at Coronel I was patched up sufficiently to take a passage to Valparaiso. Thus it was I never visited Concepçion or saw the railway between it and Santiago.

There are two lines of coast steamers, one belonging to the P. S. N., the other to the Chilian Company, which, as well as the German Kosmos steamers, ply between the most southerly ports of Chile and along the coast up to Panama in rather needless competition. The ships are built and engined in England, commanded and officered by Englishmen, though they sail under different flags, and as the railways run inland from the coast, the boats have generally fair cargoes and full cabins. Communication between the towns on the seaboard, which are the seats of commerce and industry, is mainly carried on by the steamers, which have a large local passenger traffic, and which are chiefly used in the transport of produce, and of the purveyors of supplies, to the inhabitants of the rainless and barren region north of Coquimbo.* The scene presented by the main deck of a coast steamer filled with sheep, goats, pigs, poultry, hay, straw, beans, cabbages, potatoes, locusts,

* See note, Appendix

bananas, fruit, vegetables, maize; in the midst of which are packed ponchoed vaqueros, cardsharpers, broken-down emigrants, miners, Mexicans, Indians, Bolivians, and their wives and children, of infinite variety of dress and hue, playing cards, gambling, and smoking, the women often engaged among their families in household work of the kind which monkeys love—offers a series of admirable subjects for an enterprising artist, but Chile has not as yet produced a native painter of eminence. The steamers are the market places of the pacotilleros or itinerant traders, who pay their fares as passengers and a high toll as well on the produce, animal and vegetable, with which they fill the waist of the ship. The purchaser of course has the amount added to the price of what he buys; but withal the gains are uncertain, and to judge from the aspect of the "merchants," this coast business cannot be very lucrative. In bad weather the live stock perishes—in very bad it is thrown overboard, and is, poultry especially, sacrificed wholesale. At the best the cattle have miserable times of it. They are slung by the horns, and are lifted and lowered on board by cranes, in pitiable fright and pain. Indeed, the stranger is not long in the land before he has reason to feel shocked at the usage of animals. The only mode of carrying poultry is by the legs. Half-a-dozen cocks and hens are tied together and taken through the streets, head downwards. The oxen are driven by men armed with long poles, furnished with sharp goads which are used relentlessly, and the bits of the bridles are terribly severe, but the formidable looking spurs of the riders are not more punishing perhaps than an ordinary hunting persuader.

The expectations I had formed of the coast scenery were grievously disappointed. On the run from Coronel to

Valparaiso the Andes were generally hidden from view by clouds, and the coastline of rocks and bluffs, on which the never-ceasing swell broke in foam, had little variety of form or colour. The nights were clear, the stars shining brightly; but with the morning, fogs rolled down from the mountains and settled on land and sea. Steamers when approaching a port are often obliged to lie to.

The *Chiloe* was thus detained some time off Tomé, the first port she made the morning after we left Coronel. When the fog lifted off the sea, revealing the lower slopes of the mountains, and the town itself prettily situated at the base of a series of rounded hills, covered with brushwood, rising in gradual terraces from the beach, the summits of the range behind them were still invisible. A few small craft riding uneasily to their anchors, a white margin of surf, the Chilian flag, blue and white with a white star (colours which have been taken by Colonel North as his own on the turf), flying over a little Custom-House, a mole, some low houses, apparently of wood, along the beach, rounded hills covered with brush gradually swelling up into the bare ridges of the Andes—that was Tomé.

People who go down to the sea in ships along this coast must be thankful for small mercies in the gift of safe anchorage. Tomé is considered the best port in the great bay of Concepçion, the points of Lobelia and Morro del Tomé affording ships some protection from the sea.

It was a fishing village till the establishment of large flour-mills in 1842 gave such an impetus to the place, that it has now attained the dignity of being classed as a Puerto Mayor, although it has less than five thousand inhabitants

The appearance of the steamer was the signal for a rush of the people to the jetty. The port authorities, followed by a flotilla, put out, and, as soon as they were allowed to board us, men and women clambered up the ladders and made for the open market between decks, whilst the more luxurious inquired after their consignments of oysters, which come, I believe, from the island of Chiloe, and which, if somewhat inferior in contour, plumpness, and flavour to an orthodox "native" or Ostender, are by no means to be despised. They have, however, a disqualification in the eyes of very sensitive people, in that they squirm dreadfully at the contact of lemon juice or vinegar, but the daintiest ladies are not deterred by these outward and visible signs of suffering from eating them with gusto.

There is a good rough wine produced in the district which was sold for 20 centavos, the fifth part of a dollar, now worth about 2s. 3d.; a hundred eggs cost 5s., fowls 1s. 3d. a piece, and of these we laid in store. *Per contra*, our vegetables were in great demand as well as the oysters

A couple of hours sufficed for the business transactions between the port and the ship, and off we steamed to the adjacent roadstead of Talacuhano, which is the port of Concepçion, the imposing and picturesque-looking city we had seen from the left bank of the Bio Bio when we visited the railway bridge. There was but little in the appearance of the Talacuhano to justify its Indian name, which means, I was told by one of my fellow passengers, "a ray from heaven." The same obliging gentleman was surprised when I confessed that I had never heard of the celebrated siege of the town by the Patriot army under O'Higgins, which lasted six months, nor of the deeds of the Argentine sailor, Blanco Encalada, when in command of a Chilian flotilla hastily fitted out at Valparaiso, he boarded and captured the Spanish frigate, *Maria Isabel*, and two consorts in the bay, or of the gallantry of the

Royalist Colonel, José Ordonez, who commanded the garrison with great ability. Every Chilian gentleman is acquainted with the details of the War of Independence, and my friend was naturally rather disappointed at my ignorance.

The *Chiloe* anchored close to the *Huascar*, the ironclad ram which played such a conspicuous part in the war between Chile and Peru, but my interest in the little ship arose from her encounter with the *Shah* and the *Amethyst*. The *Huascar* is brig-rigged, her funnel was lowered, yards squared, rigging taut, marines paced up and down the quarter deck and bridge, and as she lay close to us and was low in the water, we had a good look at her and saw everything was ship shape and in strict man-of-war fashion. A formidable ram projects from her bow, and if she struck a wooden ship she must send it to the bottom. The result of that engagement unquestionably diminished British prestige along the coast. Pierola when summoned to surrender declared he would fight if he were attacked. Admiral de Horsey did attack, and although it could not be said he was beaten off by the *Huascar*, he failed to take her, and her escape is counted by Peruvians, and, I fear, by Chilians too, as a victory. I cannot think Admiral de Horsey exercised a sound discretion in demanding the surrender of the *Huascar* without considering the means he had of enforcing his order if Pierola refused to obey. The *Huascar* was an iron-plated vessel, small indeed, but quick and handy. She was armed with 300-pounders, one shot of which would have disposed of the *Shah* or of her consort, the *Amethyst*, which was a light, slightly-armed, wooden corvette. The boilers of the former were in a bad condition. The skipper of the *Huascar* was fainthearted or unskilful, and the futile attempts he made to ram the *Shah* enabled de Horsey to damage her turrets with his big guns, but he could not take or overtake his enemy. Much as the British residents felt the fiasco they were very thankful indeed that the *Huascar* was not taken, and they are firmly convinced to-day, as I heard from many of them, that had the *Huascar* been captured by the *Shah* there would have been a massacre of the English in Callao and Lima and all the towns along the coast. Pierola, who is now living quietly in Lima, biding his time, it is said, to head another revolution, became, by his resistance to the British ships, an object of popular admiration, and the anniversary of the action is kept as a national festivity in Peru.

I may here observe, anticipating a little the order of my notes, that the mercantile community on the Pacific coast of South America complain bitterly of the want of "protection," and contrast their treatment with that of Germans, French, or Italians. They do not blame naval officers or consular authorities so much as the Government at home, which allows grievances to remain without redress. They say that when they make representations that wrong has been done to their interests, the Foreign Office sends an intimation that inquiry will be made. Presently a ship of war comes in; the officer in command lands and sees the consular officer and the sufferers. Then the ship of war goes away and no more is heard of the matter! Let an Italian or a German be injured and on representation made to the Government reparation is made at once, although there is no German or Italian ship within measurable distance. Probably British merchants on the coast expect too much protection. According to their own account they get very little indeed. During the late war, houses, ships, warehouses, goods, property of all kinds were destroyed, and compensation has been stingy and tardy.

Whilst it is undesirable that our vessels should be at the beck and call of mercantile communities, apt to assume a high tone with the local authorities of feeble governments, when they have a fleet at their back, it is the worst possible policy to permit any outrage upon our fellow-subjects to pass unnoticed.

In the old books of travel there is no mention of Talacuhano — probably two hundred years back it was only a small Indian fishing village, but Concepçion was one of the greatest of the cities founded by the Spaniards in their South America colonies It was described as a maritime port in the early part of the eighteenth century. The town of to-day is about six or seven miles from the sea.

The little town of Penco now marks the site of the original Concepçion, a conspicuous city in the time of the long struggle with the Araucanians, which ended in the overthrow and almost complete destruction of one of the finest native races that ever existed.

The awful earthquake and the tidal wave on 20th February, 1835—the most terrible of which there are full records, save that of Lisbon—which united to overwhelm both the towns, not only laid them in ruin, but permanently altered the face of the country and the islands in the Bay of Concepçion—upheaving the land for several feet all round the Bay. The ruins of the cities were still to be seen on the beach and on the shore near the town.

When I beheld the evidences of the force of those irresistible convulsions spread out before me I could not but reflect on the consequences of a similar commotion to the magnificent bridge which by the end of this year is to span the Bio Bio.

F

We steamed out of the spacious bay of Concepçion towards sunset, and, for the first, and a short, time, as the last rays shot across the sea and lighted up the summits through the rifts of cloud, we got a good view of the snowy chain of the Andes in the distance.

CHAPTER V.

VALPARAISO.

The Harbour and City—The Scenery—The Hotel de France—The "English Corsair," Francis Drake — The Defences—The City as it is—European Influence — Foreigners and their Work — French, German, American, and British Clubs—The Chilian Press—The Suburbs

NEXT morning the *Chiloe* came to her moorings in the roadstead of Valparaiso. I was surprised and pleased at the appearance of the city. At the foot of a deeply-indented and rugged-looking bright-red mountain range,* some 1,200 feet to 1,600 feet high, which comes quite close to the shore as if threatening to squeeze it into the sea, there is a long semicircular curve of white buildings, church spires, warehouses, and public edifices bordering the bay behind a forest of masts. This mountain range, over which peers the frosted head of the giant Aconcaqua, 23,000 feet high, is furrowed by deep cuts, which were doubtless the beds of torrents when the drainage of the upland continent was in progress, and which are still watercourses in the rainy season; between the ravines, and on the shoulders of their moraine-like banks, houses are built, tier above tier, thrown up, as it were, in clusters, from the long main street, which extends for miles along the shore, which is bordered by quays and factories. The roadstead is open to the north, and as the water is very deep the anchorage is insecure in winter when the north winds prevail, but

* See note, Appendix

it is well sheltered on the south, west, and east There is a battery near the south entrance, redoubts at various points, and a fort on the hill near the Naval School, but at the beginning of the war the town was open to attack, and it is strange that the Peruvians, when they had supremacy on the sea, did not take tithe of Valparaiso. Until the traveller lands he has no idea of the extent of the city which is bravely struggling—and successfully too—to win vantage ground from the ocean. Valparaiso is ceasing to be like a mathematical line—length without breadth; the city authorities have already retrieved many hundreds of acres from the sea, and are busily engaged in acquiring more. Workmen are engaged in bedding out the earth into the ocean and casting in stones of which the mountains furnish near and inexhaustible supplies, and thus establishing foundations for houses already rising or built on quays similarly constructed, so that there are now short cross streets from the main thoroughfare, which has also small offshoots nearly parallel to its course at the Plaza and the Railway Station.

The landing is not as facile as it might be. There is, to be sure, a fine pier projecting from the Custom House, with boat-steps at both sides, but the steps are not all easy or in good order. There is reckless shoving and ramming among the boatmen eager to land or take in their people, accompanied by "expostulation" in many tongues, for the port is the resort of ships of all nations, the majority, however, flying the British flag. The railway runs by one side of the square* close at hand, and a tramway leads up to the main street and serves the whole of the city, stopping at the lifts or *accenseurs* by which access is gained to the towering suburbs.

* Plaza de la Intendencia, ornamented by a statue of Lord Cochrane

The Plaza at which we landed, thronged by itinerant vendors of fruit, feather brushes, and by idlers and busy people frequenting the offices and places of business which surround the square area in the centre of which rises the inevitable monument, is full of life. Our goods were taken to the Custom House and were passed very promptly by one of the officers, and here I feel bound to say that my small experience of Chilian officials inclines me to consider them as very polite and obliging.

Our hostelry, the Hotel de France, is half way up the main street. It is kept by a Frenchman, a great deal of a *petit maitre*, and, except in the matter of the bill, very little of a landlord; his wife, who was good enough to take her meals in the *salle-à-manger*, where she could criticise, if she would not attend to, her guests, was a suitable helpmate. The internal arrangements were discreditable and abominable in every way, and a fair table and the merits of a good *chef* did not reconcile us to the want of decency, not to speak of comfort, in the domestic economy of the hotel.

How dangerous it is to prophesy, unless you are sure! Miers, who wrote an elaborate book in 1826, declared that, when the internal affairs of Chile were regulated, when property was secure and confidence was established, Concepçion must become the chief port of Chile, instead of Valparaiso. It was a better port—supplies were cheaper, and Valparaiso can never contain more than 6,000 people. (The population now numbers probably about 120,000.) Sixty years ago Valparaiso consisted of one street built only on one side, and contained two shops; there was no society, no amusements, no theatre, no parade, no promenade, no road to walk or ride upon, no exit from the town except over reefs of rocks, or barren hills, or up steep quebradas (ravines), and Miers, who abuses it *con spirito*, declares that in spite of its matchless climate there was not "a more uncomfortable and cheerless place of residence for a being of sense and feeling than Valparaiso." That was after three centuries of Spanish rule and government!

When the man whom the Spaniards term the "English corsair," Francis Drake, took Valparaiso, 5th December, 1578, the place did not contain more than twelve or thirteen houses, a little church, and two shops; when Richard Hawkins landed, and sacked the town, in May, 1594, he found some magazines and warehouses, in which were stored silk, linen, wine, and provisions, and in one of the four ships in the Roads which he plundered he found a good quantity of gold.

To-day there is a great commercial port with wet docks, piers, quays, warehouses, magazines—a bustling active population—colleges, schools, well-stored shops of every kind, hotels, theatres, clubs, tramways, railways, public carriages, electric lighting, gas, the telephone. But little more than a hundred years before Miers' time Valparaiso consisted of about one hundred poor houses without any order, sheltering one hundred and fifty families, scarce thirty of whom were whites. The most Chilian of Chilians must admit that but for the enterprise and capital of the European and American, German, English, Yankee merchants, engineers, traders, &c., Valparaiso would have had to wait for many a weary year ere it would have attained to the degree of civilised activity which it presents to-day. The most patriotic Spaniard cannot deny that his ancestors were miserable administrators of the regions they won by so much expenditure of energy and courage.

Valparaiso, the supremacy of which was challenged at one time by Callao, is now, without doubt, the principal port on the west coast of South America. The roadstead is capable of containing more than one hundred vessels, with good holding ground, and they are generally pretty safe; but the water is very deep, the bay is exposed to a heavy run of the sea when the wind is from the *cuarto cuadrante*, " and vessels at anchor must ride to eighty fathoms of cable at least, with the same distance between each." Notwithstanding every precaution that can be taken, there is a series of disasters—vessels driven ashore, collisions, wrecks—every year. The wind from the south, which is mild and genial in most parts of the world, is in every way detestable along the coast from Cape Horn upwards, and its prevalence at Valparaiso is a serious disadvantage; but the port is so well placed, and it has been so much improved, and provided with such accommodation for shipping and merchandise, that its trade is likely to increase rather than to diminish. Not only the products of Chile, but those of Bolivia and Peru—sugar, wool, guano, nitrates, cotton, minerals of all kinds—find here a convenient outlet. The police of the port is efficacious, the sanitary service excellent, and the shipping expenses are declared by the authorities to be as low as possible; whereat ship captains shake their heads— if they do no worse—and shipowners and merchants are entirely incredulous.

The most serious blow to the rising prosperity of Valparaiso was delivered by the hand of Spain. On 31st March, 1866, the Spanish squadron bombarded the city, effected great ruin, and destroyed property to the amount of 12,000,000 dollars, some say far more.

To guard against a similar visitation the Government have constructed a series of forts at dominant points commanding the bay, named Rancaqua, Talcahuano, Yerbas-Buenas, Valdivia, Bueras, Esmeralda, Covadonga, Andes, Pudeto, and Callao, armed with heavy guns, but the pieces are ancient smooth bores, columbiads, Blakeleys, &c., inadequate to deal with ironclads.

A double line of tramway runs round the city, and an excursion in one of the cars gives the stranger a very pleasant tour and enables him to form a good idea of the place. At certain points there are lifts for the convenience of the suburbs, if so they may be called, perched on the spurs of the hill right above the town.

Many things might be said to the disparagement of Valparaiso—the atrocious pavement of the streets and trottoirs, the exorbitant prices in the shops, the foul purlieus and the drinking dens on the quays; but there is much to admire in the well-conducted hospitals, the charitable and educational institutions, the libraries, schools, and public buildings; the facilities for locomotion, the lighting and police of the streets, the extension of electric lighting and acoustics, the telephone, the tram-car, and the railway.

Some authorities assert that it was named by the founder, Saavedra, in memory of his birthplace in Spain, but Chilians who have taken trouble to inquire into the origin of it are of the opinion that the name was given by the first Spaniards who visited the port in a ship from Peru in September (1543), in the beginning of the spring, when the hills were covered with green and the valley of the Quintil, now the Almendral (Almondry), was in full bloom of flowers and rich vegetation, so that the strangers who had just coasted the dry, brown, waterless shores of the long stretch from the north, struck by the contrast, believed that they were in a very Vale of Paradise.

It would, perhaps, be impertinent to inquire how much

of the present prosperity of the port is due to the foreigners, who constitute to-day an important section of the citizens and inhabitants of the place. There are three iron foundries; whom do they belong to? To "Lever, Murphy, and Company"; to "Harper"; to "Balfour, Lyon, and Company." There are hospitals—English, French, and German. There are also four Chilian establishments, one of which—the Caridad—is very well spoken of. There are four telegraph lines, one, the Transandino, in communication with the Argentine system; another, the American, with the coast towns; another, that of the State, which is under Government; and the fourth, called the Nacional. There are three Chilian newspapers, the *Patria*, the *Union*, the *Mercurio;* an English newspaper, the *Chilian Times;* a German newspaper, the *Deutsche Nachrichten.* There is a crop of clubs, Athletic Sports, Cercle Français, Aleman, Junior, Union, Valparaiso, Iberico, the Literary Society, the Sanger-bund, the Swiss Sharpshooters (Schutzerverein), the Harmonic, German, Deutscher Turnverein, Deutscher Liedernkranz, Cœcittianverein, &c. There are three Protestant churches to make face against nine Catholic churches and seven convents. There are three theatres. There are nine Masonic lodges and, wonderful to say, four lodges of Oddfellows. Here, as in every town of any size in Chile, there is a large fire brigade—no less than eleven companies—in addition to the military garrison quartered in eight barracks in the town and suburbs. Here is centred the administration of the army and navy, subordinate to the Ministers at Santiago, the Commander-in-Chief's office, the headquarters of the Commandant-General of Marine, who is the superior chief of the National Army, and who, moreover, controls all the maritime authorities of the

Republic, a Major-General, the Maritime Governor, a Judge of Commerce, one civil and two criminal judges, a Police Department commanded by a "Sergeant-Major" of the army.

It is difficult to ascertain the number of inhabitants; it varies from 116,000 on the authority of one gentleman, to 180,000 on the less reliable assertion of another. It is certainly an *officina*—the lower part of the town, indeed, is a *cloaca—gentium*. Crimes of violence are, to say the least, not rarer here than in places of the same character in other parts of the world.

When Monsieur Frezier made his remarkable voyage to the Pacific coast of South America he found in every port the visible signs of the enterprise of his countrymen in the form of merchantmen, mostly from St. Malo, flying the flag of France.* The Spaniards were watchful and jealous. They placed every impediment in the way of French commerce and enterprise, but the commercial energy, now almost extinct, which then directed Frenchmen to the new world, both north and south, was so powerful that the governors of the great colonies of Spain on the Pacific coast, were at their wits' end to check the subjects of the French King in their efforts to gain a footing upon it. The situation to-day is changed indeed. As a colonizing and commercial power France has ceased to exercise any considerable influence in this part of the world. She still

---

* Frezier mentions that he found at Talcuhano, in 1713, the *Mary Anne* of Marseilles, Commander Sieur Pipon of Villafranca, and the *Concord*, Sieur Prauclet Daniel, of St. Malo, with booty from Rio, sent by M du Guys' squadron; the *Virgin of Grace* and the *Concord* at Valparaiso, loading corn for Callao, at Arica, a ship of freight, *M de Russy*, at Pisco, the *Princess Conde Martin*, from Emoi, in China, and the *St Margaret* from St Malo, at Callao, two ships of St Malo, and the *Mary Anne* of Marseilles again, and a prize the Sieur Brignon of St Malo sold to the Viceroy for 1,000 pieces of eight. Of course these names are anglicised from the French text.

asserts herself in her own way. Her language is the common vehicle of intercourse among civilised Chilians in all the large towns. French modistes, tailors, shoemakers, perruquiers, hair-cutters, French musicians and dancing masters, French restaurants are in the van, but as merchants and bankers Frenchmen are in the rear. There are some great French commercial houses in the copper and nitrate trades, and in all that decorates life Frenchmen are potent agents, but they have relinquished their grip on the West Coast. In walking through the streets of Valparaiso one sees on the brass plates on the doors, which denote the seats of custom, but few French names. For one French there are three German, and as far as I could judge there are more Germans than there are English; all other nationalities, Italian, Spanish, American together, do not equal, perhaps, either the German or the English. Insurance, life and fire companies, banks, agencies, are largely in the hands of Chilians. Americans like Wheelwright, Meig, and others, have done much for Valparaiso, Chile, and themselves, in railways, public works, and manufacture, but English and Germans, I should think, "hold the fort" and have the largest grasp of the inner life of the country.

It is only natural that the foreign communities in the large towns should generally keep very much to themselves. It is certain that they do so in Valparaiso. There is a German life quite distinct from the English life. The Italians stand apart from both. Perhaps the French do the same. The English Club is not frequented by any but English, and the German Club is used only by Germans. There are English, German, Italian and American doctors with their national *clientèle* There is a Chilian Club very hospitable to strangers. But strangers visit it as rarely as natives visit the clubs of aliens in their midst.

At the exchange, the bourse, and the quay all these gentlemen, foreign and native, meet as business men, but out of business they have generally no relations. It is said that the Germans have a remarkable facility in learning Spanish, and I believe the saying is true. But I have reason to think that the number of Englishmen who marry Chilian women, though it is small, is far greater than the number of Germans who seek wives among the natives of the country. They have their musical reunions, their kneips, and their fire brigades, and as far as they can, they carry about the manners and customs of the Fatherland with them, but they are not quite so prone as the English to marry and settle in the country. English names are borne by men high in the service of the State, and by politicians and landowners the descendants of English, Irish, and Scotch, who married Chilian ladies and settled in the country, and who for the most part, if not always, became intensely Chilian in feeling, and generally adopted the religion of the people.

There is a very well-informed and enterprising public press, with able writers and correspondents, and at a *dejeuner* given to the representatives of the Valparaiso newspapers at the Hotel de France by Colonel North, I made the acquaintance of several gentlemen who were types of the best sort of American journalist. Although the papers represented different shades of Chilian politics and opinion, they all agreed in strong opposition to the Government of the day.

Looking up and down the long table in the *salle-à-manger* I was struck by the intelligent heads, bright expression, and pleasing faces of the company, faultlessly dressed, white-cravated and black-coated. And what a gift of speech these gentlemen had! One after the other they started up, glass in hand, and rolled out in sonorous phrase what they thought it was incumbent upon them to say on the occasion. Words, mere words, perhaps, but finely sounding and ear-catching! How much better, for example, "caballeros" sounds than "gentlemen"? How pleasant it was to be able to recognise old Latin friends under the rich mantle cast over them in a country where it had undergone not ungraceful or inharmonious mutations.

It is in remote places, Cuba, Manilla, &c., that a traveller first learns to appreciate the range and influence of the Spanish language. On the South American Continent it is paramount. With the exception of Brazil, where the younger, and as the Spaniards say, illegitimate, brother of the Castilian, has his way, Spanish is the mother-tongue over the whole Continent of South America, of Central America, in Lower California, and in Mexico.

With the exception of one gentleman on the staff of *La Union*, there was not one of our press friends who spoke English, and very few could converse in French.

It is averred that though the Chilians write Spanish very well, they speak and pronounce it badly; but it would need a practised ear indeed to detect any difference between a Chilian and Peruvian using the same words. Nevertheless, each province over the whole continent has its characteristic phrases and pronunciation. Though the liberty of the Press in Chile is absolute, it is not above the law, and there are ways, it is said, of "nobbling it" known to politicians.

Nothing can be prettier in their way than some of the little *maisons de campagne* of the merchants, built châlet-wise in the midst of gardens which are bevelled out of the side of the rising ground, girdled in with trees, the trelliswork and verandah bright with flowers, haunted by twittering humming-birds, hammocks and easy-chairs outside, and the comforts of home within, a rivulet babbling at the foot of the hill by the boundary hedge, lawn-tennis ground, conservatories Such I saw at Las Sorres, Mr. Berry's "the Foxes" [they actually had a pack of hounds and hunted the Chilian reynards over the worst-looking country that ever lamed horse or dog], and at Mr. Raby's, &c. There is an unuttered emulation I think among the owners in the production of fruit and flowers on the hillsides These are so steep that you see your friends' houses above, or below, as you make your way on a round of visits, and a pedestrian striking down the paths through his neighbour's grounds to the road where the tram-cars to the city bring up, will walk in twenty minutes from point to point, over what a carriage will take three-quarters of an hour to accomplish by road.

Before a visitor can reach one of those pleasant retreats he must pass through several ordeals. I am aware that there are to be found nearer home scenes of misery, squalor, vice and drunkenness, but the purlieus of this city offend every sense at least as much as those of any I have ever seen. They are peopled by a heterogeneous mass, indigenous and foreign. They seem to have come in swarms like insects, carrying with them the débris of rotten tenements, of dust-heaps, deserted slums, rag shops, marine dealers' stores—all kinds of odds and ends of planks, doors, window-frames, pieces of zinc, and corrugated iron, sacking, tiles, iron piping, &c.—to have cast them down on the hill spurs and in the ravines—and to have established their suburbs as they listed, each swarm in its own nook. The inhabitants are various: there are industrious working men for several days till they have earned a few dollars—then laborious drunkards till the money is gone; artificers, muleteers, sailors, boatmen, carmen, loafers—no doubt honest but poor people—swelter in and about these shanties like bees round a hive; flies innumerable, children almost emulating the flies; dust ever rising, ever falling; drinking-shops hemmed in by mules and horses awaiting

A Wayside Inn, Chile.

their riders; men speechless on the road-side or reeling about in the street.

That and the like was what I saw when I went to visit friends whose charming villas, luxuriously furnished, the centres of pleasant gardens fenced in by belts of natural forest, offered a contrast to the suburbs through which I clombe to reach them—clombe is the word—and visitors or the horses must " climb " to reach the recesses of the Foxes or of the Beautiful Retreat, and must, if they be nervous, prepare for disagreeable experiences as they descend to the level of the city on which they look down. I was told on each occasion that what I had witnessed was not to be seen every day, but it was admitted that it might be pretty often—at this season once a week at all events! There was a combination of religious observances and popular fête days at the time, and besides that there was a great mortality among the children, and the Chilians—so I heard again and again—are quite content when their children die, and celebrate the decease by liberal entertainment and carousal.

There is one drawback from the formation of the land which the rich and poor experience in common. It is not inconsiderable. The hills are of red clay, and in many places there is little vegetation to bind the surface. A house or a garden or a shanty settlement now and then will slide down a hill-side or ravine, and tumble in ruin at the bottom, carrying along whatever is in the way. The construction of the poorer edifices offers facilities for such collapse. Many of them are only lath and plaster or adobe (sun-dried brick) whitewashed, roofed with tiles, rushes, or palm-leaves. But botanists find many interesting plants and flowers in the quebradas or ravines, and inland the sides of the "collines" are covered with brush and forest.

CHAPTER VI

"CHILE FOR THE CHILIANS."

The President Balmaceda—Visit to Viña del Mar—An Interview—The President's Policy—The *Esmeralda* Shield—Stud-horses from England—Exchange—The Dollar—Early Intelligence from Europe—The Cable—The Copper Syndicate—The Hôtel de France

SOON after our arrival the President came to stay for a few days at the house of a friend in the pleasant suburb of Viña del Mar, and intimated that he would be glad to receive Colonel North, who was at Valparaiso awaiting his arrival. Señor Balmaceda was on his way to Santiago after the progress through the centres of Chilian life and of European industry and enterprise, in the course of which he had delivered the speeches which, as I have said, had been regarded as the pronunciamientoes of a new policy—"Chile for the Chilians." It was known that Colonel North had come from Europe to solidify and to extend interests, in respect to any increase of which President Balmaceda's programme, as reported, might be taken as adverse. It was not known how far the reports of the President's discourses were correct, but it might be inferred that they were not all accurate, because he had already found it necessary to make a formal correction of, and to explain away, one important passage which had caused serious uneasiness.

On the day named Colonel North, Mr. Spencer, Mr. Prior, and myself went by train to the station of Viña del Mar, where the senior aide-de-camp was in waiting to receive and conduct us to the villa in which the President was lodged. There was no show of sentries at the gate; in the hall there were two officers in undress uniform, by whom we were shown into the boudoir on the ground-floor, where Balmaceda was awaiting his visitors. He is a straight, spare, well-built man, with a keen, finely-cut face—an intellectual forehead, and quick, penetrating eyes—a *mobile* mouth with a subtle little smile, and he has the most easy, charming manner possible, and a cordiality which made us quite at our ease in the *causerie* which ensued. The conversation was carried on in Spanish and English, which Mr. Dawson translated for both sides. The President does not speak any language but Spanish, but he said he understood French. "After compliments," as they say in the translation of Oriental documents, the President declared that he was desirous of giving every facility to the introduction of foreign capital in developing the resources of the country, and the gist of the interview was that he had not the smallest intention of making war on vested interests. He was especially full of praise for the Nitrate Railway, which he had visited at Iquique, and he said "he considered it a complete model of good management and organization."

Colonel North was very much gratified by the assurances of President Balmaceda, and, in view of the interpretation which had been placed on the speeches to which I have alluded, the interview was, in fact, most satisfactory to him. There were, however, signs and tokens that the early declarations of policy respecting the State properties, attributed to Balmaceda, were considered by the press to be the guiding principles of the Government, and that for the future railway extension was to be reserved for the State.

All the papers in Valparaiso were, at the time, in opposition. Each had some particular grief against that particular minister or measure, and called upon the President for redress. Except in the heat of electioneering and party contests, personal attacks on the President are not common —he is smitten through the body of the minister. Ere I had been many days in the country, I had occasion to remark the frequency and number of decrees issuing from the Ministers' bureau signed "Balmaceda," many of them of very great importance. Considering how nearly despotic the President's powers are, there is rather an excess of courtesy than a want of moral courage manifested in the criticism of Government in the Chilian newspapers. Ere I left the country there were signs in the press of a strong feeling that the powers of the President were exercised in a manner, especially in decrees touching expenditure and finance, which trenched upon constitutional rights.

When the *Esmeralda* was sunk off Iquique in the famous action of which the Chilians are so proud, Colonel North conceived the idea of converting the capstan which had been taken out of the wreck into a trophy and of presenting it to the President of the Republic. He had it mounted accordingly by Messrs. Elkington as a shield, with relievos of great artistic excellence representing the incidents of the combat. It was arranged that the President should receive this shield in the name of the State and deposit it in the Hall of the National Assembly at Santiago. The brass top of the capstan is surrounded by a silver border decorated with raised stars, inside which are small discs bearing the names of those who perished in the action of the 21st May, 1879, which date is inscribed at the top of the shield. Four allegorical figures in relief surround the capstan, the centre of which bears the Chilian star, and the words, "Esmeralda—Chile." Below the capstan two figures, "Peace and Prosperity," sustain a shield bearing the names of "Piat—Urribe, Serrano—Sanchez—Wilson—Fernandez—Zegerz—Riquelme, and Hurtado." A replica or two intended for the Municipality of Iquique, &c., were lost in the *Cotopaxi*. Colonel North also brought out from England, in the *Galicia*, to improve the breed of horses, a thorough-bred stallion and a very fine sire of the Cleveland type, purchased from Mr. Burdett-Coutts' stud, which he designed for the public service, and these were later on handed over to the Government at Santiago.

The President was good enough to say to me that when I came to Santiago he would take care that all the information in the possession of the departments of state would be placed at my disposal. "We desire nothing more than the publication of the truth, and are anxious that Chile should be made known to the world as it is."

Excursions, the theatre, correspondence, visiting, and receiving visits, luncheons and banquets, balls and dances, enabled the party to spend a week at Valparaiso without taking much note of time. Every day contact with our mother earth at home was renewed by the electric telegraph, which brought us news of the price of stocks and shares in London and Liverpool, and regulated the rate of exchange.

During the American War I lived for some months "on my exchange," that is, I received so much paper for the gold I brought out that I paid my expenses. It is said that there are people who live on the "exchange" in Valparaiso. But that is quite a different matter. I daresay that a person of ordinary intelligence who applies himself to the subject may come to understand the *rationale* of Chilian exchange. I confess it was beyond me. The results were plain enough, the mode of arriving at them mysterious. One day, I went to a banker to change a circular note of Messrs. Coutts, and I received the equivalent in paper of Chile at the rate of 27½d. to the dollar. A few days afterwards I changed another circular note; the exchange had gone down or up—the dollar was reckoned at something less than 26d. The exchange question, therefore, enters instantly and closely into every business transaction in every town of Chile.

The firm which has early and exclusive intelligence of the rates in Europe holds a trump card, but the arrangements for the daily diffusion of telegraphic intelligence on this head are so good that the general public have, as a rule, as good information as the great merchants. When the paper is posted up in the club there is a great rush. "What is copper? How are nitrates?" and so forth. It was an anxious time. One of the great industries of Chile was threatened with serious harm; the news of the mischief done to the copper market by the operations of the Paris syndicate was most alarming. And the circumstance that it was a French combination which had occasioned so much loss and disturbance did not mitigate the strong expressions which were committed by Germans and English to its doors.

When we had exhausted all the resources of Valparaiso in the way of amusement, and, as far as I was concerned, of information, it was time to proceed to Santiago, where some of the ministers were already in residence to arrange the business which Colonel North had in hand ere we proceeded to the Pampas of Tarapacá So when the customary tribute of sittings to the photographers had been paid, and groups and portraits had been duly ordered and paid for too, we shook the dust—and there was plenty of it—of the Hôtel de France off our feet, and took train for Santiago. I have already alluded to the proprietor of the hotel. The descent of the Assyrian on the Colonel was certainly rude, and when his bill was discharged his cohorts might well be gleaming in purple and gold. Mine host of the Hôtel de France, in reply to an expostulation addressed to him respecting his charges, simply and smilingly observed, "It is not every day I have a Nitrate King and such a party as this in the Hôtel de France." He was quite right perhaps to make the best of it. It is not very likely he will ever get the opportunity again.

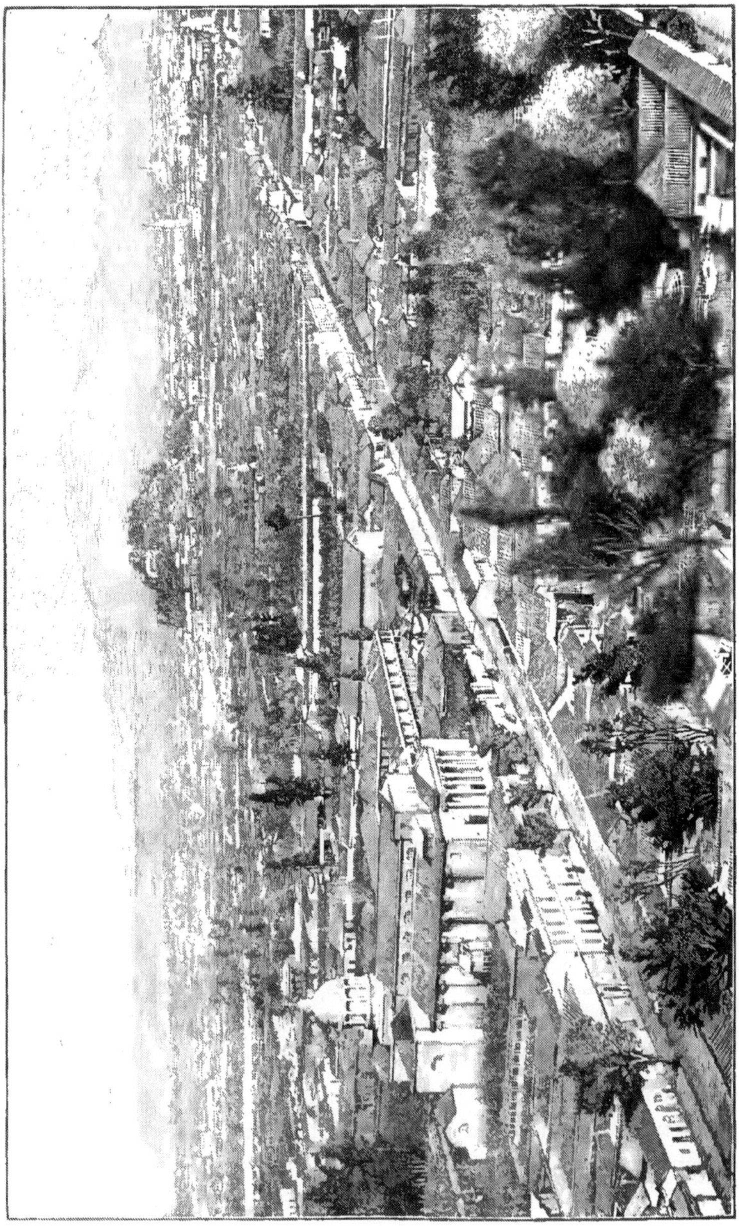

CHAPTER VII.

VALPARAISO TO SANTIAGO

The Railroad to Santiago—The City—The Streets—The Hotel Oddo—The Petitioners—Santa Lucia—Colonel North's Reception by the President The Cousiño Parque—The O'Higgins Statue—Gubler and Cousiño's Brewery — German Machinery — Macul—A Picnic —The Vineyards— The Stud—Macul Wine—The Club—Señor Maciver—The Cauquenes Station—The Drive to the Baths—Giant Cactus—Cauquenes Baths— The Establishment

THE railway from Valparaiso to Santiago, winding for a short distance along the sea-coast, after passing through a rich and well-cultivated country with here and there rocky patches, strikes off to the north-east and east, near the river, by Quillota, once the chief town of Chile, and still famous for its fruits and vines; mounts over water-courses which, in the rocky passes, have the aspect of deep ravines towards the hills; and, climbing up from Llai Llai, boldly ascends the mountain side, which it breasts for miles in a well-engineered, many-curved, and sharply-gradiented line, till it has crossed the outer chain of the Andes, and presently, after four hours' journey, you look out and see below you plains spread out like the sea, hemmed in by another chain of the Cordilleras, and make out the spires and domes of Santiago in the distance.

The city is 187 kilometres from Valparaiso, and the distance was traversed at times at an average rate of 30 kilometres an hour, which seemed quite as fast as was consistent with safety.

When Valdivia laid the foundations of Santiago on

24th February, 1541, he divided the ground into squares, each containing 1,096 toises, a fourth of which he allowed to every citizen; and to protect the infant settlement he built a fort upon the hill of Santa Lucia, which the Indians never ceased to assail for six years, keeping the Spaniards closely besieged and compelling them to live upon loathsome viands and on the little grain they could raise under the cannon of the place. Molina thinks the site and the city injudicious, and that it should have been placed fifteen miles further to the south, on the Maipo.

There were many friends assembled at the station at Santiago to meet Colonel North, and the value of such a mark of their attention could only be appreciated by those who drove from the Railway to the Hôtel Oddo; the jolting is frightful, the fracture of springs and wheels and the breakdown of vehicles constant. There are, no doubt, very considerable difficulties in the way of laying down good street pavement in Santiago; the soil is soft sand; there is no rain for months. The mode of paving in favour with the authorities consists in laying water-worn stones, which are procurable in any number from the bed of the river, round, of course, and about the size of a six-pound shot, on the surface of the ground without any binding. Very naturally they are soon disarranged by the traffic, and in the rainy season terrible sloughs of despond are formed in the very centre of the thoroughfares. There are attempts at the Alameda and in other places to complete a chaussée with cut blocks of granite, and no doubt in the fulness of time the streets of Santiago will be tolerable for man and beast, but now they are very much the reverse.

After the bustle, noise, dust, and the commercial hubbub of Valparaiso, where workmen are busy cutting down mountains and winning back space from the ocean with incessant clamour, where tramcars are for ever rolling and railway trains passing through the streets with funereal toll, the aspect of Santiago was tranquil and, so to speak, gentlemanly or aristocratic. To be sure there were tramcars and omnibuses, but there were also private carriages and many hackney cabs, with well-appointed coachmen, well-dressed crowds in the streets, fine public buildings and private houses.

I will take the liberty of transcribing a few pages from my diary, which have at all events the merit of being the record of impressions formed at the time.

"*March* 28*th*.—As soon as the doors of the hotel were opened, ladies of mournful aspect, their heads wrapped in mantas, some with babies in their arms, filled the corridors and passages, all provided with petitions and supplications for the boundlessly wealthy, generous English Colonel. They have persistence and faith here as well as hope. After breakfast Señor Zegerz, Señor Vergara, and others called, and we drove with them in open carriages to Santa Lucia, a remarkable hill or rock, very much like that upon which Edinburgh Castle is perched, in the suburb rising out of the plain. The place, which is under the guardianship of a committee, is approached by a broad carriage-way, engineered at an easy gradient from the base to the summit of the rock, where the inevitable, but not always unwelcome, Restaurant is erected on a fine plateau. The rock, now the scene of breakfasts, dinners, festive meetings, and dances, and which has moreover an enormous theatre close to the restaurant, has special historical interest for Chilians, as it was the main stronghold of the Spaniards against their implacable enemies the Indians in the early days of Santiago. Where the rock descends sheerly down to the city it is fenced in by walls, at the angles of which are placed absurd little towers, mock fortifications, and gazebos. I never saw a panoramic effect like that which is to be seen from Santa Lucia: you look for the place where the canvas is joined to the foreground. The city is spread at your feet as a map in relief, or on a gigantic chess-board. It was a very fine day, but floating over the Cordilleras, towards the base of which the plain spread like a sea, there were clouds; fortunately they were not compact, and the fleecy veil floating away southwards revealed from time to time the stupendous fronts of the mountain range, and the snow peaks glistening brightly on the horizon.

"A déjeuner which did not remind the visitors in any way that they were in full sight of the Andes rewarded them after their rambles up to the look-out places and round the rock.

"A message from the President, who is back in Santiago, to say he would receive Colonel North to-morrow.

"*March 29th.*—It was decidedly, but not intolerably, hot this morning Under the auspices of Señor Vergara I paid an early visit to the Union Club. A good house, well lighted, commodious rooms, reading-room well provided with newspaper and other literature, surrounding an ample patio, the finest billiard-room I have ever seen, with a great array of tables, six or eight at least, and ample space between. Colonel North, Mr. Dawson, and Mr. Manby, &c., were received by the President, and had a long interview. Señor Balmaceda thinks that the property which Colonel North has bought from a Chilian gentleman—whose right to sell it is disputed by the Government—is worth very much more than it has been arranged to pay for it. At the same time he is very anxious to encourage foreign capitalists to push forward Chilian railways. Señor Zegerz was kind enough to send a charming victoria, with a pair of white Arabs, for our disposal later in the day. It is cruelty to animals to drive over the pavement and tramways of Santiago, so we directed our course to the park which has been given to the city by Madame Cousiño, the Alma Diva of Chile. Passing by the western side of the fine Alameda, we arrested our course to contemplate an egregious statue, which may challenge comparison with any eccentricity in bronze or marble in any part of the world, to Don Bernardo O'Higgins, the hero of the revolution of 1814, the victor at Maipo, the Supreme Director of Chile. No man ever was in greater danger in his life than the hero who is represented on an impossible horse at an angle of 45° tipping over on his rider. I was just reading a biography, which states that his father, Ambrose, was born at Summerhill, County Meath, where he was postillion to Lady Bective; that the lad was sent to Spain, went to Peru as an engineer, fell in love with, but did not wed, the mother of Bernardo, and ultimately became viceroy. It was a relief to find ourselves on the smooth, level roads of the park, with clumps of wood and groves of tropical plants on either side, and glimpses of a little lake winding through shrubberies and gardens, furnished with kiosks and bridges near at hand; and then, looking up, to see, faint and hazy, and, indeed, almost cloud-like, the snowy summits of the Andes. In the evening we went to the Theatre, a very large building, like a bull-ring, boxes almost empty, pit full. The piece was Suppé's *Donna Juanita* ; the *prima donna* was elderly and obese, with a strident voice ; orchestra very fair, choruses noisy ; general result unsatisfactory.

" *March* 30*th.*—Devoted to an excursion to Gubler and

Cousiño's great brewery, six miles outside Santiago, which was followed by a picnic at Macul, the country seat, vineyard, and breeding establishment of the latter. A *cortège*—two breaks, a char-à-banc with French coachman, fine horses, drivers and postillions in livery, provided by our hosts—set forth from the hotel early in the morning. But when we got out of the town and off the pavement, which is bad enough, the dust prevented much enjoyment from the sight of the surrounding country. Teams of oxen, heavy carts, streams of horsemen passing along on the tracks, which it were flattery to call roads, between *adobe* walls, in this rainless season fill the air with wool-like dust. The suburbs are squalid exceedingly; a slattern population, women with black matted locks, many with their heads and jaws bound up, ill-favoured and ill-dressed, with a fierce look in the eye and a defiant air, coffee-coloured children in coffee-coloured rags; a cry of dogs, mongrels of low degree; men lounging about the grogshops; broken windows; ragged poultry skirmishing in the highway or around the common baking-oven of the quarter; kennel-like huts of reeds, lath-and-plaster, patched with bits of corrugated iron and zinc.

"It was pleasant at last to leave the main road, with its vast commerce of waggons and oxen, to find ourselves amidst fields of Indian corn and vines, irrigated by the river Mapocho, which, fed by streams from the Andes, seems to enclose the town in a sweep from the north-east to the south-west.

"Passed the great works on which the Government is engaged for the canalisation of the Mapocho, west of the city. Three thousand men are now combating the floods—at least they are throwing out the fortifications which are to oppose the devastating inroads of the river—now but a network of shallow rivulets threading their way between widespread stretches of stone and shingle—when the snows are melting, an awful flood! We pass the new Orphan Asylum, a fine building, so extensive that one is led to inquire how there can be so many orphans in the city of Santiago.

"In an hour more the *cortège* and cavalcade passed through a gateway into the vast enclosure surrounding the brewery. Gubler and Cousiño brew Pilsener and strong ale, which my thirsty, dusty friends thought as good as Bass's best. Señor Gubler will never become a Chilian equivalent of Lord Burton, nor will Señor Cousiño be ennobled as Lord Macul; but, if making large fortunes and good beer and plenty of it, entitle respectable brewers to patents of nobility, these worthy Chilians are unlucky in being residents in a Republic where the magnates of the maltocracy do not procure seats in the House of Lords, and cannot secure for their children the noble position of hereditary legislators.

" Our friends compete here with the Andes and discount the glaciers of the Cordilleras; they make not only much beer, but supply the city, &c., with ice. The breweries are directed by Germans and Swiss; there are French *employés* and French stud directors. All the machinery is German From these spacious buildings issues the great flood of Gubler and Cousiño's beer which forms deposits in every drinking-shop throughout the republic of Chile. From the brewery, where we halted for nearly an hour, we drove to Macul, an outlying property of some 1,200 acres belonging to the Cousiño family. The farm, which is approached through a fine avenue of elms from the gateway up to the site of a house not yet complete, but with rooms sufficiently furnished to serve as a comfortable summer residence, is very interesting—well wooded and furnished with pens and enclosures for wild animals, aviaries, and a garden and pleasure-grounds, green alleys, the undulating grounds hemmed in by strange forms of vegetation, novel trees, shrubs, plants, osiers, laid out in the Lota style with artificial rockeries and labyrinths, ponds, and lakelets, girt with tropical vegetation—Kew in the open air—all very pleasant, through which we sauntered till déjeuner was announced.

"In a natural *salon* of magnificent fig-trees draped with flags a table was spread for a liberal repast, where the delicious white wine of Macul, like a full red Burgundy, made on the spot, refreshed and prepared us for a long defilade of English and French stallions of race, Normandy percherons and Clydesdales led by English and French grooms. These were followed by a train of admirable native horses—well-made, spirited little beasts—and then there was a procession of famous bulls bought at great price from England and France. Next we went off on a visit of inspection to the vineyard—one enormous field, a sea of vines with streamlets of clear water running through it—where men and women were busy loading tram cars with masses of grapes on the iron way running from the fields to the crushing vats, for the presses. Nearly all the wine that is made in this enormous establishment is sold at good prices in Chile; very little, if any, finds its way to Europe. Señor Cousiño said it would bear transport well, as had been proved by the dispatch of consignments to France. The inevitable photographer came on the scene and had a shot at us just as we were departing. After spending a delightful day at Macul we were driven back to Santiago as we had set out, and arrived at the Hotel Oddo rather tired, but much indebted to Messrs. Gubler and Cousiño, the most attentive and agreeable of hosts, for the excursion.

"*March* 31*st.*—I woke up with a start! Rattle! Rattle! Rattle! The windows shaking, the glasses on the wash-

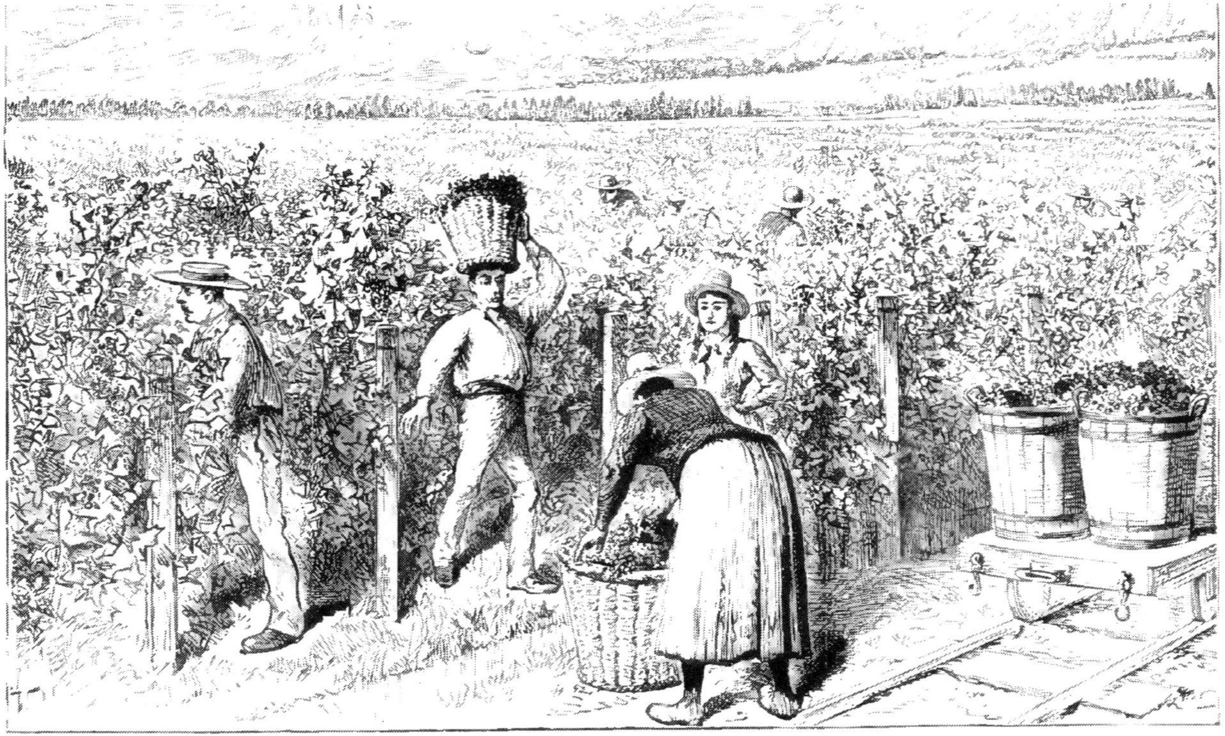

hand-stand clinking—the very room trembling: a sound like the rumbling of an underground train. The dresses which were hanging up against the wall were waving. It was over in a few seconds 'This is a good one, indeed,' said Mrs. Russell, with the air of a connoisseur in earthquakes—only a little frightened perhaps· 'I knew it would awake you!' All was still at once. It was six o'clock. When I went in to breakfast I was told only one of the party had felt it The landlord said it was 'only a *temblor.*' Only! It was an earthquake! Went to the club where the news of the wreck of the U.S N. *Trenton, Vandalia,* and *Nipsie;* of the *Olga, Adler,* and *Eber,* Imperial German Navy, in a hurricane at Samoa, and of the escape of H.M S. *Calliope* had just arrived. 'Ah!' said a Chilian gentleman, 'you see after all we are the best sailors in the world! We and the English.' He spoke with conviction. Another gentleman observed that he thought it was a proper rebuke to the European powers for interfering with matters so far away from home. In the afternoon the ladies borrowed *mantas* from some friends and went to the Cathedral. They were late for High Mass and for the imposing religious ceremonies which they expected to see, though I daresay they were much admired by the congregation, for they looked very well in the universal Sunday head-dress, but they were not much edified.

"*April 3rd.*—A banquet to Colonel North and his friends at the Union Club, given by Señor Maciver, one of the leading politicians of the very composite Opposition. He is not a violent party man, but, as he is a strenuous Republican and advanced Liberal, he is opposed to the policy of the Government which appears to him to favour Conservative, or aristocratic, reaction. He is an able speaker, but his ancestors would not understand a word he uttered, for he has lost all touch with the ancient clan in the western Highland, of which I told him some interesting auld-world stories, derived from personal acquaintance with its members.

"The dinner was excellent—deputies, ex-ministers, Señor Martinez, once envoy to London, &c.; many speeches and much cordiality."

The days passed very pleasantly at Santiago, although there was not much to see, or to do, as far as we were concerned. We visited churches, the House of Representatives —a very fine building, with a chamber which puts to shame our "House" at home—sat in the Plaza listening to the band, and prowled about the shops, and so the time wore on.

I would have willingly remained at Santiago, though it was not "the season," a circumstance which is important to fashionable natives, but which does not concern foreign visitors to a great city. Americans generally select the time when there is "nobody in London" for their descent on our capital, just as English people go to Paris, Rome, Berlin, and Vienna, when these cities are deserted by all who can afford to leave them. But it was a duty to make an excursion to the Baths of Cauquenes, one of the institutions of Chile. So, on April 5th, at nine o'clock A M., our party left Santiago for a resort of which, I am not ashamed to say, I had never heard in my life.

The Chile Euston is very commodious. The ample roof over the offices and platforms, supported on lofty columns, is well provided with all the European accessories— passages, waiting-rooms, the usual departmental bureaux, not forgetting the weighing-machines, where the travellers' baggage is gauged as accurately as if he were going from

London to Paris. There is a very animated scene on the arrival and departure of the trains. The majority of the crowd may be country people—the men in ponchoes of many hues, sombreroed, heavily booted and spurred; the women in the long, loose, and bright-coloured dresses which they affect when they leave off the city *manta*. The platforms are open to all the world, the *salle d'attente* being a development of civilization which would only be tolerated in a few favoured countries. As a race they are a bundleiferous people, next to the Maltese and Hindostanees, more addicted to carrying shapeless bags and sacks than any I know. The migratory disposition of the Chilians yields rich returns to the railway companies.

As the Americans were the original promoters of railway enterprise in Chile, it is natural that the cars should be on the American principle, and that an American express agency should take charge of the passengers' baggage. We were installed in a handsome and commodious carriage called "La Esmeralda," in which nothing was wanting to comfort and even luxury.

Emerging from the suburbs of Santiago, the line strikes across the great plain which, well irrigated by runnels from the Maipo, spreads to the foot of the Andes. The vast fields were rich with crops of maize and vines, also with prodigious forests of thistles, busily engaged in propagating their species by sending out seed on the wings of the wind all over the country. There is a story that the thistle was unknown in Chile till a Scotchman imported it "for love," but that is of course untrue. The plant is indigenous. It thrives in a fashion that would excite the admiration of a Sutherland crofter. There were on each side of us pasture lands where horses, herds of cattle, and flocks of sheep were enjoying themselves in the expanse of vineyards, cornfields, and thistles. Poplars and *eucalyptus* screened the villages, and clouds of dust from the hoofs of oxen and the ambling cavalcades of mounted travellers marked the course of the roads.

The line runs in the valley between the sierra or ridge of the outer chain, which lies generally at some distance from the sea, and the inner chain of the Andes, most charming glimpses of which were revealed to us through the cloudy mist on their slopes.

At one place the two mountain chains approach so closely that there is only just room for the line on the margin of the moraine-like bank of the river which, compressed between great boulders, rushes impetuously towards the sea. Then the mountains open out again, and the plain spreads once more into an expanse of cultivated fields. It is obvious that more ground could be cleared and tilled than there is if there were hands to do it. Narrow as the strip of country is between the Cordilleras and the ocean there is but a scanty population. The men and women working in the fields—and there are less of the former than of the latter—are a fine, strong-limbed race, but there are few boys or girls to be seen, and there is reason to think that the accounts of the indifference—and worse—of parents to their children's health—nay, life itself—are in some measure well founded, though they have no burial clubs or children's insurance companies to reward their neglect.

At the various stations groups of people were invariably waiting for friends or for places—idlers for whom the arrival of the train was the event of the morning; women and boys with fruit, bread, milk, and water to sell, saddle horses tied up to the trees, and country conveyances to order or for hire; there was also, be it observed, full information for the stranger on every station wall—the name of the place, the distance from Santiago, the distance from the next large town, the fares. And there were telegraph offices. And, mark this! letter-boxes!

Beyond the pleasant village of San Bernardo, where Barros Arana, the learned and modest historian of Chile, resides, the plain expands in spreading folds of green, and rejoices in many well-cultivated fields studded with villas and houses. Presently we come to the valley where the Maipo brawls over its stony bed, which is marked by rocks

A Railway Station.

and boulders invading the fields on both sides, in channels now quite dry.

At Buin, the chief town of a district the natives of which gained a high reputation for bravery in the field during the war, there was a gathering on the platform to bid good-bye to a young married couple. The name on the luggage of the bridegroom, who was in uniform, suggested an Irish origin, but the owner could not speak either Irish or English. It was only the other day I observed in the list of successful candidates for the naval school, published by a Chilian crammer, the names of Tito McSorley, Daniele Stuardo, Patricio Morgan, O. Urquhart, Hen. Jones, S. Sykes, Wilson, Barry; but, as I have observed, the descendants of British subjects in Chile are *Chilenis ipsis Chileniores.*

It is said that the line to Cauquenes, which is connected near the station of Hospital (47 kilometres from Santiago) with the line from Concepçion, is expensively laid out and badly engineered, and there are various tales of the mistakes of the makers told by the natives, but I am bound to say that the former have at all events given Chile a most picturesque and interesting route.

There was a good, if rather garlicky breakfast served at Rancagua, where Darwin slept the first night of his two days' expedition from Santiago to Cauquenes — we had traversed the distance in three-and-a-half hours. A run of less than an hour more brought us to the end of our railway journey at Cauquenes Station—several hours distant from the baths. In the yard outside the station Dr Espejo, the proprietor and doctor of the Baths, awaited us with all the resources of the establishment—a light caleche with two horses—a wagonette with four horses (abreast), a coach on high wheels and old-fashioned springs drawn by four horses in the same fashion, and a carriage for the luggage—just sufficient for the party.

The doctor—driving like Jehu, the son of Nimshi—led the way, and the Chilian coachmen, whose skill and nerve we had occasion to admire with an awful joy, as we were bumped and thumped in our bounding vehicles, were worthy of their leader. Despite dreadful bumps and jolts, the drive from the station to the baths was charming. The general direction is indicated by the course of the Cachapoal, which rages furiously in the stony bed it has torn through the Andes amid gigantic boulders, or flows placidly in broad streams over the shingle in the valleys, which are marked by the devastation of its floods. For some miles indeed there was a good highway through cultivated fields.

In some places the much-pebbled rutty track, here and there provided with mud holes, and occasionally traversed by little streams, ran close to the river bank, and we looked down on the torrent one hundred feet below with speculative anxiety; then it would take us down a steep descent to the bed of the Cachapoal, and again climb boldly up the face of the mountain. But when the travellers could bestow their attention on the landscape they were rewarded by its ever-varying beauty—grandeur, perhaps, would be too "big" a word to apply to the scenery—till we were near our destination. Then the Andes stretched out giant arms to meet us. The valley deepened, and there were now and then glimpses of snow patches through rifts in the mountain chain, but there was nothing "towering" or grand—no awful cliff like the Gemmi, or fearful ravine like that of the Tête Noire.

Many men and some women passed on horseback, the former in the universal poncho, for which so many merits are claimed by the wearers, without the mention of the greatest of all, the picturesque look of the bright-hued blanket, deep seated in their saddles on the ambling steeds which seemed in no need of a touch of the tremendous-looking rowels on the massive spurs; the latter, coarse-haired, swarthy ladies, without charm of face, figure or costume, riding in pillion or *en amazone*. A hardy oak laden with acorns was common by the roadside, and the hill-tops were guarded by cactuses of the "candlestick species," which were infested by a parasite which bursts into a scarlet flower, like a sponge full of blood.

Twice did we meet small processions of ox waggons laden with wood or rushes for thatching. Pedestrians there were none, save a fatuous and very ugly mendicant at the

Giant Cactus.

village of Cauquenes, who informed us he was 120 years old.

At a store of the American type, modified to suit Chilian requirements, we changed horses. One of the party of an inquisitive turn—*sicut ejus est mos!* came on piles of English books in one of the rooms, and on asking whose they were, was answered by a quiet bearded gentleman whom he took to be a native, "Mine." The owner proved to be Mr. Reed, a well-known English naturalist who had been professor of natural history to the Naval School at

Valparaiso, and who is still a collector of birds, beasts, butterflies, &c., the present proprietor of the storehouse.

The baggage carriage came to a halt later on, owing to the collapse of one of the horses. The driver unharnessed another of the team, mounted it, cantered up to some horses grazing in a field near the road, and lassoing one of the most likely, put it into the harness of the disabled animal, which was turned adrift to the doubtful pleasure of liberty. After a good deal of flogging he induced the captive to take up the running, but it was in a very riotous spirit.

The evening was drawing on as we came in sight of the white walls of the Baths nearly buried in trees, on a cliff overhanging the river. Some of the guests were assembled to inspect the new arrivals on the rocks outside, inscribed with names in black, red, and white paint. There was a gate, a gateway, with a slough on one side, an avenue of trees, and a road up to the courtyard, and the squares of single-storeyed buildings which formed the *establecimiento termal.*

"The buildings," says Darwin, speaking of his visit to Cauquenes, "consist of a square of miserable little hovels, each with a single table and bench." They certainly do not answer that description to-day, but the establishment does in some respects fall far short of the requirements of civilized life. The outer court, which is surrounded by coach-houses and stables, and accommodation for "the hands," is littered with refuse, amid which pigs and poultry hold high festival; a portal opens on a passage to the quadrangle, where are the office of the establishment, a store, and a telegraph-office whence messages can be sent all over the world. A paved and tiled walk runs in front of the one-storeyed rooms, the doors and the windows looking out on a garden with a fountain in the centre. The walk is covered in, and a verandah clothed with creepers and vines affords shade from the sun.

In one side of this quadrangle, which is intended for boarders who cannot afford the higher priced rooms, there is an archway, to a wide flight of steps to the spacious bath rooms—those on the right for ladies, and those on the left for gentlemen. There is an ample swimming bath, broad and deep, with suitable chambers for the bathers. Portraits of the most famous physicians of Europe and America decorate the walls of the hall—the names are painted underneath for identification—amongst them not one English. The baths are marble, the usual apparatus of pipes, cocks and taps is not wanting.* The water is served piping hot and tempered down as may be desired. Another passage leads to a similar quadrangle, of which three sides are occupied by rooms, the fourth being formed by a low hedge-row, fencing the garden from the cliff, below which foams the Cachapoal. The dinner saloons, billiard-room and kitchens are off the outer quadrangle. There is a reading-room and a drawing-room for ladies, with piano, &c. The bedrooms were not luxuriously furnished, but there was no want of beds, chairs, glasses, tables and wardrobes, and if Chilian servants could be taught the most rudimentary principles of tidiness and cleanliness, visitors to Cauquenes would have no reason to complain. Except the raw material for boiled and roast (often raw also), all edibles must be brought to the hotel; there is a country-made wine used at table, which Chilians can and do drink, and Santiago Pilsener is abundant. A German who preceded the present master managed to keep the grounds and rooms in good order, but the domestics now

* See note, Appendix

use the angles of the garden as slop-basins, and throw the dirty water from tubs and basins, as well as waste paper, vegetables, &c , into them. Presently there will be electric lights in the public apartments, and bedrooms, and the baths, garden, and in the promenades, in the pleasure ground or park, which is gained by a suspension bridge thrown across a deep ravine, through which a small tributary runs to join the Cachapoal. Darwin in his "Naturalist's Voyage round the World" (p. 263, New Edition, 1870), says:—

"The mineral springs of Cauquenes burst forth on a line of dislocation, crossing a mass of stratified rock, the whole of which betrays the action of heat. A considerable quantity of gas is continually escaping from the same orifices with the water. Though the springs are only a few yards apart they have very different temperatures, and this appears to be the result of an unequal mixture of cold water, for those with the lowest temperature have scarcely any mineral taste. After the great earthquake of 1822 the springs ceased and the water did not return for nearly a year. They were also much affected by the earthquake of 1835, the temperature being suddenly changed from 118° to 92°. It seems probable that mineral waters, rising deep from the bowels of the earth, would always be more deranged by subterranean disturbances than those nearer the surface. The man who had charge of the baths assured me that in summer the water is hotter and more plentiful than in winter. The former circumstance I should have expected from the less mixture, during the dry season, of cold water; but the latter statement appears very strange and contradictory The periodical increase during the summer when rain never falls can, I think, only be accounted for by the melting of the snow, yet the mountains which are covered by snow during that season are three or four leagues distant from the springs. I have no reason to doubt the accuracy of my informer who, having lived on the spot for several years, ought to be well acquainted with the circumstance, which, if true, certainly is very curious, for we must suppose that the snow-water, being conducted through porous strata to the regions of heat, is again thrown up to the surface by the line of dislocated and injected rocks at Cauquenes; and the regularity of the phenomenon would seem to indicate that in this district heated rock occurred at a depth not very great."

The waters contain chloride of calcium and of sodium, a trace of chloride of magnesia, sulphate of lime, sesquioxide of iron and alumina and of silex, bromide of magnesia, chloride of potass, &c. According to the guide book, and the advertisements, they are most potent in rheumatism, throat affections, and eczema—in fact, in most of the ills that flesh is heir to or that it acquires for itself. Although there was nothing in particular the matter with me, to pass the time I took one of the mineral baths every day, and was none the worse for it. There were many people at the establishment, and at night there was music and dancing in the salons, but no gambling or, as far as I saw, any cards.*

* See note, Appendix.

CHAPTER VIII.

BATHS OF CAUQUENES.

A Chilian Carlsbad—Señor Soto—Mr Reed—The Corral—The Vaquero-Lassoing—The Samacuecca—Chilian Horsemen—An Equestrian People—Humming Birds—The Valley of the Cachapoal—A Picnic of Two—Farewell to Cauquenes

IN this Chilian Carlsbad we passed a week, making those excursions which are supposed to be necessary in such resorts, lest life should pass too peacefully—to have a picnic at one place, to see a fine view from another. The English and the Chilians soon after our arrival organized a fête champetre at a romantic spot near the village of Cauquenes. Supplies of provisions were sent on in advance. The visitors set out in country carts, into which beds and cushions were placed to ease the jolting. Each waggon was drawn by six oxen, which went at a fair trot. The men took their guns in expectation of sport, and got a few partridges. The natives and the strangers fraternized most warmly, and song and dance wound up the pleasures of the day—indeed the people we met in our travels always seemed ready to join in any junketing in their way.

The proprietor of a large estate in the neighbourhood, Señor Soto, whose brother was at the picnic, invited the strangers to come over to witness the herding and lassoing of cattle, of which he owns many thousands, and to give us an insight into Chilian country life, and the following day we set out from the hotel on wheels and horseback accordingly. As our *cortège*, enveloped in the inevitable dust, after an hour's drive, came in sight of a plain in which there was a large lake fringed deeply with bulrushes, thirty or forty horsemen emerged from the cover of a wood, with loud cries, and galloped in single file towards a long wall, above which we could distinguish a forest of horns. These cowherds, or *vaqueros*, managing their spirited, active, little horses with perfect skill and ease—every man with a lasso on his saddle bow—wore many-coloured *ponchos*, and were dressed with sashes round their waists, short jackets, big boots or many buckled gaiters, and heavy spurs, in a picturesque fashion. Señor Soto and Mr Reed, the naturalist and owner of the English books we had seen at the store house in the village, were awaiting our arrival. Señor Soto has travelled much, is well read, and speaks several languages; and as his estates adjoin the road to the much-frequented baths of Cauquenes, he is in constant touch with the world, living, it is true, somewhat apart from it, content with the management of his flocks and herds—the horses in the plain and the cattle on the hills.* He wished first to show how the *vaqueros* separated any particular animal from the herd, and how the cattle—all but wild, as they were driven in from the mountains where they pastured—were coralled—driven into enclosures, surrounded by walls of adobe, to be branded and marked or to be picked out for dispatch to the market towns. The manner in which a couple of *vaqueros* riding into a corral, among a herd of half-wild animals, managed to extricate, so to speak, from the agitated herd any one animal which we indicated was a triumph of united action of man and horse, for the two

* Señor Soto has good cattle—1,150 horses on feed These are tended by 190 *vaqueros* Each of these has two acres of land to cultivate, and is paid wages for his work There are 500 families on the estate There are also many thousands of sheep on the farm

worked together—the horsemen pressing their way through the herd, keeping one at each side of their victim till it was, after repeated attempts to get away, headed and forced out of the corral. But they were not always successful at the first attempt, and the other *vaqueros*, who were drawn up in line like a wall, to prevent the animals breaking through, enjoyed the failure. The work was accompanied by considerable shouting * Man and horse are to the manner born; there cannot be a finer raw material for cavalry than the Chilian peasantry in the world.

Then we rode to a knoll, wooded at the base, commanding a view of the plain and of the marsh, over which flocks of divers and duck were wheeling and rising out of the tall reeds, but, as our sportsmen found, inaccessible to shot Among the beds men, deep in mud and water, were cutting and stacking the reeds, which are now fit for the market. They are most valuable in a country where walls and houses are constructed of reeds, plastered; and we met many ox carts laden with piles of them from Señor Soto's lake.

In the plains there were herds of wild-looking cattle at pasture, and *vaqueros* were sent down to lasso the runaway cattle of different tempers—some resisting passively, others fiercely and actively, when caught by horn or heel at discretion. The operation has been often described, but to understand the precision of eye and hand, the judgment of distance and of speed, and the neatness of it, one must see it in practice. When many illustrations of the skill of the accomplished cowherds had been given we had an exhibition of their cleverness in collecting or dividing the herds

Luncheon in a shed on the hill followed, and then two women, one rather good-looking, and aware of the fact,

* See note, Appendix.

and both attired in European fashion, who were seated outside, guitar in hand, sang middling well two or three songs over and over again, and presently the song was hushed, and gave place to the dance—the Samacuecca, the very pretty and characteristic dance which English people call "the quaker," for a description of which see everyone's travels *passim*.

I asked a friend "if there was a house on the estate?" for I could not understand why we were entertained in a barn. "Yes, of course! Señor Soto lives there." "I suppose it's a long way off?" "No! not at all." "I wonder why he does not invite us there?" "Hush, it's never done in Chili—at least, most rarely—and probably the family are not at home." Our host, with an escort of *vaqueros*—galloping madly in clouds of dust, accompanied our party back to Cauquenes, and whilst the horses were resting at the village the Chilian horsemen amused themselves and us by playing at "barriers." The game is played by two men or two parties who strive to force their horses, jammed as close as they can go against a wall or a fence, inside those of the other side. The horses enter into the sport, and it was delightful to watch one clever little mare putting her head below her rival's neck, and then prizing her head up, to win the victory for her rider. The champion in these games was a picturesque and dirty old fellow, who said he was seventy, and looked more, but who danced the "quaker" as well as anybody. He had his horse in perfect control, and though he was nearly unhorsed in one violent scrimmage, recovered his seat gallantly.

In England we are too apt, because our squires and farmers are fond of hunting and our breed of horses is unrivalled, to consider ourselves an exclusively equestrian people, but the ordinary English peasant or labourer knows as much of a horse as a horse knows of him, and we are not to suppose that because immense crowds scream themselves hoarse at the Derby or the St. Leger that we are all Centaurs In Chile the population generally lives in the saddle, and in such a country these horsemen ought to be invincible under good leaders, and they proved that they had courage as well as skill before Lima.

By the time we entered the avenue of the Baths after a break-neck drive down and up and across rivulets and over river beds, very much pleased and very tired, with many kind recollections of Señor Soto's reception, it was late at night. There was, nevertheless, a ball in the hotel *salon* to wind up our pleasures.

"*April* 9*th* —A fall of snow in the night! The hills and the ground were clothed in white. The sun presently peered over the hill tops into the valley, and soon the thaw filled the tiny rivulet outside our quadrangle, and made the ground sloppy. Our friend the bold humming-bird very active about the clematis this morning; I fancy he knows us.* He sits on a dry twig close at hand and takes no notice of me or of my wife, but if anyone else appears on the verandah he is off at once.

"*April* 10*th*.—A delightful drive, *solus cum soli*, up a steep mountain road to a point some eight miles distant and 2,000 feet higher than the baths, whence is seen a profound valley, issuing through which the Cachapoal, joined by a tributary from the giant Andes which tower in front of us, rushes over its stony bed far below. The scene was very peaceful and pretty, but in the depths of winter the place must be an awful solitude.

* See note, Appendix.

"The bark of the shepherds' dogs reached us from the depths. Overhead soared in easy graceful sweeps a couple of condors, pretty finches to me unknown, and larger birds of the thrush kind hopped and fed near at hand, and all around among the rocks enormous cactus with blood-red parasite flowers reared their eccentric stems and bulbous branches. The snow peaks are visible as far as we can see

Leaving Cauquenes—General Baquedano, Colonel North, &c.

in serried lines. There are passes to our right which are used by the natives, and one of which in Darwin's time, or a short time before, was the route by which Pincheira, the robber leader of a band of Araucanian Indians and half-castes, was wont to descend on the estancias for plunder and murder. We had passed two of these farm-houses on our way, and there was one down at our feet embowered in trees with pasture and cultivated fields—the last up the valley.

"Opened our baskets and lunched, and so home, where the indefatigable Colonel was busy in arranging for more festivities to wind up our visit to Cauquenes. Our dinner was a triumph of an expectant *chef*. A farewell dance and

Country Carts.

supper in the evening. Europeans and Chilians fraternized once more, and Colonel North paid the piper. General Baquedano, the Commander-in-Chief of the Chilian army, bracing himself up for his impending visit as chief of a military commission to Europe, arrived, and joined the evening party."

CHAPTER IX.

SANTIAGO ONCE MORE.

Return to Santiago—President Balmaceda—St Dominic—The Cemetery—The Holocaust of the Campaña—Banquet at Valparaiso—Mr Woodsend—The *Cotopaxi*—Hotel Colon—Difficulties—A Manta Difficulty—Don Luis Zegers—St. Vincent da Paulo—The University—The Esmeralda Shield—The Stud Horses

On the 12th the party returned from Cauquenes to our old quarters, the Hotel Oddo, at Santiago, where we remained till the evening of 20th March. Once more a few leaves from my diary will give my readers an idea of our lives and of the incidents of the time.

"*April 14th.*—*Domingo de los Ramos.* President Balmaceda—in evening dress, ministers ditto—opened the New School of Medicine in state. Three open carriages, drawn by fine horses, a well-mounted escort of fifty cavalry of the Guard, equipped exactly like French hussars, a capital brass band in front. Some of our party who went to look on were invited by the President very courteously into the hall, and seated near him.

"*April 15th.*—Went out with my wife and spent the day visiting sights, under the auspices of a Chilian gentleman. The Church of St. Dominic not yet finished, simple and grand, fine proportions, very noble marble columns, pictures on the walls covered (I'm glad to say) with crape. To the Cemetery, a vast necropolis, a forest of marble sepulchres neatly kept, the walks bordered with orange trees in full bearing The quarter assigned to the remains of the upper ten thousand abounds in instances of lavish expenditure not always in good taste. I should think there are hundreds of tons of the finest Carrara marble devoted to the glorification of the living and to the memory of the dead. Some of the inscriptions were curious; over the door of one tomb was engraved, " *Casa de la Union por los restos de la famiglia*

The Manta.

Delpuente." O'Higgins and other heroes of the War of Independence and of the later war with Peru, some known only to their own countrymen, repose among many less famous people.* The memory of Matthey is perpetuated by a quasi-Egyptian edifice of great size, with a nymph at each side of the portal, sphinxes, the winged globe, &c., a strange conglomerate. There are reserves of burial-ground for the various nationalities, notably the Italian. In con-

* See Note, Appendix.

trast to the ostentatious monumentation of these caballeros, may be seen close at hand in the same ground the humble graves of the forgotten poor, uncared for and unnamed. The two thousand three hundred victims of the dreadful holocaust in the Campaña, the ancient Church of the Jesuits, twenty-six years ago (that inflicted a lasting stigma on the whole body of the clergy in the popular mind because of the selfish cowardice of a few), lie together in a great trench, near which a column records their fate. I hear it is intended to erect a suitable memorial to the innominate dead, whose fate filled Chile with so much mourning, and was justly regarded as a national calamity. The Campañia has been closed ever since.

"*April* 16*th*.—Yet another function! It was a veritable struggle for the weaker vessels to get off by the 6.45 to the Woodsend dinner to Colonel North and his friends at Valparaiso. Train stops at 10 at Llai-Llai for breakfast. 'How,' asked a wondering cockney, 'can this place be called Yay Yay? Its name is spelt with two hells, a hay, and a hi.' Valparaiso at 1 o'clock. The dinner took place at the Union Club, in a room adorned with flags, the table covered with exquisite flowers. It was very successful, the English colony mustered in force, and late into the night there were toasts and speeches. The chairman and giver of the feast, Mr. Woodsend, one of the foremost merchants of Valparaiso, dwelt with feeling and force on the career and work on the West Coast of the guest of the evening, and on the results they had all experienced from his energy and enterprise, and Colonel North made a characteristic speech in acknowledging the toast and in returning thanks for the ovation he had received from his countrymen.

"There was only one cloud over the enjoyment of the

evening, but it was heavy indeed. The *Cotopaxi*, one of the finest of the fleet of the P. S. N. C., was long overdue from Europe, and reports which had reached Valparaiso of her having been in collision, &c., in the Straits of Magellan, were very disquieting The daughter of Mr. Lyon, the vice-chairman, and relatives or friends of nearly every one of the company at table were on board the vessel.*

" Long before the dinner was over the last train had left, and we had to sleep in Valparaiso. We put up at the Hotel Colon, in the main street, for the night.

" *April 17th.*—The landlord, Karl Beinhardt, very indignant when I asked, naturally enough, if he was a German. The possibilities, judging from his name, were that he was a Jew of Alsace. '*Allemand! comment donc? Non, monsieur! Je suis Breton! je suis le B r e-r-r-eton des Bretons!*' Anyway an excellent host. He told me he was the great Sarah's uncle, '*une gloire pour la France! une honte pour sa famille!*' After the experience of the Hotel de France, it was quite a surprise to the Paymaster-General to have a moderate bill to discharge when we were leaving.

" Up again at 6.45 o'clock A.M., and walked to Station. Train at 8 o'clock back to Santiago. Arrived at Hotel Oddo at half-past one o'clock Legal difficulties in connection with the title to the nitrate fields at Las Lagunas, which Colonel North has bought, are spoken of The Government questions the validity of the title of the owner.

" *April 18th.*—(Our Maunday Thursday). Universal holiday in Santiago. The strictness which formerly characterised the observance of Passion Week has yielded to secular

---

* News of the total loss of the *Cotopaxi* was received soon afterwards. Fortunately no lives were lost, and great credit was given to the captain for the coolness and conduct he exhibited both on the occasion of the collision which preceded the wreck, and on her foundering in the Straits of Magellan subsequently

influences now that the Church has lost its power in the land. Shops, except confectioners' and 'sweets' sellers', shut, but the people were not all dressed in black as of yore, and the coaches and tramway carriages ran as usual. Our ladies in mantas, borrowed from friends for the occasion, went to the Cathedral, which was crowded. The doors were never shut, service was going on and people were passing in and out incessantly all day, so that there was neither silence nor repose within the sacred edifice.

"*Good Friday*.—I came back from my morning visit to the club to the hotel at noon; I found my wife at home with a troubled air. When I left her in the morning she was going to Mass at the Cathedral, and not having a manta she thought it would answer as well to wear a black bonnet, veil, and shawl. She entered the Cathedral and knelt down quietly in a nook near the entrance to pray. She was dressed entirely in black. Presently she was touched on the arm, and looking up she saw a man in priest's vestments who pointed to the door and made signs that she must leave the church; he left no room for doubt about his meaning, for he caught her by the shoulder as if to turn her out. She shook off his hand and walked to the door, the priest by her side gabbling about 'manta.' My wife was very indignant. So was I. I was going to write to the Archbishop, who is said to be enlightened, but my wife persuaded me not to take the trouble, and perhaps she knew best. We resolved to say nothing about it to our friends.

"*April 20th*.—Don Luis Zegers, Professor of Physics, &c., at the University, called, and took me to the Escuela de Medecina, inaugurated by the President last Sunday. The building is imposing—with a fine portico and pillared frontage, which must have cost a large sum of money, spacious quadrangled courts or patios, lecture-rooms, professors' apartments, worthy of an institution which would do honour to any capital. There are thirty professorships, and when the school opens there will be six hundred students in attendance, but at present it is out of session and the lecture and demonstration rooms are empty.

"Thence we went to the Hospital of St. Vincent da Paulo, the walls of which abut on those of the Escuela, and were rewarded by the inspection of one of the best managed, sweetest, and cleanest establishments of the sort I have ever seen, and they are very many.

"Originally intended only for soldiers, the Hospital has been enlarged, and there are now beds for 600 patients for all classes. The rooms are on the ground floor, looking out on square courts, with flower beds, shaded by trees, oranges, &c. The Sisters, who seem to have the control and care of the staff of assistants and of the patients, full of zeal and work, moved about noiselessly, and evidently exulted in showing the results to a stranger, 'aiblins a heretic,' like myself. This and the four other hospitals in Santiago are maintained by a Board of Charities, which owns large estates and has other sources of revenue. I spent an hour most instructively, and I left with the conviction that in no city in the world could the sick and wounded be more tenderly or skilfully cared for than in the Hospital of St. Vincent da Paulo in Santiago.

"Next my good young Mentor took his elderly Telemachus to the University on the Alameda. It is a plain, uninteresting edifice. I was much interested in Señor Zegers' perfect installation, comprising the newest work of the best makers of Europe in electrical, astronomical, and chemical, &c , apparatus in all their various branches, on a most liberal scale, for the instruction of the students in physical science. Signor Zegers is a young man; he has studied under the most celebrated physicists of France and England, and it may be predicted that he will add to the reputation he has already acquired as one of the most instructed of the band of learned and accomplished men who are preparing the Chilians for the place they must fill in South America as the leading nation on the Continent."

Before we left Santiago Colonel North, at a formal audience, delivered the Esmeralda shield to the charge of the President, who took charge of it on behalf of the State. He also gave over the two sires—the coach-horse stallion, "Captain Cook 2nd," and the hackney stallion "Copenhagen," from the Brookfield stud—which he had brought out from England for the improvement of the native breed of horses, to the State breeding establishment. The proposals he submitted to the President for the extension of Chilian railways, and for the promotion of industrial enterprise in the country, were received with promises of full consideration. As nothing could be done, however, to carry them into effect till the ministers returned to the capital and till the Chilian Parliament met in June, Colonel North resolved to go back to the coast, to prepare for our visit to Iquique, and to the Nitrate *oficinas* on the Pampas. We left the Hotel Oddo with a very kindly impression of the good landlord Herr Flindt and his family, and quitted Santiago for the pleasant suburb of Viña del Mar, near Valparaiso, on 20th March, to await events.

CHAPTER X.

VALPARAISO—VIÑA DEL MAR.

Viña del Mar—Petitions and Petitioners—A Scholar in Distress Excellent Askers, Givers, and Takers—Drink for the Church—A Herald of Winter—Farewell Festivities—How Small the World is!—The Great Ball—Captain Simpson—Departure from Viña del Mar

WE remained at the excellent hotel of Herr Luttjes in Viña del Mar till April 1st, and the time did not pass, by any means, unpleasantly. The young people rode or walked out in the day, and danced in the evening; the elders read books and papers, toddled about under the trees, visited or received visitors, were photographed singly and in groups, ate and slept. The weather was what we call "glorious" at home: no rain or wind, a warm sun, a clear sky and mild air. Day after day the sun sailed in its course seawards, through the rainless blue, and next morning found us as it left us. The episodes in our *pastorale*, as far as we were personally concerned, were few. But there were weighty matters for Colonel North to arrange at Santiago, and he hurried to the capital, and came back, at short notice. One morning it was, "Where is the Colonel?" "Gone to Santiago." "When do you expect him back?" "I can't say." Next day it was, "Who is this coming from the station? Why, it's the Colonel!"

As at Coronel, Valparaiso, Santiago, so at Viña del Mar, the doors and passages of his hotel were blocked by gaping petitioners, and his mail-bags were sure to be heavy with their prayers, supplications, and requests. Women, young and old, with and without children, sat on the steps, each with a written statement of "a most urgent and deserving case." They rustled past you in their black silk mantas and thronged the staircases and waylaid the doors, and it needed much craft and subtlety to evade them in the corridors and lobbies. One lady "had three charming children ; she was beloved by a young man of an honourable family, who would marry her and acknowledge the dear ones as his own if the generous and great-hearted English lord would let her have a *dot* of $5,000. If she could not repay him on earth, he might rest assured he would receive ample compensation from the angels in heaven." Another needed "a small sum to complete the education of a family left fatherless in the war." A third had a mine of wealth which she could not work. but which, to meet pressing necessities, she would sell for a tenth of its value. All human needs had their spokeswomen. Sisters wanted help for their hospitals, nurses for their foundlings, music mistresses for their schools One gentleman urged the Nitrate King to finance a revolution in a neighbouring state. The papers had published biographies and portraits of the Nitrate King in every town, and the report of his enormous wealth had gone abroad among the people.

One morning, there came an old gentleman—the only one of the many who appeared day after day—that I would have helped. He had, after an adventurous career in Portugal, &c., settled in Valparaiso some half century ago and founded the first English seminary in the city. He obtained an excellent position, was held in much esteem by the leading men of the Republic, amassed a little fortune, and then. carried away by the rush for mining enterprises, which swept half Chile off its legs, embarked his capital, which foundered and sank, in shafts and lodes somewhere near Antofagasta I think, and left him struggling for dear life. He fought for years, but never won, and now, having lost all his early friends—"Harry Keppel, I know, would be sorry to hear of my situation"—he was reduced to poverty, and was selling off the little that remained of the possessions he had acquired in prosperous days, some Latin classics, a Milton's "Paradise Lost," second edition, published in the lifetime of the poet, a Galignani Byron, &c.—on which he placed an exaggerated value. The Milton alone found a buyer.

Touched by sympathy for a countryman in distress, our party made up a small subscription, which Mr Blank took, I suppose, without reflection, for in a day or two the notes came back with a letter of thanks of the curtest—"he wanted to sell his books"—*voilà tout !*

A Chilian gentleman to whom I mentioned the *chasse au Colonel* thought it quite natural. "The people are extremely charitable among themselves. They help each other to the utmost when in distress. The result is mischievous. A servant or a workman will throw up his place on the smallest provocation. He knows he has only to go to his friends and he will have food and shelter. No Chilian feels humbled by such help, nor does he hesitate to ask for it, and nothing seems more reasonable to these people of whom you speak than to apply to a rich man who has made a fortune in Chile to give them what they want. But they will not feel very angry if they are refused. They are excellent askers, givers, and takers."

There was a felicitous illustration of the value of the precept to be all things to all men afforded in the case of two respectable ecclesiastics who came one day to ask for a subscription—black sombreros, black cloaks, black knee-breeches and stockings complete—intensely clerical, and Jesuitical enough to drive an Ulster Protestant village into frenzy. One, I believe, was an Englishman, or English-speaking Spaniard, the other an American. They sent in their petition and waited motionless as statues in the hotel garden. Presently there came through the open window a concise utterance, equivalent to a rejection of their prayer. But that they might not go away without some show of civility, they were invited to enter the room. They did so, and when they had made their bow they were offered the usual drink of the country. They drank. "Will you take another?" They did. They were evidently good fellows. A subscription of $50 was given. "Would they have another drink?" They would, and they did. And finally they took leave quite steadily with $200 in hand towards the accomplishment of their work! "Though, I confess," said one of them to a friend afterwards, "I was exceedingly ill next day." They seized the opportunity in the spirit of martyrs, and prevailed. We are all on the move to the Nitrate Kingdom, or preparing for it. Mr. Vizetelly and Mr. Prior made ready to-day to proceed to Iquique on Saturday next, in advance of the rest of the party.

"*April 25th.*—The appearance of a dark and rather large humming-bird, almost the size of a wren,[*] which is regarded as a herald of the coming winter, was signalled this morning in the garden. This fellow, like most of his race, is exceedingly pugnacious, and drives away all rivals from his hedge. Once a pair of them, engaged in a desperate scuffle, fell like a ball of feathers on the gravel close to my

[*] *Trochilus galeritus?*

feet. Of the three or four kinds I have remarked, none exhibit the metallic brilliancy and gemlike appearance of those we saw at Rio. Hitherto, since our arrival, we have been generally in excellent health, but among so many it was not to be expected that the happy exemption would last. One of the ladies, who has not been quite well for some days past, was visited by Dr. Breedon and pronounced to have typhoid fever, and as the doctor strongly recommended her removal to the English Hospital on the heights above Valparaiso, my wife accompanied her to town, and saw her comfortably installed in the excellent institution, which is chosen by the English physicians for all patients, no matter what their rank in life, in preference to their own homes. Mr. Gilling will consequently have to remain behind with his daughter when we leave for the north, in solitary watch

"*April* 26*th*—Several farewell festivities are in preparation. As the time of our departure for the rainless region of Tarapacá draws near, entertainments and visits and engagements crowd upon us

"*April* 27*th*.—How small this world is nowadays! I sat this morning at Las Zorres in a charming garden belonging to Mr. Berry, talking to Mrs. Young of her gallant brother, in whose house at Pretoria I had spent so many happy days when he was Governor of the Transvaal, and in the train in which I travelled from Viña del Mar to Barno station on the way to Las Zorres I met an old friend whom I had last seen in Calcutta! On the platform of the same station, as we were returning to Viña del Mar, I encountered an old Crimean acquaintance whom I had last seen in London, when I returned from India in 1876! *La Epoca*, one of the leading papers of Santiago, which has published a portrait and a flattering notice of Colonel

North, has also been busy in transmitting to posterity the features and history of all of those who are travelling with him, so that the 'Comitiva' are tolerably well known in Chile by this time.

"*April* 28*th*.—A very grand banquet was given by Colonel North in the large room of the Hotel at Viña del Mar, to the principal English residents, the Consul, merchants, bankers, &c., of Valparaiso. Admiral Uribe, who distinguished himself in the war with Peru, and several Chilian gentlemen and Chilian ladies were among the guests.

"*April* 29*th*.—A great ball at the hotel wound up the long chain of festivities at Viña del Mar. Special trains from Valparaiso—the best band that could be hired—and a most elaborate supper. The rooms were brilliantly lighted, the floor smooth, the dancers many and merry, and the music good. Many speeches at supper. Then more dances. What more could be done? To bed, but not to sleep. Close at hand there was the special blocking the line, the engine blowing off steam, and making the morning hideous with its shrill whistling to summon the loitering guests, who hurried at last, in the garish light of day, in long streams from the hotel to the railway.

"*April* 30*th*.—The last day of our pleasant sojourn at Viña del Mar. Colonel North went to Santiago by the early train at 7.45, which, considering that the jovial threat of the refrain, 'We won't go home till the morning' was being thoroughly well executed 'for the last time' about 6 A M., would have been rather a trial for anyone of less energy. He went to see his lawyers and friends, among them Señor Toro, who was one of the passengers of the *Cotopaxi*, and who exhibited, in the moment of shipwreck, the courage he had displayed before on the battle field, where he received more than one wound in the last campaign. A Chilian officer, named Simpson, appointed to the naval command at Valparaiso, who was introduced to me by Mr. Hicks, gave us some very interesting information about the surveying work in the Straits of Magellan and in the Archipelago of Chiloe, in which he had co-operated with officers of the English Navy, for whom, especially Captain, now Admiral Mayne, he professed much regard. He was far more Chilian than English, as are most descendants of Englishmen born and bred in Chile, and he would fight us with the greatest readiness, I am afraid, if he had a chance.

"*May 1st.*—A turning of keys and a grating of locks, a cording of trunks and nailing of boxes—Frank, the Colonel's *factotum*—in charge of baggage, presiding over the movements of an army of porters on the way to the railway-station, the Hungarian major-domo, and the German landlord acting on the admirable maxim 'speed the parting guest.' But it looked doubtful whether we could get off in time, for the chief was missing. Colonel North did not make his appearance till the morning train from Santiago arrived at Viña del Mar, but he was in time It is only half an hour's run to Valparaiso, and the steamer for Iquique would not start till the afternoon. Then there was a hurried leave-taking of friends at the hotel and station, and in an hour later we were 'all aboard' the train for Valparaiso."

CHAPTER XI

VALPARAISO TO IQUIQUE.

Departure from Valparaiso—The *Serena*—Aconcagua—The Coast of Chile—Birds and Fishes—The *Cotopaxi*—Dr Tyndall, R N —Coquimbo—A Cosmopolitan City—The Copper Crash—Drive to Serena—"English Corsairs" Early Visits to Serena—Huasco—Its Grapes—Carrizal—A Visit to a Workshop—Caldera—Spoils of War—Pacific Rollers—Antofagasta—Mr. Hicks' Anchor—Candidissima Causa Belli

MANY of the English colony, and a goodly number of Chilian friends, were waiting at Valparaiso to bid Colonel North adieu. My friend, Captain Harris, had his gig alongside the jetty steps, and put my wife and myself, after some difficulty in shipping the feminine part of his cargo, safely on board the Pacific Steam Navigation Company's steamer *Serena*, of 2,500 tons, Captain Vaughan. She was crowded with passengers, many going to Europe, which, in the case of most of them, meant the Paris Exhibition. The revellers at the ball of the night before, the members of the clubs, the friends and acquaintances of Colonel North and his party crowded the quarter-deck and filled the saloon to say "good-bye." Then came libations of the *vin d'honneur* and feeling speeches, kindly words, and the final adieux.

At six o'clock p m., the *Serena* moved ahead, with a flotilla of boats filled with people cheering and waving hats and handkerchiefs, in her wake. She stood out to sea, and having given a good offing to the projecting headland, steered north on her course. Once past the northern headland of the bay we encountered the gentle roll of the Pacific, which was blazing in the rays of the declining sun to the west like a sea of fire. To the east the snow-white crest of Aconcagua was just visible, towering high above the mist on the lower ranges of the Andes. It might well have been a patch of cloud floating in the grey air All next day we ran northwards along the coast. There was little to see save black reefs and the red beach, and sandhills beyond them. The uniform dulness and the monotonous appearance of the shore are irritating. A brick-coloured wall of irregular contour and height, rising from the sea in slopes or terraces, or abrupt cliffs, a fringe of rocks and reefs at the base of which the surf rolls for ever! No sign of vegetation or of life! We searched the recesses of the chain with the glass for sign of habitation or cultivation in vain. Inside that wall of brick-coloured rock there are mines of copper, hills covered with sheep, and in the plains between the mountain chains there are fields of wheat and barley, and all these find outlets in ports close at hand, such as Los Vilos and Papudo

Vast flocks of divers, gulls, and pelicans indicated the abundance of fish, of which shoals now and then flecked the surface, tormented by porpoises and swordfish. "It's a derned place for sharks too," said an American; "but I never heard of them eating any humans." At intervals precipitous ridges of rock rise from the sea appearing as if they were heads crested with masses of white hair—these are inchoate attempts of the sea birds to establish guano beds, and they are carefully watched by the Government.

One of our passengers, Dr. Tyndall, who was appointed to H.M. storeship at Coquimbo, had been wrecked in the

Cotopaxi, and his account supported the theory of Colonel North that the vessel had not struck upon a rock, but that when she "opened out" the plates with which her rents had been patched after the collision with a German steamer previously, gave way.* Dr. Tyndall said he was leaving the saloon with the purser when he heard cries and saw smoke and steam issuing from the hatchways on deck. Immediately afterwards there was a slight explosion and a rush of steam, which showed that the sea water was putting out the fires. The conduct of the Captain was admirable, and he was well seconded by his officers. In eight minutes every soul on board—men, women, and children—were in the boats escaping from the sinking steamer, which disappeared bodily in a few seconds after the Captain left her. They were rescued after several days' severe privation on the desolate shores of the Straits by a German steamer, without the loss of a single life.

May 2nd.—It was night when the *Serena* reached the port of Coquimbo. Presently the shore boats clustered alongside. There came from one a hail in English, "Have you got a passenger named Dr. Tyndall, of H.M.S *Liffey*, on board?" "Ay! ay! here I am all right!" "We have come from the ship to take you off! Have you got much baggage, sir?" "Confound them," said the Doctor, "what a question! the fellows must know I have lost everything! They are making fun of me!" And, in fact, the Doctor was saved with the clothes on his back only, and had to get a temporary refit and rig-out at Valparaiso for this voyage to his ship.

May 3rd.—The doctor bade us good-bye this morning

---

* It was subsequently ascertained, however that there was a rock *in situ*, one of the German steamers found and determined its position, close to the scene of the catastrophe.

and went on board H.M.S. *Liffey*, the supply ship for the British Pacific Squadron and station, to which he was appointed from the flagship at Queenstown.

Most of the party landed early and paid a visit in the forenoon to the vice-consulate, where we were hospitably entertained, and where we read the papers and telegrams and learned the latest news, whilst the posting resources of the town were being called into activity to furnish carriages for an excursion to Serena.

There are between 5,000 and 6,000 people in Coquimbo, among them French, German, Spanish, and Italian, and the English names of Edwards, Grierson, Lloyd, Steele, Spencer, Stephens, James, Raby, &c., denote the presence in the town of the Anglo-Saxon

The number of insurance companies is remarkable. I counted the South British, London Imperial, London Corporation, Lancashire, Queen, Commercial, Union, Northern, the Chilian Valparaiso Company, &c. There are several banks, two lines of telegraph. There is a large staff of officials, a civil governor, a commandant, a judge of the first instance, a marine governor, a commandant of the troops, an administrator of customs, and a postmaster, &c

The "Coquimbinos," as a friend of mine called the natives, judging from their praise of the air and even of the scenery, are very well content with their town. The advantages of the port in comparison with most of the sea towns on the coast are considerable. There was an active trade here, copper, silver, cobalt, coal, and manganese; but, owing chiefly to the copper crash, it is at present diminished The great foundries and smelting works are silent, the chimneys of most of the factories are smokeless.

Coquimbo has all the apparatus of civilisation and of government, with such luxuries as the electric light and telegraph, the telephone, and a railway. A canal fed by the river which trickles into the sea by many devious channels, provides the town with drinking water, and serves to irrigate the patches of garden around it. I should have thought Coquimbo rather a dismal place, but it appears that it is not considered at all bad—that is, by comparison. There is a good climate; there is some sport to be had and even a little society, and as it is a port of call, the bay is enlivened by the steamers and by the men-of-war which have a fancy to look in from time to time.

We had to wait some time till the tide was sufficiently low to allow us to drive out by the sands to the ancient city of Serena. At high water the ground close to the shore is swampy, and carriages cannot cross the river. Close to the sea, the sand is hard and smooth and the horses, accustomed to the roar of the surf, do not fear an occasional sweep of a breaker up to their knees. It was a novel and very interesting excursion—on one side the beach and the Andes—on the other the deep sea. The coast is dotted by old batteries and earthworks, constructed during the war to prevent the Peruvians landing, in some of which small guns are slowly rusting away, but a much more effectual protection is permanently afforded by the surf and shoals.

Our carriage halted at a restaurant near the railway station outside the town, and after a brief delay for refreshments, we set out to see Serena. We made an excursion through the principal streets in a tramcar under the control of a very pretty young lady. The employment of women as conductors is universal, and as far as I know it is free from inconvenience.

It is not owing to the good offices of our countrymen that Serena exists. Spanish historians record that the "English corsair," Francisco Drake, made an attempt on the place in December, 1578, and that Richard Hawkins sought to take it in May, 1594, but that they both "desisted in face of the resistance offered to them by the inhabitants." The "pirate, Bartholomew Sharp," was more successful, for he entered the town in September, 1680, and after he had sacked all the treasure in the place, burned it. Edward Davis, the buccaneer, made an unsuccessful attempt in 1686 to repeat the exploit of his piratical friend. But the forces of nature were more formidable than corsair or buccaneer, and the earthquake of 8th of July, 1730, destroyed the greater part of the town. However, the natural advantages which commended the site to Valdivia, one of the greatest of Spanish governors and conquerors, enabled it to maintain its position, and if somewhat sombre and dull, it presents to-day the appearance of a well-ordered town. Serena is built in the usual Spanish fashion in rectangular blocks, one hundred and twelve yards square, and is gifted with well-paved streets, an alameda, a plaza and boulevards lined with trees.

We were introduced to the Club, and presently a number of gentlemen, anxious to do the honours of their city, came there to welcome us, and were profuse in expressions of desire to be of service. We had, however, to return before dark, and so we took the train back to Coquimbo. When we got back to the *Serena* we found there was an addition to our passengers between decks and a considerable diminution of the stores. A fog came on soon after we left Coquimbo, and our speed was reduced at night.

May 4th.—At seven A.M. anchored in the roads off Huasco. The Pacific rushing on the reefs and on the shore, where two small piers marked the landing-place, sandhills in front, sandhills on the flanks, sandhills in rear, the Andes and clouds behind. A little heap of houses huddled together in the midst of some large buildings, furnished with tall chimneys, now smokeless. Why Bartholomew Sharp and Davis harassed the place two hundred years ago it would not be easy now to determine, unless Huasco has been greatly changed, or that they were very fond of fruit. The country around this arid spot is noted for its fertility. Excellent wine of a generous quality is produced in the valleys, and the raisins are considered by the natives equal to those of Malaga. There are mines of gold, silver, copper, and cobalt in the hills, and the plains yield rich crops of every description of grain.

Weighed again at eleven A.M. Observed at sea curious patches some miles in length, irregular in form, but generally in narrow strips as white as snow, seemingly of a creamy or a buttery character, floating on the surface, probably foam off the rocks on the coast collected under conditions of atmosphere which, as far as I know, do not exist elsewhere —at least, I have never seen a similar appearance.

A short run along the coast brought us next to Carrizal (Bajo), a port not too commodious or safe, to judge from appearance. In the good times that have disappeared, before the operations of the copper syndicate, Carrizal had considerable trade. The moles and quays are now deserted; the furnaces are blown out; the export of ores which two or three years ago amounted to more than two millions of kilos, has fallen one half, and the two lines of railway have but little to carry or take for Carrizal. But for one of the party this little place possessed an absorbing interest

In a building which he pointed out to us from the deck was the workshop in which Colonel North was first employed after his arrival in the pursuit of the fortune which he finally captured on the coast, and scarcely had the anchor reached the bottom ere he hastened to visit the scene of his early labours. He led his friends to the deserted workshop. "There is the bench at which I worked! There is the place where I kept my tools! Here day after day for many a month I worked as an engineer at four dollars a day!" I believe there was a fellow workman whom he recognised at the place. A *rencontre* of that kind, you may be sure, is generally to the great advantage of one of the parties. There is not a town along this coast which has not some point of interest or some reminiscence for Colonel North, but I think he had more pleasure in his visit to Carrizal than he found in any of the other places we touched at. Apart from such associations and from ties of business, property or family, there are generally few more dreary and uninviting localities in the world than the little ports on the Pacific coast of South America.

May 5th.—At eight A.M. the *Serena* anchored in the Puerto Mayor of Caldera, two hundred and eight Spanish miles (*millas*) from Valparaiso. Landing at the moles to-day was not easy. Although there is a lighthouse on a little hill at the point, a skipper would do well to wait for day before he ran in to take up his moorings. The town is purely commercial, and its prosperity depends on the mines near at hand. There are the usual factory chimneys, towering above the low houses of wood disposed in streets ankle-deep in sand, at right angles, with the universal background of sandhill and brick-coloured mountain. Close to the quay are rows of guns of great size and small power, Columbiads, Rodmans, the spoils of the arsenals of Lima. Why they were brought so far and why they were left at Caldera, I could not find out. There is a lighthouse and there is a railway—the first of any importance constructed in South America—to Copiapo,

Pabellon, &c. There are telegraphic lines and a submarine cable. In fact, there are few towns of 3,500 people in Europe so well provided with everything, except water, for which the people have to depend upon the condensers of the railway, which produce 27,000 litres a day. The country around is exceedingly arid One attraction Caldera possesses, but it is only when there is a perfect calm at a certain time of the year—August or September—and then there are frequent displays of the *fata morgana* of unusual beauty. A southerly wind with a point or two west in it brings in a heavy roll. The surf beats heavily on the rocks. Remained here till half-past two in the afternoon. Our vegetables were in great demand, and it was with difficulty the ship's officers could get the purchasers into their boats as the screw was turning ahead.

Monday 6th.—We had rather an unpleasant experience last night of the rolling power of the Pacific in the run from Caldera to Antofagasta, where the *Serena*, passing the ports of Chañaral, Taltal, Caleta Oliva, Paposo, and Caracoles, anchored at eight A M. To the eye there is but little to commend Antofogasta. Nevertheless I surveyed the place with great interest. Here arose the quarrel—a cloud not larger than the hand of Mr. Hicks—which, charged with the thunder of war, spread over Tarapacá, burst in storm on Peru, and when it receded left the Chilian flag waving all along the coast northwards up to Arica. There was a fleet of vessels at anchor tossing and rolling uncomfortably in the long swell, and certainly I was not tempted to land by the experiences of my companions, but very much preferred to be tossed about in the *Serena*. A large anchor traced in white on the face of a hill over the town marks the line of safe anchorage. Antofagasta has a church, a hospital, a public slaughterhouse, a band of music, a philharmonic society, a club, hotels, restaurants. Squares of gaily painted wooden houses, built upon sand, a garden, in which a few flowers and plants are sustained at the cost of the municipality in the Plaza. Such is the town as it is seen from the sea. But it rejoices in the full apparatus of governors, commandants, and officials. There are three Alcaldes.

We are getting close to the borders of the Nitrate Kingdom, and the first great oficina or manufactory of the prized material which, more than "villainous saltpetre" itself, was a factor in the war of 1879, is at Antofagasta. On the discovery of the rich silver mines of Huanchaca, of Calama, San Pedro, &c, and of the salt fields in the neighbouring districts, Antofagasta became important. Mr. Lewis, of Valparaiso, has large smelting works here.

Notwithstanding the bad character of the port, open to seas from many points of wind, and the consequent difficulty of loading and unloading vessels in the roadstead, there is now considerable trade—more, I believe, than there was when the Republic of Bolivia rejoiced in it as its only port—and railways run to various points in the desert of Atacama, and to Ascotan on the Bolivian frontier.

It is only a run of eighteen hours to Iquique, to which our steamer, without touching Cobija, Tocopilla, Guanillos, Pabellon de Pica, and Punta de Lobos, proceeded from Antofagasta direct.

CHAPTER XII.

IQUIQUE.

Iquique—Friends in Waiting—The Railway Station—The Water Boats—Festivities on the Coast—Mr Rowland—Our Quarters—Anglo-Chilian Cuisine—Chilian Diet—Steamboat Fare—A Chilian "Crewe"—The City of Iquique—Its Wonders, The Fire Brigade—Living on Nitrate of Soda—Iquique in 1835—Iquique in 1885—Visitors from Above—Projectors—Mining Speculations—A Bird's-eye View from my Balcony—The March of the Trams—Up and Down the Andes.

Tuesday, May 7th.—At 8.30 A.M. fired a gun, no land visible, fog or thick mist on sea, slowed, and presently anchored. Iquique at last! It was not easy to make the shore out at first. But the veil of cloud or vapour drifting upwards revealed what I was not prepared to see—a town with pretensions, an imposing sea frontage, public buildings, the brightly-hued cupola of a Cathedral, a Custom House. Close at hand, in the roadstead, a number of large ships, lying in regular tiers, full rigged barques, three-masted schooners, one large four-master. Steam tugs plying with lighters in tow between the shore and ships, factory chimneys, giving out abundance of smoke, and a well-defined line of railway striking from a mass of great magazines and workshops, right up the side of the mountain, the summit of which was hidden by the clouds, behind the city.

The English colony and Chilian friends were waiting to come off to welcome Colonel North. But the people in general, who intended to give a great reception to the man who had done so much for Iquique, congregated at the Custom House pier, as it was expected he would land there.

Iquique.

(To face page 138.)

The Wooden Bridge, Santiago.

To face page 139.

There was a good deal of sea on—not an uncommon incident here—and it was considered advisable, especially for the sake of the ladies, to land at the Railway Jetty, some distance from the Custom House pier, and close to the house of Mr. Rowland, the chief of the Railway, in which we were to have our quarters. Even the easier landing-place was difficult enough. So Colonel North's friends on shore, band and all, were disappointed, and that which would have been a collective demonstration resolved itself very pleasantly in due time into individual greetings after he had landed.

Immediately on landing at the Railway Pier, we proceeded along the branch line in a carriage drawn by a tiny engine to visit the Railway Station, and to inspect the workshops, the Iron Foundry, and the water reservoirs, before we settled down in our quarter. It was difficult to believe that the busy scene around one was what a well-known writer calls "one of the unnatural abodes of men on the shores of the Pacific," which has become the centre of activity and life in the space of a few years. But it could not have held many people till some means of supplying fresh water had been provided. There are frequent mentions of the place in old books, and the rocky island opposite the town on which the Lighthouse stands is frequently spoken of in voyages as "the island of Iquique."

Iquique, Pisagua, and the other ports in the rainless region of the Chilian coast and their dependent populations on the pampas, extending from 19° to 27°, are unique in the nature of their relations to the world. They tax the resources of all parts of the earth, and in return they sell that which enriches exhausted fields, and gives fresh life to the worn-out agricultural lands of Europe.

Out at anchor beyond the Railway Pier you see one of the three water-ships belonging to Colonel North; vessels of

800 or 900 tons burthen, some of which make fourteen trips a month between this and Arica and the coast, where they take in water to supply Pisagua and Iquique. I believe I am not wrong in assigning to Colonel North the credit of a clever arrangement of the water tanks by which the dangerous cargo is confined and carried with safety. The reservoirs on shore are filled by 5-inch rubber hose from the water tanks in the ships. The Tarapacá water business was at one time in Colonel North's hands, but he sold it some time ago for £100,000, or about three years' purchase of the returns.

I have not thought it necessary to give particular accounts of the hospitalities and festivities which were inaugurated at Coronel, continued at Valparaiso, at Viña del Mar, at Santiago and at Iquique, and which did not come to an end till the party left Callao for Panama on their way home. These were pleasant at the time, and they have left pleasant memories in the minds of those who renewed old friendships, or formed new acquaintances at the merry meetings. But though the banquets afforded evidence that the resources of civilization are abundant and various in Chile, and the balls proved that where there are light hearts, nimble feet, and plenty of partners, nothing is wanting for the enjoyment of the dance, I think my readers will not care to read of the gaieties of people they do not know, or to study the *menus* of dinners at which they did not assist. The entertainers and most of the guests at these reunions were Europeans, the majority of them English, and, with the exception of one very large and luxurious banquet given by Señor Maciver, a Chilian Senator, to Colonel North and his friends at Santiago, and the entertainment of Señor Cousiño and Señor Gubler at Macul, there was no marked departure from the reserve which generally governs the social relations of the people to foreigners and to the stranger within their gates, during our sojourn in the land.

When the President was *en voyage* public banquets were given in his honour at the great towns; and the foreign residents, who often played a part in the preliminary preparations, were naturally invited to be present; but if it be the custom in Chile to entertain distinguished citizens on suitable occasions, as it is in Europe, the newspapers did not notice the entertainments, and I can only recollect three or four *vins d'honneur*, *dejeuners* or dinners of native origin being given whilst we were there. Considering the love of the Chilians for making and hearing speeches, it is rather remarkable that they do not indulge more largely in opportunities for the display of post-prandial eloquence.

Mr. Rowland and his wife received Colonel and Miss North, Miss Wentworth Smith, my wife and myself, and installed us most comfortably in their house, whither at breakfast, lunch and dinner there flowed in an uncertain contingent of the party, Mr. and Mrs. Spencer, Mr. Melton Prior, Captain Brough, Mr. Power, &c. Mr. Dawson gave shelter and a gracious and ample hospitality to others of our fellow-travellers, Mr. Beauclerk, Mr. Vizetelly, &c.; and Mr. Buckland, the acting consul, gathered the rest under his friendly wing. It must have been a great strain on the household administration of our good hosts to provide so large a party with accommodation and food in such a place as Iquique, but there were no signs of it. Well, the sea yielded fish, the corbino, the congrio and the lissa, and when it did not, there was the dried salt cod, "bacala" (not for me), to fall back upon; there were vegetables and fruit in abundance, delicious bread and good eggs, wine, beer, milk, butter, pigeons, turkeys, poultry, beef and mutton (all imported), the invariable *picante*, and many other dishes.

It is astonishing how the progress of civilisation is sweeping what are called national dishes before it, greatly, I think, to the general advantage of the human constitution. There are, to be sure, notable exceptions—an Indian curry—let Madras and Bombay contend for the honour of the best and most delicate—a Bouillabaisse or a Matelotte à la Normande, a Paprika-huhn. But the list is long. Suffice it to say, that there are exceptions to be highly valued and to be thankful for, but I hope I may not offend if I say I do not think that these abound in Spanish cookery; and though a Portuguese "boy" can turn out eatable things when he is far away, it appears to me that the inhabitants of the Peninsula revel to excess in Provençal cookery, and that the Chilians inherit the tastes of their ancestors in Europe. They love their casuela, a chicken broth with vegetables, served at breakfast, and not absent at lunch, dinner, or supper, which perhaps affords as favourable a medium for discussing tough poultry as any other, and they greatly affect a kind of mutton pie, only it is not always made with mutton, and is not round, simply meat enclosed in thick paste and baked to a turn. But in roast and boiled they are primitive, and in made dishes are given to ways which induce the stranger to prefer their simpler exercises in the culinary art. The mutton would not take a prize in any British market, but Chilian beef is excellent, the poultry plentiful, but worn to a thread by misery and want of food. Turkeys, on the contrary, flourish, vegetables and fruit are excellent, the Chilian potato the best in the world, Chilian flour incomparably the sweetest I have ever eaten. So with milk and butter, bread and wine, as Disraeli said, "Man's two first luxuries and his best," life is worth living for the rich. As for the poor, they have *peroto* or beans, on which they thrive and throw out muscle, and they have also all kinds of vegetable products wherever a drop of water flows or rain falls. No one is long in Chile before he is invited to praise the kingfish, the pescarey, which is rather like a champion gudgeon, and which split open and fried is not altogether tasteless, with something of the flavour, or want of it, that characterises the whiting. Like our whitebait, the kingfish thrives in brackish waters, and affects shores where fresh-water streams mingle with the ocean. The congrio, a large fish of the sea, is held in much estimation; but of the fish on the coast of which I made the acquaintance at table the best was unquestionably the lissa. In Tarapacá food and drink are exotic, but the stranger would be ignorant of the fact if he were dwelling in the house of one of the hospitable residents.

The tables on board the coast steamers are very well served; an early cup of coffee or tea, biscuit, toast and butter, are ready for the earliest riser on his way to or from his bath. At nine o'clock an ample breakfast, the inevitable casuela, pescarey or other fish, picante, cutlets, beefsteaks, omelettes, fruit. At one o'clock the hardier people can indulge in lunch. At five there is a repetition of breakfast on a large scale, with wine instead of tea and coffee, and then supper at nine enables a man to retire with the consciousness that he has supported nature for the day. On landing at Valparaiso or Iquique you find the same meals varied slightly, at least as plentiful, with as many, if not more, dishes, and perhaps more enjoyment on the part of the partakers You have only stepped from a floating home to one which would be called solid, but for those terrible earthquakes, with which we were destined to make early acquaintance soon after our arrival at Iquique, having had an introduction to the sensation at Santiago. The wines of the country are so good, that it is not to be wondered at if the natives drink nearly all that is produced, and leave very little of the better vintages, of the Urmeneta, Macul, and Paquerete for export. The better qualities are by no means cheap, and the poorer classes are content with beer, by no means despicable, and with chucha, a preparation made from grapes, which I did not find palatable, but it is commended by its cheapness, for it is quite intoxicating, and a man can become very drunk at a trifling expense.

Iquique, where we resided for several weeks, was the scene of many convivial gatherings and social reunions during the whole of our stay. The large British colony warmly welcomed Colonel North as one whose enterprise and energy had largely contributed to the development of the commerce and industry which had raised the port and city to a capital position, only second to that of Valparaiso.

No doubt the sandy plain could be made to teem with vegetation if the supply of water and of labour were adequate, but for the present, at all events, the 20,000 people living on the shore receive the means of life and provisions for its wants and luxuries by sea.* With money in your purse there is very little you can desire which you cannot buy in Iquique. Day after day the wonder of this artificial existence was at work under our eyes, but it was only on reflection that its strangeness struck you, and that you were led in a vague way to think what would happen if water and food failed, if the condensers and steamers ceased to

---

* The Water Company is now laying down mains from Pica on the W of the Tamarugal Pampa to supply Iquique, and the pipes are already serving Pozo Almonte and the Nitrate Railway.

Nitrate Railway Goods Yard, Iquique.

work owing to want of coal, and if the provision stores gave out; and to recognize that this town has literally struggled on through flood and fire, for it has been nearly swept away by tidal waves, shaken down by earthquakes, and converted into blackened ashes by conflagrations.

At the station of the Nitrate Railway you see a bustling staff of English clerks, engineers, and drivers; piles of jute-bags from Bremen or Dundee; Heath's patent fuel, Cardiff; machinery from Leeds and Glasgow; Fowler's and Fairlie's engines; American carriages—a little Crewe full of life and energy. A couple of hundred yards off you see the chimneys and hear the clang of machinery of the Tarapacá Foundry. You enter and find three or four hundred men busily engaged in making machinery for the *oficinas* and for the Railway, boilers for the nitrate works, and castings for all the iron work that is required on the Pampas above—steam-hammers going, lathes boring, wheels revolving, furnaces discharging streams of molten metal. The iron ore comes from England, why I could not quite understand, as there is much of it at Lota and at other places along the coast. Adjoining the Railway, and close to the Foundry, the carriage works and carpenters' department in full activity invited and rewarded inspection. The spacious sheds were filled with men busy with repairs, for nearly the whole of the work of the Nitrate Railway is executed in the shops. In connection with this establishment there is a magazine containing brass castings and material for every description of metal work, as well as necessaries for the workmen. The superintendents are English, the workmen natives. It is said that Chilians are more manageable than our own countrymen and quite as efficient, but I could not hear that they were exempt from the besetting sin of their class, or that they were indifferent to the attractions of the grog-shop.

The city, like all towns in Chile, is built in rectangular blocks. The main streets running to the sea are sixty-five feet wide, and are cut at right angles by others. There are some two-storeyed houses, but the great majority are only of one storey. The houses are constructed of timber, and covered with cement and stucco, which is coloured generally with some bright wash, cream, orange or blue, the doors, windows, sashes, &c., being painted in darker hues, and the general effect of the town, with its gazebos and cupolas rejoicing in the sunshine, which is rarely absent, is certainly very light and pretty. It is in virtue of a prescription from Madrid in the time of the Spanish domination that Chilian cities and towns are laid out in straight lines, crossed by others—and it is a very comforting way for strangers—so that seen from a height they present the appearance of a chessboard. Another feature in these Chilian towns, dear to the natives, which they have inherited from Spanish ancestors, is the Alameda, with its Plaza sacred to the fame of some local native, whose statue is often a doubtful adornment to the centre of it. Iquique is gifted with one large plaza, which is bordered by trees as yet young and literally reared by hand. In the centre is a monument to Arturo Prat, captain of the *Esmeralda*, whose body was laid on the spot for a time, ere it was conveyed to Valparaiso. There are two smaller plazas, one named after Charles Condell, a naval commander in the late war, the other after Manuel Montt.

For those not occupied by business there are not many resources, but in comparison with an average European town of the same size, Iquique has no reason to be ashamed of itself. It is provided with banks, shops, hospitals, public schools, barracks, prisons.—It supports two or three newspapers, *La Industria, Il Progreso*, &c. There are excellent saddle horses and carriages, open and shut, for hire; there are tramway cars, there are three clubs and many restaurants, and at the corners of the streets are popular "Bars" and exchanges, and there is a theatre for any itinerant troupe that may visit the coast; there is a well-patronised racecourse and a cricket ground, and there are the lungs of the city lying two miles outside on the seashore in the shape of Cavancha, of which more hereafter. The streets need no paving—they are laid down with some kind of cement and sand, and the sidewalks have pavements of artificial stone, or are formed by planks. The wood does not decay in this rainless region. The telegraph and the telephone are in full play; the houses are provided with electric bells—the Lighthouse and other public places with the electric light, which has ascended the Andes and which illuminates the Pampas from the towers of the *oficinas*. Gas is supplied at fair prices by a flourishing company, founded in Peruvian times, in which Colonel North is interested, for the streets and houses. The Intendente of the Province resides here, and Courts of Civil and Criminal Justice and a High Court of Appeal sit to administer the law. There is a garrison of an artillery detachment, a squadron of cavalry, and a battalion of foot, and there is a regiment of the National Guard to protect the place. There is an excellent and vigilant police, and there is a large and well-proved fire service, mostly supported by the merchants of different nationalities. But strange to say there is no English or British section, and Colonel North, who brought out the prize Exhibition fire-engine from England to present to the town, had no British Bomberos to whose charge he could consign it

Very soon after my arrival at Iquique there was a parade of the Brigade of Bomberos, which was really a remarkable spectacle; the different sections were in uniform, the engines displaying the flags of the country to which they belonged. They indulged in a practical proof of working efficiency which made the streets unpleasant, for they turned the earthy deposit on the wood sidewalks into mud. The town, being built of wood, has suffered severely from fires, and in no country in the world with a population of the same size are there so many towns provided with efficient fire-brigades as Chile. In addition to the ordinary causes of conflagrations which abound in cities built of wood, where many inflammable materials are stored, there is in nitrate of soda a certain danger of combustion ; the causes of which are not, I believe, thoroughly understood. But ships laden with nitrate have taken fire on their way home so frequently that Lloyd's have been making anxious inquiries about the matter. Several vessels have been burned in harbour, and bags of nitrate have caught fire on shore, notably at Pisagua, and have blazed up almost as fiercely as nitrate of potass itself. Once the material is well alight, it is scarcely possible to extinguish the fire or save the ship.

Iquique, as it is, owes its working existence to nitrate of soda, and its prosperity to those who make and deal in it, the latter, seven out of ten perhaps, being foreigners. The occupation of Tarapacá by the Chilian Republic gave Iquique a better administration and an assured form of government. It is assumed as an axiom along the coast that "Chilian officials are honest and that Peruvian officials are the reverse." I do not know how far the remark is true, but there can be, I think, no doubt in the mind of a visitor from Europe that the Chilians are seriously in earnest in their endeavours to improve the condition of their country, and the improvement of the towns in it is necessarily included in that object. There was no effort to render the streets walkable till the town passed into the occupation of Chile.

Darwin's description of Iquique when the *Beagle* visited it in 1835 says:—

"The town contains about 1,000 inhabitants, and stands in a little plain of sand at the foot of a great wall of rock 2,000 feet high, here forming the coast. The whole is utterly a desert. A light shower of rain falls only once in very many years, the ravines are consequently covered with detritus, and the mountain sides covered with piles of fine white sand even to a height of 1,000 feet. During July a heavy bank of clouds stretches over the ocean; it seldom rises above these walls of rocks on the coast. The aspect of the coast is most gloomy. The little port, with its few houses, seemed overwhelmed, and out of all proportion with the rest of the scene. The inhabitants live like persons on board of ship. Every necessary is brought from a distance; water is brought in boats from Pisagua, about forty miles by water, and is sold at the rate of 4s. 6d. an eighteen-gallon cask. Very few animals can be maintained in such a place. I hired with difficulty, at the high price of £4, two mules and a guide to take me to the Nitrate of Soda Works. These are at present the support of Iquique."

Captain Castle, whose excellent "sketch," as he modestly terms it, published in 1887 (he visited Iquique in 1885), may, *mutatis mutandis*, be taken as a good account of the port to-day, after quoting Darwin's description, says:—

"The population of the town, including shipping, is now about 16,000, 30 per cent. of whom are foreigners. The inhabitants still live as persons on board ship, inasmuch as that provisions of every kind are carried to them, either in coasting steamers or sailing vessels. Arica, a port 95 miles north, supplies water, and every class of food; the southern ports of Chili send horses, mules, cattle, poultry, vegetables, fruit, &c. Native sailing vessels supply barley, fodder. Foreign sailing vessels bring hither coal, coke, spirits, wine, machinery, steel, iron, wood, and corrugated iron (for building purposes), jute bags for nitrate of soda and borax, besides every description of general cargo. Abundance of coal, such as Orrell Steam, West Hartley, Australian, and from Lota (South Chile), is imported in enormous quantities, and sold at moderate prices. During the year 1884, 300 sailing vessels, amounting to 223,537 tons, and 33 steamers, amounting to 45,286 tons, entered and left the port. The steamer tonnage does not include the ordinary bi-weekly coasting service of the Pacific Steam Navigation Company and the Compañia Sud Americana de Vapores. In addition to drinking water conveyed in Mr. J. T. North's steamers from Arica, it is distilled in the town. I was informed that the condensing apparatus, &c., patented by Mr. Provend, C.E., and erected by a company formed by him, is capable of making, theoretically speaking, about 26 lbs. of water for 1 lb of the worst description of coal; and can condense 40,000 gallons daily. Mr. J. T. North has also erected an apparatus which I am informed can distil 30 lbs. of water for 1 lb. of coal. There are many other smaller apparatuses for distilling. All exhaust steam is condensed, and used as drinking water for man or beast, or washing purposes.

"A large number of cattle can be maintained in the place: about 700 being imported monthly, 14 oxen and 40 sheep are slaughtered daily, for town consumption, while the remainder are sent to the nitrate districts in the interior.

"Horses and mules are imported and plentiful. Carriages can be hired in the streets at 20 cents. the course, or 2 dols. the hour (the paper dollar is worth 24d., or half the value of the American dollar). Saddle horses stand at five different livery stables, and are let out at 1 dol. per hour on week-days, at 5 dols. an afternoon on Sundays or feast days."

We were some time in Iquique before our party was ready to visit the Pampas, the unseen region whither all the current of supplies was flowing up and whence so much wealth was coming down, but from time to time some of the managers of the *oficinas* came to see Colonel North and to partake of Mr. Rowland's hospitality, and I could form some sort of idea of the clear-headed, energetic, laborious and scientific men who were engaged in the *oficinas* above. Not to be wondered at that nitrate of soda and iodine, the prospects and prices of the markets, the output of the various establishments, furnished the main topics of conversation; for now that "copper is dull," that the effects of the *degringolade* of the French syndicate are felt all along the coast, and in the heart of Chile, and that guano is played out, Iquique depends on nitrates, as indeed does the Railway itself. But there were visitors, too, who had mines to sell and various projects to recommend. One enthusiastic gentleman came to work out nothing less than a rebellion in a neighbouring state, and made an application to Colonel North "to finance a revolution in Peru" as a most legitimate and profitable employment of his spare capital.

Notwithstanding the uncertain nature of mining speculations, the people on the coast, natives as well as foreign, have a great hankering after ventures in quest of ore, and proprietors of mineral property there are always ready to offer it, and wandering prospectors, engineers, and promoters ready to form companies to work it. Some, indeed, have made fortunes. Others have lost them in the quest. There are rich mines near Iquique, and there are those who believe that even in mines long since abandoned there is abundant return to be obtained for the employment of capital, as the Spaniards and Chilians who worked these mines were not able to reduce what they got, or to utilise the deposits. But I think the Chilians who own good mines like to keep them. There were indeed close at hand outward and visible signs and proofs of the existence of silver in the mountain range above us. We could see and judge for ourselves of the richness of the ores of Huantajaya, Descrubadara, Constantia, Paquanta Colorado, and by visits to the "Amalgamating" Works at Cavancha, or to the "Beneficiadora" in Iquique. At the latter I not only walked on a carpet of powdered ore spread over a large enclosed square, but walked down an avenue between walls which were built up of silver bricks! These works are managed by a worthy "Captain" from the west country, long resident on this coast, where he has made many friends and acquired, I hope, a fair fortune, for the family he has reared up in Chile with the help of his good English wife. Although there are certain processes which are not revealed to every visitor, the amalgamation and reduction of the ores are effected, as far as I could judge, after the methods in vogue at Leadville and Denver. The utmost care is taken to guard against the fumes of the quicksilver, and the most recent improvements are applied for the protection of the workmen employed in the amalgamation and reduction. It is said there are fewer cases of mercurial poisoning here than in any similar establishment in Chile, but the hands are careless, and there are now and then patients for the hospital.

Before the party went up to the nitrate fields I had ample leisure to look around me at Iquique, and to observe the ways of a community which lives from hand to mouth on a strip of sand between a restless ocean and a frowning mountain side, with tidal waves to dread outside it, and earthquakes below it, and I must say the people appeared to do very much as they would have done if they had a limpid river at their doors to supply them with water, a full harvest in the fields, pasturage for flocks and herds, and fruit and flowers and pleasant groves around them. They buy and sell, marry and, when the times are good, are given in marriage, dance and sing and enjoy themselves and have their sports, games, and amusements, like other folk.

I was wont to spend many an hour on my balcony, finding never-ending interest in the scene below. In front there is the Cricket ground, an asphalted quadrangle. Not many yards distant from longstop's whereabouts, and within range of a good drive for three, if you are by my side, you may observe a mound of earth like the semi-circular top of one of the village ovens, in the sandy plain in which the shoe would sink ankle deep. There are generally two or three, sometimes more, women in black, kneeling devoutly before the mound, and if you walk over you will see that there are lighted candles flickering in a vaulted space enclosed by adobe walls. The women are worshippers at the tomb of a saint. Who he was I never could ascertain. Possibly I asked the wrong people. Indeed, some worthy residents of Iquique could not tell me the name of the great church in the plaza! But the story I heard was that some years ago the body of a man was found on the beach and carried to this spot and buried. Lo and behold! The leg of the dead man presently popped up out of the grave! It was put under ground once more. But it came up as before! Repeated interments could not keep the uneasy limb in its place. So the people concluded that the man was a saint! They erected a semi-circular wall round the grave. And now in time of trouble, believers repair to the shrine and pray, and votive offerings and flaming tapers attest the sincerity of their faith, and the performance of cures effected, and wishes gratified, by the intercession of the agency of the holy castaway. Irreverent people laugh at all this; they say that the body was that of a drunken English sailor who fell overboard from one of the ships in the harbour. But they did not account for the irrepressible leg or the miracles! For myself I thought it very touching to see these poor worshippers kneeling and praying before their shrine, caring little for the shouts, "Run! Run! Throw it up! Well caught!" and the like from the cricketers and the spectators in the Cricket Clubhouse. There is a tall wooden cross near the mound marking another grave, but no one pays any attention to it.

Two sides of the cricket ground are enclosed by shanties in which the Chilian labourers live. Above the roofs of these rise the iron cranes of the Railway Pier, the cisterns and water tanks of the condensers, and the chimneys of the Iron Foundry and of the workshops of the Railway Company. On a steep hillock, beyond the scraggy little suburb, there is a look-out station on a high mound, with a flagstaff and a fieldpiece, which ought, it is supposed, to be fired by some one or other at noon. There was generally a group of soldiers near the gun about that time. Sometimes they fired it, sometimes they did not. It seemed to me that any of them who liked touched off the piece when he thought it was time; ten minutes before or after made no difference. Occasionally the report coincided with twelve o'clock.

Separated by a wall from the cricket ground you see the offices, storehouses, the passenger and goods stations, the sidings, platforms, locomotive and carriage shed, and workshops of the Nitrate Railway—"worthy," as Captain Castle says, "of any city in Europe"—all on a grand scale, lofty and spacious, covering many acres. Nearer to you down below is the court of the house and the wee farmyard, with a covered fountain in the midst for the delectation of the ducks, poultry and pigeons, and goats, of which Mrs. Rowland superintends the welfare, and therein, in the tiny garden, the green of which is most refreshing to the eye, are some bravely struggling trees, creepers, rose-bushes and flowers. To the left are the roofs of the houses of the town, the Church of the Immaculate Conception, cup and ball, pediment and dome painted in many hues—at least five distinct colours—and farther away there are the pier and the signal tower, which indicates by flags and a ball the state of the surf, safe or otherwise, and Lighthouse, the Island which protects the roadstead and the town from the sea. The chimneys of the Gasworks meet the eye farther southwards, and beyond the limit of the streets and across a little bay, you catch sight, on a rocky spit, of the buildings of Cavancha, a conglomerate of wooden shanties, eating-houses, and restaurants, on platforms built over the sea, to which the Iquiquetians resort in tramcar, carriage, on foot or horseback, to bathe, or to eat and drink, with the salt spray in their faces, and the breakers boiling at their feet.

The contrast between the stony face of the rugged Andes

frowning sullenly through the veil of mist which hangs, like a Turkish lady's yashmak, across it, and the heaving breast of the blue Pacific girt by iron reefs, fringed with white surf, is very striking. The huge vessels in the harbour, for the most part full-rigged ships and barques, rolling lazily at their anchors, the barges moving between them and the beach, the busy little tugs, the small sail-

The Nitrate Railway. Iquique to Mollé.

boats beating in or out of the seaward channels between the spit of mainland on which the city is built and the rocky island that guards the anchorage from the southern and western gales, occupy the foreground. The roll of cart-wheels, the clang of tramcar bells and bugles, the whistle of the locomotive, the hum of men, the animation in the marts and street, are so strange when one looks around and sees that all this bustle is going on in a veritable wilderness of sand, without visible means of subsistence or *raison d'être* whatever, fenced in by the sea on one side, and the inexorable mountain on the other

Every day I saw from my room in Mr. Rowland's comfortable mansion, the Nitrate Railway trains ascending and descending the steep mountain side, those going up laden with jute bags and supplies for the oficinas, which depend on the port for food, clothing, the necessaries of life and machinery; those coming down, charged with the result of the labour of the nitrate manufacturers. They were as regular as clockwork in their rates, each train keeping its prescribed distance from the other, as if they were fixed parts of a machine. As each train passes a station the clerks in the office at Iquique are notified by the telegraph of the exact time, and the manager has under his eye, as it were, the position of every engine and waggon on the line. The railway can be traced stretched like a narrow black riband on the greyish-brown mountain side from the Reversing Station outside the town some two miles away, to which the ascent is not very steep. As you look eastwards to the Andes, you see near the skyline a faint small white cloud like the smoke of a gun. But it moves—the puffs are intermittent Straining your eyes you make out a dark object on the black thread. It is a locomotive descending from the Pampas, drawing its appointed load of waggons and carriages. It seems almost stationary—but it is creeping down. As you are trying to count the trucks in the train, another jet of vapour from another black speck at the summit behind, announces another train in the wake of that which is now visibly gaining ground towards you. Presently a third train comes in view. You have now the three before you at the exact same distance one from the other, so well timed and kept that as the first is running into the Station close at hand the second is reversing above you, and the third will be at

158   CHILE AND THE NITRATE FIELDS.

the Reversing Station by the time the second has arrived at the platforms, and each comes in within a second of its regulated schedule. A similar exactness is maintained in the movements of the ascending trains. I used to watch them daily through my glass toiling up the steep till they vanished one after the other over the summit, and I never

Nitrate Railway, with Iquique in the Distance.

could detect any variation in their orderly progress. The nitrate bags are unloaded at the bodegas or warehouses on the seashore close to the pier and custom house, where are accumulated what is needed by the oficinas and their people. The powerful Fairlie engines (eight wheeled—Fairlie and Fowler's), from eighty-two to eighty-five tons each, are masters of the situation and haul up their seven

12-ton cars with the greatest ease. At the beginning of 1889 the Railway and branches could boast of $230\frac{1}{2}$ miles of rail, all of steel, 64 lbs. to the yard, fish plated and tied, 5 ties in 24 feet. The rolling stock consisted of 45 locomotives, 8 first, 9 second class carriages, 1 inspector's car, 2 baggage vans, 1 engine van, 1 breakdown car, 16 cattle, and 834 trucks, but of course the stock is augmented from time to time. As to the facts and figures, are they not written in the annual report? Some fine day no doubt the line will be double.

CHAPTER XIII.

IQUIQUE TO THE PAMPAS.

The Ascent—The Fight off Iquique—The *Esmeralda* and *Huascar*—The Moving Mountain—Molle—A Silver Mine—The Salt Pampas—Darwin's Description—The Central Station—A Nitrate Clapham Junction—The Nitrate Kingdom—Pozo Almonte—The Resources of Civilisation—Saturnalia of the Salitreros—The Scenery—Maquinas—Buen Retiro San Donato—Ramirez—The Liverpool Nitrate Company

A WEEK after our arrival at Iquique we started (May 13), for the Pampas. The special train, composed of an American saloon carriage, a truck for baggage, and the engine, preceded by a pilot engine, was in charge of Mr. Rowland, and we felt quite safe in his hands.

The engines are necessarily powerful, for the gradients vary from 2.50 to 3.85 per cent., and there are curves to be overcome of 450 feet radius. The favourite type in general use is, I believe, a Fairlie of from eighty to eighty-five tons, with double boilers. The line climbs up, due east, the steep mountain side from the terminus to the Reversing Station two miles distant. There the engine is transferred to the other end of the train, and thence strikes the line south to the slope of the Andes. On the left hand as you mount there is the oolite rock of the mountain range seamed with ravines which are filled with drifted sand; to the right there is the steep slope of the hillside, descending sheerly to the sandy strip between its base and the beach. Not more than a mile across from the base the strip of flat land is bounded by the beach and the reefs and the breakers of the Pacific. As we mount the view becomes more picturesque, in the true sense that it is very like a picture. Not many minutes pass before the passengers in the train look on the town of Iquique, which is spread out below, like a chess-board with large squares, seemingly so near that you make out the Alameda, the Cathedral, the Station, Cavancha and the Racecourse, the Hospital, the Silver Refineries, the Gas and Water Works, the Lighthouse and Custom-house, the houses of your acquaintances, set in a framework of brown desert, with a fretwork border of rocks on which the surf beats eternally. As the train ascends, the lines contract, and the ships in harbour between the island and the shore are dwarfed to cock-boats.

You are now looking down on the scene of a great event in the history of the late war. For a Chilian this is classic ground, and below is classic sea. Iquique, then a Peruvian port, was blockaded by the Chilian vessels *Esmeralda*, Captain Prat, and *Covadonga*, Captain Condell, when the Peruvian ironclads *Independencia* and *Huascar* came down to raise the blockade, and on 21st May, 1879, a combat which ensured Arturo Prat a Chilian immortality ended gloriously, if fatally, for the blockaders. The wooden corvette, *Esmeralda*, was rammed by the *Huascar* after a vigorous defence of four hours, and a gallant attempt to carry the ironclad, in which Prat perished on the deck of the enemy, and sank with 120 of the crew of 180 officers and men with which she began the action. You can see the point (Gruesa) off which the *Independencia*, chasing the little *Covadonga*, was lost. The Chilian steamer, to escape her formidable foe, ran inside a reef off the point close in shore, and the Peruvian, following with more eagerness than judgment, went on the rocks and was wrecked. The anniversary of the fight is kept as a national holiday.

About six miles from the Reversing Station there lies, on the right hand side of the line as you ascend, a remarkable ridge of sand "in the shape of a cornucopia," says one eye-witness, "with the narrow end next the slope of the mountain, and the broad or truncated end towards Iquique." "It looks," according to another, "like some monstrous animal couchant, a great lion with ribs and sides and mane of sand, menacing the plain." Travellers have related that this sandhill, variously estimated to be 600, 800, and 1,000 feet high, is slowly moving southwards, and have prophesied woe to Iquique, but I could not find any verification of the story that the hill moves onwards year by year. At all events the progress of the hill is slow, and it may not be sure. Once a man managed to get up to the top of the mound, and it was with great difficulty he was rescued from the sand.

As the line mounts we cross old mule-tracks from the shore, not yet altogether abandoned, as cattle for consumption at the mines and oficinas are still driven up by the herdsmen to the plateaux above, and some of the ore is sent down by these routes to the reducing works, under the superintendence of Mr. Nichols, and to the works of the Chilian Company at Iquique. At Mollé, where there is a small station, about 1,600 feet above the sea level, a *débris* of bottles, meat tins, leather, rags, and bones, on the desert near at hand, marks the site of a Peruvian encampment, and gazing on the scene around us, we can realise the nature of a campaign in such a country. The winter plateau before Sebastopol was a very blooming parterre—the desert between Kassas-

Iquique, from the Nitrate Railway.

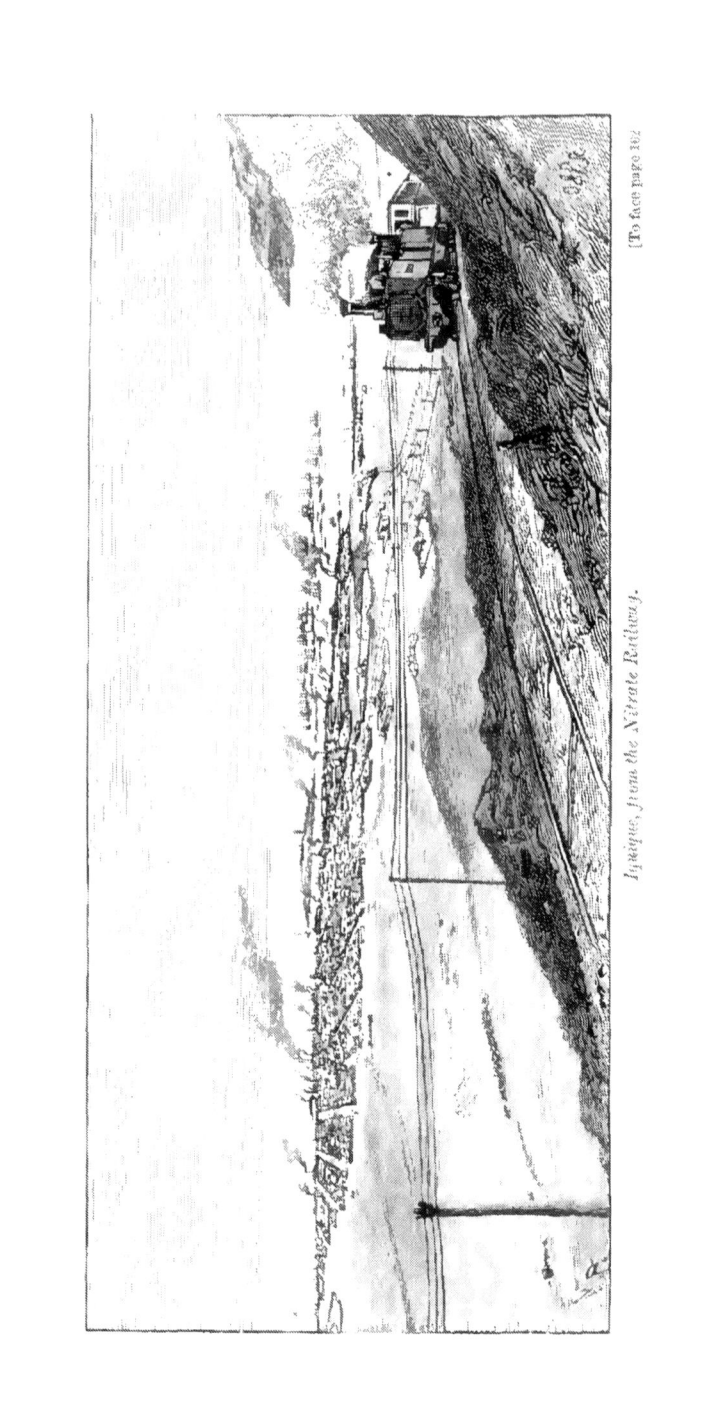

[To face page 162.

sin and Tel-el-Kebir, a garden of Eden—compared to the sandy, salty, waterless waste before us, bestrewn with belts, old shoes, cooking utensils, &c., and scarred by trenches, the broken walls of camp ovens and gun emplacements. How and where the men got water I know not, unless it was brought by rail from below, or by mules from the wells far away on the pampas. There seems to have been a force of several thousand men on the ground, but it is possible that some of the rubbish and refuse was contributed by railway "navvy" detachments or miners on their way to the Pampas. When the Peruvians evacuated Iquique after the Battle of Dolores or San Francisco, November, 1879, they halted here on their way to Tarapacá, where the allied forces of Peru and Bolivia hoped to make a successful stand against the Chilians. Both sides claimed the victory at Tarapacá, but after the battle the Peruvians retreated to Arica, and their march across the desert was one of the most trying and terrible recorded in history.

At Mollé the line curves sharply to the eastward. A few miles further we pass Santa Rosa, 17½ miles from Iquique, some 3,200 feet above sea level. Santa Rosa is not cheerful to the eye, but in relation to the mines of silver ore in the district, for the produce of which it affords an outlet to the refineries of Iquique, it has its past and its future. Huantajaya, in its immediate neighbourhood, is a name to conjure with among mining adventurers. Not a great way from the station lies the mining ground of one company, which has as yet made no great external show. On the sand-covered rock on the right of the line there was a small, a very small, wigwam settlement, the inhabitants of which, some score of men and women, Chilian or Bolivian, and various skittish goats, gathered in front of their village to look at the train. The passengers got out for a minute or two to look down two small shafts of culvert-like proportions, and to walk a few yards on the plank incline, which was the "railway siding" on which stress was laid in the prospectus of the Company. Whatever silver ore may turn up can certainly be carried away with ease to the beneficiadores below. Of a verity there is need of mineral wealth here to make amends for the sterility of the land in everything else.

We are on the plains—"the pampas," at last—but as yet the view is limited. The sea is invisible; on the right there is the railway embankment and sandhills; on the left a rough waste of greyish red earth, bounded by a line of hills to the east. Assuredly there is nothing to charm the eye in the scenery around us. I remember nothing like it save the bed of the Bitter Lakes at Ismailia before M. de Lesseps opened the flood gates and let in the sea water on the basin of salt and sand. The description of Darwin in 1835 will apply to what we gazed on to-day :—

"The appearance of the country was remarkable from being covered with a thick crust of common salt, and of a stratified saliferous alluvium, which seems to have been deposited as the land slowly rose above the level of the sea. The salt is white, very hard and compact; it occurs in water-worn nodules projecting from the agglutinated sand, and is associated with much gypsum. The appearance of this superficial mass very closely resembled that of a country after snow, before the last dirty patches are thawed. The existence of this crust of a soluble substance over the whole face of the country shows how extraordinarily dry the climate must have been for a long period."

The simile is excellent. The plain was exactly like a field covered with the "dirty patches" of snow which are left by a thaw in level country at home.

There was some tough engineering and navvy work for several miles through this region, from the summit of the first plateau.

The Central Station, 29 miles from Iquique and 3,220 feet above the sea level, is a veritable surprise. There is a large station with sidings and platforms, a telegraph service and post-office, a hotel, a restaurant, a general store —a "merchant's," they would call it in the Highlands— trucks filled with nitrate drawn up for carriage to the port, and trucks laden with jute bags and cases, in readiness to be hauled to the oficinas to which they are accredited. There are around the station—marvellous to see in such a place!—Norwegian frame-houses—wood and zinc with high sloping roofs—and the walls are covered with familiar names and advertisements, which recall the old world beyond the sea.

Here is the junction of the line to Pisagua on the north, and of the Iquique line, which continues as a main trunk with many branches, to the nitrate works, to the south. From the Central Station the oficinas of Sebastopol, Paposo, San Carlos, San Vicente, Sacramento, San Pedro, Peruana, San Fernando, Solferino, and Argentina, lying close together, are provided with communication and transport. It is a Nitrate Clapham Junction. The branch to the west serves Nueva Soledad, San Juan de Gildemeister, Esmeralda, Balta, and San Lorenzo, where it halts. The branch to the east serves San Pablo, Virginia, and turning sharply to the north, ends at St. Elena. It is from the southernmost part of this branch that the projected railway will run to Lagunas.

Whilst our giant Fairlies were being unharnessed here, and lighter pampas engines were tackled to the train, we walked about the station and heard the local news from the master and the gentlemen of the nitrate oficinas, who had come to meet Colonel North. These large stations are centres of life to the circle of nitrate fields around them, and groups of workmen assemble to hear the news, inspect the new arrivals, and enjoy themselves after their fashion.

As the train entered into the Nitrate Kingdom, the lieges assembled sought to testify their loyalty by firing off squibs and crackers, cheering and waving flags. The visitors had an opportunity of seeing the natives in their most festive mood. When we looked around we had reason for wondering where they lived when they were at home, and where they would go to when the train moved off.

I had a most interesting account from a fellow passenger of the manners and customs of the people, among whom he has worked for many years, and I am obliged to say, that with all the stamp of authority and truth on what he told me, I was rather loth to accept the statements he made respecting the immorality of the priesthood, if not of to-day, of times not remote, and of the consequent degradation of their flocks. Gallenga and others have given accounts of the shocking profligacy of the clergy in some South American States, not, it seems, inapplicable to this part of Chile. The Peruvian episcopate held very loose reins, and its members were by no means strict in discipline or practice. The peccadilloes of the *padres* were matters for village gossip and amusement. "*Non meus sermo, sed quæ præcepit Ofellius*"—my informant—a very good fellow indeed. He left us at the Central Station, to my great regret. A geologist, naturalist, physician, philosopher, and man of sense, his lot seems not to be cast in pleasant places, but he has accepted it patiently if not cheerfully. Lord Palmerston told the late Wingrove Cook that if a stranger desired to be thoroughly misinformed he would "listen to a man who had been thirty years in the country and spoke the language like a native." My friend had these qualifications, but he was entirely trustworthy. He did not give me leave to use his name. I am sure he would not have refused it had I asked, for he is as fearless as he is truthful. His father, who fought under Napoleon, is in his ninety-fifth year, in possession of all his faculties, and his son related some of the reminiscences of the veteran, which will, I hope, find permanent record.

Continuing our course northwards from the Central Station, we see the Pampas spreading out on either side of us like an inland sea, or the bed of one, with ochre-coloured shores, above which, on the right, rise cloud-like Andes, with snow patches on the summits, roseate in the rays of the declining sun. The ruins of adobe walls and chimneys around us marked the sites of abandoned native manufactories of nitrate, but without help I could not have guessed what they were. They mostly date from the days when the raw material was boiled, under the old system, in large shallow cauldrons, one or two of which were still to be seen lying about.

I have been continually reminded of the African desert and of the western shore of the Red Sea since I visited the pampas

The train passed the next station, Montevideo, $36\frac{1}{2}$ miles from Iquique, and 3,811 feet above the sea, without stopping. This is the highest point on the railway, and is therefore selected as the site of the great reservoir, where the water pumped by steam from the wells at Pozo Almonte is stored for the supply of the Central Station, and stations and oficinas dependent on it, till the Tarapacá Water Works Company can complete the line of pipes from La Pica, 44 miles distant, in the foot-hills of the Andes.

At 2 5 p.m. the special drew up at Pozo Almonte.

Now the first large oficina is in sight. The word " oficina " is of liberal application—it may mean the counting house of a banker or a merchant, the bureau of an advocate, a workshop, a place of business or a manufactory. On the pampas it signifies an establishment for the manufacture of nitrate of soda and iodine. The outward aspect of an oficina does not contribute to the ornamentation of the scene in which it is placed In the tall chimney, in the boiler arrangements, and in the mounds of refuse outside, which afterwards we learned to speak of and to know as *ripio*, there is a general resemblance to gas works, with the adjuncts of a coal mine. The surface of the ground near at hand is scarred with excavations like rifle pits.

Pozo Almonte, or the Well on the Hill, 3,371 feet above the sea level we had so lately left, is provided with a corrugated iron or zinc hotel and restaurant neatly painted and well furnished—prints on the walls and carpets on the floors, all kinds of tinned luxuries on the shelves, a bar, many varieties of drinks in bottles, Stein-wein in box-beutel, Cabinet hock, and Chateau Lafite, and every appliance for the reasonable requirements of civilized man, and swarms of flies. This height of 3,371 feet is nothing to speak of as an elevation compared with the heights of the Andes, not far off; but when we think of Snowdon, Ben Nevis,

Benmaedhui, and our insular mountainous aspirations, Pozo Almonte stands fairly well up in the world.

At the station there is the pumping establishment, by which 6,000 gallons per hour of a highly mineral water are obtained for the railway locomotives, &c , but the quality of the fluid is unsatisfactory and it crusts the boilers with deposit Pozo Almonte possesses a workshop, engine and carriage shed, ample platforms, and stores. It is the point on which the routes and branch lines from Buen Retiro, Calacala, La Palma, Peña Chica, San José, La Serena, Normandia, and Tegethoff converge. There is an excellent dwelling-house for Mr. Watts, the station master, and suitable accommodation for his staff; and the dusty, hungry, and weary traveller—and I think it likely any stranger who is voyaging in these parts will be well described by these adjectives—will, I am told, find a triumph of civilisation in the shape of the before-mentioned hotel, good rooms for living and sleeping, and abundant meals, to which additions can be made from the store, where foreign delicacies, wines, liqueurs, aerated and mineral waters, potted and preserved meats—yea, even *pâtés de foie gras* and truffles of Perigord—are arrayed on the shelves, or, if he desires economy, from the market-women, by whom fruit, native pastry, chucha, and the like are sold. There is another traffic carried on in the great collection of hovels and huts made of wood, corrugated iron and zinc, of which least said is soonest mended. I dare no more than hint at the orgies here, of which drunkenness is the most innocent incident, when pay day, Saints' days, or holidays liberate the workpeople, and attract them to the joys of Pozo Almonte Saturnalia.

The train moved off to the sound of vivas, cheers, and crackers. A few miles from the station there appeared away on our right a welcome sight. There was something green to look at. A great plain stretching for miles to the foot of the second range of the Andes, of which the higher crêtes were white with snow, had, under the impulse of a flush of water from the hills in a sudden

Fruit and Cake Sellers, outside a Pulperia.

thaw some years ago, thrown up a crop of "tamarugal," and other shrubs. In the distance, where the flood, after it had cut channels of escape for itself over the slopes in the plain, had loitered and found rest in the hollows, were clumps—yea, even little groves and avenues of trees. There were now many oficinas in view, each in the centre of its nitrate ground—all with a common garniture, the branch railway and line of trucks loaded up with nitrate bags, ripio heaps, mounds of caliche, chimneys, boilers, tanks, the residences of the overseers, the pulperia, or stores, and the—truth to say—squalid-looking settlements where the workmen and their families abode. They were to be to seen on the plains far in front for miles, chimneys smoking, railways working, banks of ripio, trains of carts and mules.

Close to Pozo Almonte is Buen Retiro, and we left our carriage at the siding and walked over to inspect the works. The external aspect of the oficina was not unlike that of a north-country coal or iron mine—tall chimneys and machinery, corrugated iron buildings, offices and houses, the shanties of workmen, a high bank of refuse.

The Buen Retiro was established by Colonel North, in conjunction with Mr. R. Harvey, some years back, and was subsequently transferred by them to the Colorado Nitrate Company.

After glancing at the huge boilers, one of them turned out from the foundry established at Iquique, the Blake crusher with its ceaselessly-wagging iron tongue, the 8 boiling tanks, 18 feet long, 6 feet broad, and 7 feet deep; the 28 bateas, each 24 feet long, 12 feet wide, and $3\frac{1}{2}$ feet deep, steaming like so many miniature geysers, some filled with orange-coloured or crimson *caldo*, and others with precipitated nitrate, we entered the residence of the manager. British furniture and faces, and a *ménu* comprising such items as "Bouchées de roi à la Godard," "Aspic de foie gras en bellevue," and "Dinde truffée aux marrons," went far to convince us that we were not in a very uncivilized region after all. The talk, or at any rate a great deal of it, ran on nitrate, and it was incidentally stated that the *caliche* here averaged 35 per cent.

Also that 16 cartloads of *caliche*, 38 quintals each, would produce from 150 to 160 quintals of nitrate. The oficina was giving a yield of 30,000 to 35,000 quintals a month at the date of our visit, but we were informed that it was equal to turning out double this amount. After luncheon we passed through the pulperia, where mercery, haberdashery, grocery, and greengrocery, to say nothing of wines, beer and spirits, are sold to the workpeople on what would be bitterly denounced in England as the truck system, and we also glanced at the iodine house.

Having had our first lesson in nitrate making, we mounted to our places, and the train started. There is certainly no attractive feature in the outward aspect of nitrate-making. It seems to be an almost invariable concomitant of manufacturing processes that the pursuit of utility should not be accompanied by any attention to decorative art. Looking in front, you see on either side slender chimneys rising above black or dun-coloured masses of machinery, vomiting out smoke, white vapourous steam issuing from the boilers beneath, and heaps of brown refuse, which enable an expert to judge of the extent of the output or the age of the oficina.

As the shepherd knows each sheep in his flock, and can detect differences between each invisible to the eye of a stranger, so the intelligent gentlemen who have brought to perfection this strange industry on the Pampas can pick out nitrate works, and show how one varies from another.

Passing on the way, Calacala, La Palma, Peña Chica, San José, Peña Grande, on the left or western side of the line, and most of them with short sidings, we continued our journey ten miles on to San Donato, where we descended to inspect the oficina.

The San Donato Company own 147 estacas, and the patches of caliche which are now being worked yield about 45 per cent. of nitrate. At present about 30 estacas are under exploitation, the rest being untouched ground. Some 32,000 or 33,000 quintals of nitrate are produced every month, but it is expected that there will be a large increase when the new manufactory is built and improved machinery erected. At present there are three boilers 24 feet by 7 feet, one Blake crusher, seven boiling tanks, 28 feet long, 6 feet broad, and $6\frac{1}{2}$ feet deep, and fifty-three buteas, 15 feet square, with a good slope Here, as at most of the oficinas in this district, there is an iodine house, of the operations in which I shall have a word to say presently.

Having inspected the buildings, looked at the crushers working, the *caliche* boiling, the mounds of nitrate stored up on the *canchus* at the base of the *buteas*, and the bags awaiting transport, we resumed our journey and after another short run halted at the Ramirez oficina, belonging to the Liverpool Nitrate Company. The works appeared to be very extensive and complete. A great collection of boilers, tanks, engines, two chimneys rising in the midst, workmen's huts and the residences of the staff, the pulperia or shop—of which a similar establishment is attached to every oficina on the Pampas. The maquina is intended to work an area of 300 estacas; it possesses six boilers, four crushers, ten boiling and sixty precipitating tanks, and can turn out 140,000 quintals of nitrate a month. Six square miles of nitrate ground, said to be exceedingly rich, are owned by the company. On the branch railway a long train of waggons loaded up with nitrate bags for the port was awaiting haulage, and the explosions of the *tiros* near at hand indicated great activity of working power.

From Ramirez the engine travelled slowly and cautiously onward. As the sun set, fiery flashes pierced the darkness, followed by heavy thuds, as if of some cannonade, and when it became quite dark it needed no great stretch of fancy to imagine that one was looking at a bombardment of some town from the sea. These outbursts were the firings of the mines. The towers of the oficinas shot rays of electric light through the waste, and as the train passed them, we heard the heavy thumping of the machinery crushing *caliche*. And so we went by Constancia, Santa Rosa, Rosario di Huara, San Jorge, Tres Marias. Then there was a run of five miles to a junction where were many trucks piled up with nitrate. Thence our little train turned down a siding or branch line, and presently stopped at the platform of a large station. We could see by the light high above our heads the outlines of the oficina, with which we were to become better acquainted. Primitiva at last!

Oficina. Liverpool Nitrate Company.

[To face page 174

CHAPTER XIV.

PRIMITIVA.

Primitiva—The Reception—Our Quarters—Mr Humberstone—The Staff—
The Workmen—The Pulperia—The Early Morning—Quo Quousque?—
A Look Round—Drive to the Calicheras—The Operations on the Calichera

"SENSATIONS" are not very common upon the Pampas, and the arrival of Colonel North produced a considerable commotion among the workpeople. Their day's labour could not be said to have ceased, for they work night and day; and the population, young and old, assembled at the station and greeted the visitors with tumultuous demonstrations of rejoicing, which became oppressive when the natives followed the party up to Mr. Humberstone's house, mounted the steps, crowded the floor of the verandahs, and flattened their noses against the windows. They were invading the hall, when they were driven forth by two little men in white linen uniforms, armed with the largest sabres—the longest and the broadest-bladed I ever saw—the hilts well up under their arms, and the scabbards clattering at their heels—members of the gendarmerie, who are, it appears, necessary on large establishments upon the Pampas to keep unruly spirits in order.

Mr. Humberstone's house is 3,700 feet above sea level. It is a quadrangle with the Spanish patio or court in the centre, on a solid base raised six feet from the ground, covered with zinc, a verandah all round, in the style of a good Indian bungalow. It has accommodation for the manager's family, for the secretary and administrators of the oficina, and the usual household offices. Although the house is many-roomed, I fear me our party bulged out, or doubled up, some of the usual residents. The works are not a hundred yards away, and as the house is on an elevation, you command a view from it of the main railway, the oficina line, the boilers, tanks, nitrate shoots and canchas, and the large village built of one-storeyed

Primitiva. Branch and Main Lines.

houses numbered in order in regular streets, a few hundred yards further on, where the workmen of Primitiva and their families live. The dwellings are of patchwork. Pieces of zinc, corrugated iron, matting, and shreds of sacking do duty as walls to some of the shanties. The workmen are Chilians, Peruvians, Bolivians — the last are the best — generally married, I presume, from the number of women and children I saw about — neither very clean nor oppressed with much clothing. They are not always orderly. Sometimes there are violent and dangerous quarrels among them — the men carry knives. When the workmen drink there is trouble, and it is not easy to keep drink from them. The men, brown as coffee, are stout, sinewy fellows, and do an immense amount of work on their favourite diet of beans—or *peroto*—which Mr. Hicks told me he considered to be a most excellent and nutritious food, but as the Irishman consumes great quantities of potatoes when he lives on them alone, so does the Chilian eat very largely of these beans. At the well-furnished *pulperia* or store they can get necessaries of every description—clothes, provisions, wines, and spirits, and there is generally a supplementary market outside the station, in which itinerant basket-men and women sell vegetables, cakes, fruit, &c. Next the village are the stables or *corrals* for the mules and horses, and then there is a wide expanse of *caliche* beds all around the oficina up to the rounded hills of moderate elevation which enclose the banks of the desiccated lagoon, where the nitrate lies under the "crust."

The administrator of the oficina, Mr. Humberstone, lives with his staff around him, engaged in his campaign against *caliche* without respite. Glancing over the books in his library I saw the most recent and approved writings of modern chemists, geologists, and mineralogists. The tables were covered with the latest papers and periodicals, and the rooms were so well appointed and comfortable that it was difficult to realise the fact that you were out of the world, in a house on a waterless desert, or to understand how in a few years so many of the conveniences and luxuries of life could have been collected on the spot. Mrs. Jones and our host's wife—ladies who did much to render our stay agreeable under Mr. Humberstone's roof—had many reminiscences of their time of trial and anxiety in the time of the war. Mrs. Jones' house, further north, became the headquarters of the Bolivian general, President Daza, and, to escape the shock of actual battle, she was eventually obliged to fly from it with her family, and to travel weary miles in the wilderness to a place of safety.

The members of the staff are intelligent, active young gentlemen, and are all well educated and well paid, and have their several departments to attend to One looks after the working parties, another superintends the transport, a third manages the personnel, a fourth has charge of the machinery, and so forth. One has been an officer in a crack regiment, another an engineer. There is also an accountant and a bookkeeper and a statistician, so that the state of Primitiva is carefully regulated and governed. The effect of the novelty of the scene and of the situation, the strangeness of the life around me, and the fatigues of the day, not inconsiderable, in wayside hospitality, and in visits to bateas and boilers, counteracted each other, and I sat up with the company rather late the night of our arrival

I went to bed with the throbbing of the machinery and the clank of steam engines near at hand in my ears. At one side of the house all was silent; at the other side there was Primitiva thundering and clanging away, for the work goes on incessantly, gang following gang, crushers grinding *caliche*, boilers dissolving it to stew in its own juice, in *agua vieja*, and nitrate of soda yielding itself up in the tanks night and day, to be sent all over the world.

Before sunrise, or indeed daylight, a general subdued uneasiness—the creaking boards, betraying a passing footstep, the opening of a window shutter or blind, the gentle closing of a door—announced that the natives of the house interior were up and stirring. Among the luxuries of the establishment was a capital bath-room, and there the last particle of dust from the steppe of the day before was got rid of before the coffee, rolls, bread and butter, &c ,

Primitiva.

[*To face page* 173.

of the *chota hazari*, which is *en regle* to precede a visit to the works, were ready.

In the daytime Primitiva,* for all the electric lighting, shows to more advantage than at night. You see that every portion of the machinery and all the accessories are beautifully kept, that the three great chimneys are bright red, that the boilers are fronted with white tiles, that the bateas or vats—drawn up like a battalion of soldiers in company columns—are painted scarlet. At the same time the more you see, the more the dimensions of the factory grow upon you. The main buildings, some sixty or seventy yards distant from the house of the administrator, run along at the foot of a high bank and abut upon it, and above them are the engine-house to work the crushers, the cabins of the attendants, and the pillar and look-out steps of the electric lighthouse. This is the centre of the *estaciamento*, the heart and head of the great nitrate-producing establishment of Primitiva.

As I was standing in front of the door of the house before we set out on our day's work, surveying the curious sights and listening to the strange sounds near at hand, I asked one of the staff, "What extent does Primitiva cover?" The answer was, "Twelve square miles." "How much of that has been worked?" "I should say about three square miles, but some of that ground has been only partially worked. We begin at the outer parts of the estate and work gradually back towards the *maquina*." "Well, how long do you suppose the *caliche* grounds you have to work will last?" "That is, a question to which no answer can be given, because we do not know what the output is to be. If the present *maquina* were worked at the present rate—that is, if the general

* See Appendix.

number of quintals per day which has been turned out on the average were not exceeded—I believe there is *caliche* enough here to last for the next thirty years. Even then, if nitrate of soda became very dear and commanded high prices, there is plenty of stuff, which it is not worth our while to deal with at present, that might be worked at a profit." "But supposing that the manufacture of nitrate of soda were pushed to the utmost, and that all the force of the *maquina* were exerted to turn it out in quantities, without reference to price or cost, how long would the *caliche* last?" "The answer must be conjectural. I could go into the figures, but even then there would be no certainty, for there can be no average of the quality of the *caliche* over nine square miles. However, I would say that with the very largest possible production of nitrate the beds would last for fifteen or eighteen years to come." "And what would happen then?" "That is beyond my ken. So far as this ground is concerned we can continue, I firmly believe, yielding nitrate of soda sufficient to pay most handsome dividends for more than twenty—ay, or twenty-five—years to come. Can the same be said of any other mining work?—coal?—diamonds?—gold?—silver?—copper? Certainly not! Here comes your carriage."

And so my wife and I set out in a two-wheeled cabriolet provided with a hood and drawn by a pair of mules, ridden by a Chilian Postillon de Longjumeau, to explore the nitrate fields and processes, under the guidance of Mr. Teare, who heedless of the fine dust, which rose like smoke from the ground on the slightest provocation, rode alongside us. The ladies, escorted by Colonel North, Mr. Humberstone, and all the riding men, took to the saddle on horses from the stables, which were well stocked with them, and with very fine mules. The moment the caval-

A Calidera, Primitiva.

To face page 18.

cade was in motion the equestrians were lost, in clouds not altogether celestial, as completely as Homeric heroes; but presently there arose a brisk breeze, as there generally does in the morning on the Pampas, and the annoyance was blown away to leeward as fast as it was made.

The limits of the various estates on the pampas are marked by slabs, like milestones, or by mounds of earth at regular intervals. In less than half an hour, driving across country to the westward, we came to the scene of operations, or rather to one of them. The vicinity of this *two* was marked by pits, around the edges of which were masses of earth in wall-like mounds. This accumulation was formed by the broken *costra*, and all that remained of the *caliche* bed were excavations resembling upon a small scale the craters of volcanoes; these pits were worked-out mines.

The technical words used in describing the section of a nitrate mine are—*chuca*, the outer covering, the surface of the ground, generally friable, varying in thickness, sometimes scarcely existent; the *costra*, or bed of harder earth beneath the *chuca*, resting on the *caliche;* then the *caliche* itself, which varies from a few inches to 10ft. or 12ft. in thickness; then, under the rock-like mass of the nitrate bed, the soft stratum of earth or sand called *cova*.

We approached a group of men engaged in breaking up the *caliche* and separating it from the *costra*. The hole into which we peered was about 7ft. deep, and for about 15ft. on either side of it the earth was heaved up and cracked in deep fissures by an explosion of the mine fired the night before. Around us were also the great blocks of *costra* and *caliche* not yet separated, which had been blown up. Two little forests of iron bars or "jumpers" were stuck into the ground near at hand to be used by-and-by. The material from which nitrate of soda is evolved resembles rock salt, sometimes seeming so white and so pure that it should need very little manufacturing to fit it for the market. In reality, however, this fine-looking stuff needs preparation as well as coarser-looking ley. The appearance of *caliche* is no safe guide; the actual quality of it can only be tested in the chemist's office. As in all strata formed as *caliche* is supposed to be, there is great difference in the thickness of the seams, so in the nitrate grounds the strata of the *caliche*, of the covering of it, and of the matter on which it rests, differ materially in depth; the *costra* may be an inch or several feet thick, the *cova* or earth underlying the *caliche* may be reached by the *barreteros* very readily, or they may spend weary hours in the *tiro* in driving the "jumper" through *costra* and *caliche* before they arrive at the *cova* where the powder is to be placed for the mine. When the hole has been made to the *cova* it is enlarged by means of a gigantic spoon till it is sufficiently wide to let down a little boy, the powder-monkey, or, as he is called, the *destazdor*, whose business it is to scrape away the soft earth under the *caliche* till he has hollowed out the *taza* or cup for the charge of powder for the breaking up of the bed. The *barretero* has sunk the shaft, the *destazdor* has scraped out the *taza*, the *particular* then charges the *tiro* with a bag of powder, to which is attached a fuse long enough to allow the men of the working party to retire to a safe distance, and fires it. In adjusting the strength of the charge considerable knowledge, to be gained only by experience, is required; the object being,—not to produce a volcanic eruption—but to disintegrate the ground thoroughly, so as to split it in every direction, and enable the *particular*, or man in charge of the working party, to judge whether it is worth while to clean the *caliche* and load it on the carts for the factory.

NITRATE OF SODA MAKING   183

When the smoke has cleared away the *particular* and his workmen come to examine the ground. As he is paid by the number of cartloads that he sends away

Primitiva. Filling the Waggons.

from the *tiro*, he has to decide whether he will load the carts from the bed or try another, because he must put good *caliche* into the carts for the crusher or he will be docked of his pay. The *corrector*, or overseer, argues with him over the price per cartload—35 to 42 quintals are a cartload—before the rate is fixed. It is said that sharp eyes are needed to prevent very inferior stuff being mixed up with good *caliche* in the loads put on the carts, but of this I have only report. The *particular*, having had the price fixed per cart, proceeds, with the help of his gang and the

Primitiva. Filling the Crushers.

carters, to place the loads in fixed weights on the carts or in the small trucks on the portable railway.

With the early morning, just at daybreak, begins the labour of loading the carts. The *caliche*, broken up into suitable blocks, is piled, when it is separated from the *costra*, in stacks by the side of the *tiro*. All the arrangements for the working of an oficina are minute in the division of labour and responsibility. The *capataz*, who has under

him mounted men, controls the carters and directs their
labour. The carts are kept going between the mine and
the *maquina* all day with very little interruption. Mules

The Crushers at Work.

when exhausted are allowed to find their own way to
the stables, their places being taken by others always
kept for the purpose. When the animals have to struggle
through very bad ground, the horsemen of the *capataz*
hitch on and help them. As each cart arrives at the

factory, the contents of it are inspected by the man (*bolelero*) who is in charge of the crushers, and who determines whether the material shall be tipped over to be crushed up or rejected. The crushers are placed a few feet below the ridge, or incline, up which the carts are drawn. The *caliche* is thrown into them by the *acendradores*, by whom it is delivered over to the *carreros* to be placed in the boiling tanks by hand or by mechanical appliances. The crushers are insatiable. Worked by steam they munch their *caliche* all day and night, and disgorge it in coarse-grained powder into the cars on the tramway, which discharge their contents into the *cachuros* or boiling tanks. In some maquinas the iron cars or tanks travel upon a railway raised over the *cachuro* with the ground *caliche*. The bottom of the cart or tank opens on hinges, and the contents fall into the boiling tanks. In these tanks commences the chemical change undergone by the *caliche*, of which some account will be found further on.

When we reached the *tiro* we found some of our equestrian friends and Mr. Humberstone already there, examining the *caliche* of the recently exploded mine. There were masses of the stuff lying about which might easily be mistaken for fragments of marble. The workmen, muscular fellows lightly clad, were chiselling away the *costra* from the *caliche*, splitting up the blocks which sometimes offered such resistance to the sledge that it is necessary to break them up with gunpowder. How they stood the smother and heat, in air filled with saline particles, and with a fine dust which settled down like a second skin in a few minutes on clothes, face and hands, was a marvel. But habit has made these men capable of enduring such and greater discomforts—"though," said one of the staff, "they do take good long drinks when they get a chance and when the day's work is over"—that is by sundown or earlier. It is then that the *tiros* are generally completed and that the mines are fired.

We went from one *tiro* to another, over the *caliche* ground, gradually taking in the points of difference as they were explained and indicated in the quality of the deposit,

Managers examining Caliche.

and acquiring some knowledge of the outward working of a maquina, till the heat of the dust, as well as the hour, suggested that it was time for the *almuerzo*, or breakfast. This is a meal which in Chile has the characteristics of a *déjeuner à la fourchette* nearer home. Ice is abundant, and the railway carries fish, fresh from the sea below, to the oficinas. When the supply fails there is *bacala*—salt cod, or ling—thirst inspiring, not always sweet to the nostrils;

but of meat, poultry, game, vegetables, butter, &c., there is generally plenty. There is, occasionally, uneasiness created in a household because a case of provisions has gone astray, or some consignment of luxuries has failed to reach its destination, but on the whole all that is necessary for civilised people is forthcoming in the *cuisine*. The bread is delicious, the potatoes are not to be excelled anywhere, the beef is particularly good. The poultry is "of the Pampas"—teal, duck, lapwing, and Chilian partridge, not unlike the Himalayan kaleege, frequently appear on the table, but the *menu* is invariably headed by "casuela"—a soup of meat, fowl, and vegetables. Nothing better than good Urmeneta, Macul, or Paquerete wine can be needed by any one, and aerated waters, Santiago, British, and German beer. The stronger distilled waters used in preparation of "cocktails" always grace the sideboard, and the table is set forth with exquisite flowers from Arica and the coast.

In the afternoon we made an inspection of the *pulperia*, the village, the *corral*, and, finally, of the *maquina*, where some hours were spent in examining the machinery of the processes, "imbibing," as Mr. Kinglake says, "the information" we received from willing and never-tiring experts. I cannot say with the historian that "the time is now come for imparting it," because I do not think those who read these pages would care to be presented with a detailed account of the manufacture of nitrate of soda and of iodine in the minutest form, and with a description, in every particular, of boilers, taps, siphons, gauges, &c. Machinery cannot be described clearly by words, and needs elucidation by engravings and diagrams, which would be suited to a treatise on nitrate-making, but which would be out of place here.

I not only do not pretend to understand generally the details of manufacturing processes at first sight — I go further and say that where those around me are refulgent with light, it requires a long time to give me an insight of an engineering interior. I have a shrewd suspicion that most people—and "most people" after all, by votes, plebiscites, or sheer numerical totals, rule the world—are as ignorant as myself in such matters—very like the Pasha in *Eothen* who had a general idea that machinery works— whizz! whizz!—by wheels. The impostors, male and female —and, ungallant as it is, I am obliged in the interests of truth (alas! she gives little interest in return!) to say that I think there are more of the latter than of the former in any given crowd who go round machinery galleries in exhibitions, and listen with rapt attention to explanations of the processes, and that those who do not understand bear to the intelligent minority—the inquiring and recipient *cognoscenti* who comprehend thoroughly—a proportion which is probably that in other things of the multitude to the man of sense.

In the work done in the oficina, however, there was no mystery, no difficulty that could not be mastered by ordinary examination and inquiry in a day. There are, as the map will show, a great many oficinas on the plateau of Tamarugal. They vary in importance—that is, in the extent of the ground belonging to each, the value of the output, the construction of the works, and of the engines and machinery, but the *modus operandi* in the manufacture of Nitrate of Soda is uniform. It may be described as a simple chemical process, depending on the relative points of saturation of water by common salt and Nitrate of Soda. Chloride of Sodium (common salt) and Nitrate of Soda are taken up— that is, they are almost equally soluble—in cold water.

The deposits of *caliche*, whether formed by the evaporation of sea water, by the decomposition of vegetable matter in the beds of lagoons, or by other natural processes expounded by various philosophers, contain common salt as well as Nitrate of Soda. If a saturated solution of common salt be heated the solution will not take up much more salt than it held before. But if a solution of Chloride of Sodium (common salt) and of Nitrate of Soda be heated, the solution will not reach its point of saturation as regards Nitrate of Soda, till the water has taken up three times as much of the Nitrate as it dissolved before it was heated, whilst there is only a slight increase in the quantity of common salt taken up in the solution. On this "differentiation"—to use the pet word of Professor Smelfungus—rests the Nitrate of Soda Kingdom. A saturated solution of common salt and Nitrate of Soda with a specific gravity of 84°, called *agua vieja*, or "old water," or "mother water," is let into a tank filled with pounded and broken up *caliche*. There it is heated by steam passing through coils of piping, as in a distilling apparatus. The solution, as it is heated, takes up the Nitrate of Sodium, leaving the Chloride of Sodium in the *caliche* nearly unmolested. Then it is let off at the bottom of that tank into another, which is also filled with *caliche*. There it is boiled up and acquires greater density. The process is repeated in one tank after another down to the last of the series, till the liquor has acquired a specific gravity of 110°, and will take up no more Nitrate of Soda. It is then called *caldo*.

The *caldo* is carried from the boiling tanks by open iron channels or gutters which conduct it to the settling tanks or to the precipitating tanks, *bateas*, where it deposits its salts. When it is considered not quite clean or pure enough for the *bateas* or precipitating pans, the *caldo* is run into settling tanks by boys acting under an expert. The *bateas*, 18 ft. square, 3 ft. 3 in. deep at one side, and 2 ft. 9 in. at the other, are placed on an elevated scaffolding to facilitate the work of precipitating the Nitrate to the drying floor below. The precipitating process commences as soon as the *caldo* begins to lose its temperature; it goes on for three or four days, and then the *caldo*, having cooled down and dropped its charge of Nitrate equitable, becomes *agua vieja* once more.

When all the Nitrate has thus been precipitated the *agua vieja* is run off into a reservoir, from which it is pumped up into another receiver placed at a higher level than the tanks. The *arrolodores* then break up the Nitrate of Soda in the *bateas*, and the *canchadores* empty it out on the *cancha* below to dry in the sun. This drying is often done so effectually that the nitrate hardens again, and then it must be broken up by the *retiradores*, for the *llenedores*, who put it in bags to be taken by the *cargadores* to the railway trucks. Then the conflict waged between the Nitrate producers and the Railway Company recommences, or indeed continues. It has been going on for years, and for very obvious reasons. The Nitrate Railway Company, in virtue of its concessions, has or had the monopoly of transport, the exclusive right to carry merchandise on the Pampas. The oficinas desire naturally that the Nitrate should be carried at the smallest cost, and as the Government has a material interest in the export, regardless of the cost of production, seeing that more than the third of all the revenue of Chile is derived from the duty levied on Nitrate at the ports, the pressure on the railway authorities is rather severe from both sides.

By the time we got back to the house the sun had set in a golden haze over the low ridge of hill which bounded the Primitiva estate on the west. The rays of the electric lights of the oficinas were piercing the gathering darkness, which seemed to roll down from the Andes on the plain—fiery flashes, followed by dull reports, sounded through the gathering night from the exploding *tiros*—the fires of the *maquinas* glowed on the Pampas around—in the deep vault of heaven above the stars shone and glowed in the sky, with the brilliancy which the air of the desert seems to give to their glory—the notes of a piano came through the open window of the drawing-room, which was lighted up as bright as day—from the workmen's quarters the sounds of a guitar and a chorus were borne on the night wind. What was a lifeless waste when the century opened was now a centre of enterprise, capital, science, and civilisation!

The administrator of the oficina is a magistrate vested with large powers in his little kingdom. He is generally regarded by his people with deference on account of his superior knowledge, and he has a quasi-paternal influence in their affairs. Though the Chilian may be more in touch with his workpeople than the European nitrate-maker is, he is certainly not more respected.

It must be confessed that if the Inquisition were to be resuscitated in the Pampas to-day, it would not be easy for the most zealous of the Fathers to discover any taint of heretical practices among the people. Sunday is not a day of rest in the nitrate kingdom. There are neither chapels, churches, meeting-houses, priests, parsons, nor ministers in the Salitreras. At Iquique there is the great Church or Cathedral of the Immaculate Conception, which is pretty well attended, and an American, or Anglo-American, Evangelical meeting-house, not much frequented. Every Sunday the church pennant flies from one of the ships in

The Primitive Ground. Men Working Explosions.

To face page 2.

harbour, and a clergyman of the Church of England—an American by birth, I believe—performs Divine Service on board, the number of the congregation from the town depending on the state of the surf. Our little friend "Rosey," Mr. Rowland's daughter, and her governess were venturesome enough, but they only got off to the ship on one Sunday while I was at Iquique, and I was not able to accompany them on the occasion. I mention these circumstances that it may be understood how little religious differences affect the relations of foreigners and natives in Chile. There might be a harvest for the missionary on the Pampas, but it would be very rude reaping.

Although the life of the staff of the oficinas ought to be conducive to health, my short experience leads me to think that the gentlemen employed on the Pampas look forward with pleasure to the prospect of leaving it. There is a constant change going on—promotions, transfers, resignations, arrivals, departures. One employé, in receipt of a very good income, said to the administrator of an oficina, who expressed his wonder at his throwing up his engagement, "Oh, yes! I know all that! But I'm sick of 'Shanks' Lixiviating' Process, morning, noon, and night, day after day, month after month, and year after year!"

It must have been, and it was, no doubt, a very agreeable apparition to the young gentlemen, to see four or five ladies at Primitiva. The time went very pleasantly during their stay—morning rides, daily excursions, picnics, nightly dances, and even balls, to which the neighbours came from the oficinas around, from Iquique and Pisagua below by special train, which conveyed bands of music and armies of cooks, confectioners, and waiters. These balls (*baile*) are institutions fostered by the want of "distraction" on the Pampas and the coast, and they are European rather than Chilian—more crowded, pretentious, and pleasant, and much more satisfactory to those who want supper—than the local *tertulia*. Our stay on the Pampas was actually shortened by the necessity, as it was represented to us to be, of attending a grand *baile* at the Filarmonica, Iquique, to which we repaired by special train from Primitiva; and similar functions, with interludes of horse-racing and smaller diversions, which are always accepted with eagerness as sufficing causes for festive migrations and gatherings "on the coast," enabled us to see a good deal of life, habits, and customs among the residents in the province of Tarapacá.

CHAPTER XV.

Various Oficinas—Agua Santa -The War on the Pampas—Caleta Buena—Rosario di Huara—San Juan—Argentina—Ramirez—La Paccha—Jaz Pampa—Chihan Oficinas—Las Lagunas

WHILST we were at the Salitreras we made daily visits to neighbouring oficinas, and took trips by train to various places on or near the Nitrate Railway towards the north. One of the most interesting of the oficinas I had occasion to visit, because of its special conditions, its extent and originality, was that of Agua Santa. We had a long and interesting ride and drive from Primitiva to the oficina, and were enabled to form a good idea of the nature of the country, which is broken up by rolling-ground, ridges and sand-hills, with cups or lake-beds in the depressions, in which were the remains of old "paradas" or native nitrate works. There were several oficinas in full work on the way, all of which, except one—the Aurora, I think—lay out of the direct route between Primitiva and Santa Agua. On the way to Santa Agua there are the remains of a nitrate village, called Germania, to which some recent historical interest is attached on account of its having been the scene of a combat, or more properly speaking, of a skirmish, between the Chilians and the Peruvians after the capture of Pisagua. Passing over such a country without a drop of water, either running or stagnant, in view, or a sight of a leaf or a blade of grass, burning sand below and blazing sun above, I could realise in some measure the sufferings of the Chilians and of the allies, who either marched triumphant or fled in defeat in one of the most trying campaigns, I should think, which soldiers ever underwent. The retreat from Iquique and Pisagua, and the flight of the Peruvians and Bolivians after the Battle of Dolores, the forced march of the Chilians and the pursuit of the enemy after the action of Tacna, called for an endurance and a patience which perhaps would not have been found in troops not to the manner born, unless under the pressure of supreme necessities. It is not wonderful that the Peruvians—of a race more mixed and of inferior physique—and the Bolivians—hardy mountaineers as some of them were—should have exhibited less persistency and endurance than the Chilians, who boast that they are the descendants of the hardy races of the Northern provinces of Spain, and assert that they have but little infusion of the Indian in their veins, though surely an admixture of the blood of the Auracanian race would be no injury to the best of their population. The Huaso, a rude Centaur, would prove, one would think, to be but a bad marcher; but the Chilians, whether Huasos or Guachos, exhibited in the field the qualities of excellent infantry, and appear, as far as results can be trusted as an index, to have produced cavalry far superior to the mounted men of the Peruvian and Bolivian enemy. However, this is a digression. The tide of war that rolled over these deserts has left little trace behind it. I fancy the sympathies of the Nitrate people generally lean towards the losing side. They had, in fact, experienced fair treatment from the Peruvian Government, and they were handed over, after the annexation, to a vigorous administration, which had a longer and stronger arm and greater national wants to supply than the Government of Peru, which had been for years an intermittent anarchy — outbursts of despotism tempered by assassination and revolution.

Agua Santa is now the property of a company, chiefly Chilian, with a capital of 5,000,000 dollars. The Administrator of the works, Mr. Whitelegg, is a man of capacity and originality. Mr. Humberstone, though he modestly disclaimed any merit for the adaptation, introduced what is called the Siphon system when he was chemist here, to convey the *agua vieja* from tank to tank. The *maquina* is to be reconstructed, if it be not so already; and although the oficina has been working for some time, and has been producing 150,000 quintals a month, the *calicheras* are so extensive and the ley so good that there is every reason for the company to expect a good return for their outlay. Near the residences of the Administrator, his family and staff, there is a town of huts—"a thing of shreds and patches"—where the workmen and the population on the estate are housed, and children, dogs, flies, and pigeons swarm around. The corral has accommodation for 800 mules, and there is room, moreover, for horses, cattle, pigs, sheep, rabbits, and poultry. The *pulperia* of Agua Santa must yield a good return, for it is stocked with provisions and materials for the settlement, which, because Agua Santa scorns contact with the railway, may be considered as a colony on an island fed from the sea.

Messrs. Campbell, Outram, and Co., the original owners, are or were the leaders in the war waged by the nitrate makers against the Nitrate Railway and its rates and claims. It is not necessary now to refer to the details, or to examine the merits of the *casus belli*. The firm, considering that they had not adequate transport provided by the railway for their nitrate, and that they could carry it in carts drawn by mules to the edge of the plateau, over the Port of Caleta Buena, and then send it down the steep hill to the sea-shore by means of an Incline Railway, obtained a concession to construct the Incline from Government, and were about to make a railway from the Agua Santa oficina to the "cuesta," when the Nitrate Railway Company stopped the infringement of their rights by an injunction. Messrs. Campbell and Co. began to make an aerial railway to Caleta Buena. But it was a "railway." They were stopped, and they reverted to mule and cart,* which take seven and a half hours to accomplish the journey, a distance of thirty-five miles, with a rise from the top of the cliff of 400 yards to Agua Santa. Captain Castle says:—

"The incline is divided into three stages. It consists of two lines of rails, on which the ascending and descending cars travel. On a platform at the top of each incline is fixed a revolving wheel, round which a single part of $2\frac{3}{4}$-in wire rope travels; the bight of which lies between teeth, which open and close alternately, holding and freeing the rope, so that should the rope break during the ascent or descent of a car, it cannot altogether fly off the wheel. A break controls the speed of the drum, the principle of the incline line being, that a full car of nitrate descending pulls up a car lightly laden with coal, wood, barley, hay, &c. Twenty-five tons of water are sent up daily, to provide for the requirements of from 300 to 400 mules and cattle that are corralled on the Cuesta. About 200 tons of nitrate can be sent down in a working day of 8 hours; the weight of a full car is seldom over $5\frac{1}{2}$ tons; the wire rope is tested to the maximum strain of 35 tons.

* It is announced, since this sheet was written, that the Chilian Government has given a concession to the Company to make a railway to Buena Caleta

"The inclines are rather stiff, the lower one varies from 45° to 53°, the middle about 38 to 43, the upper a good steady 45°. Ladies have made the ascent and descent. Some parts of the journey are disagreeable, viz, leaving the level for the incline, and again, when leaving the incline for the level, also in the descent, going from 45° to 53°; but the most timid need not be afraid of becoming giddy"

One of our party describes his experience of a trip on the Incline as follows —"A kind of step was hitched on to the back of the car that was waiting for me, and on this I took my stand. The brakesman retired into his house and set the rope loose, the attendant labourer removed the block in front of the car and pushed it forward. Another moment and it had passed over the edge of the platform, and was going down the cliff. Switchback railways and toboggan slides at home had in some measure prepared me for this sort of thing, but I must confess that when I found myself leaning forward on my stomach against the back of the car, and taking a bird's-eye view of Caleta Buena and the ocean beyond, I involuntarily gripped hard and sank into an almost kneeling position. A few seconds recovered me, and I began really to enjoy the sensation of rushing downwards through the air. On reaching the bottom of the section the car was levelled on a turn-table shifted to right angles, run along on to a second turn-table, and again brought parallel to its original position, in order to commence the descent of the second slope. Down this I went, the sound of the wire rope rattling over the roller guides placed at close intervals all along the line between the rails being the only sound marking our progress. At the second level the car was again shifted as before. This took a minute or so, and it was all but dusk as we literally shot over the cliff for the last time. 'Ouf!' I could not help ejaculating, for with a grade of fifty-three, it really looked as if the car and I were going to take a header into the water I could just make out glittering below me. But it was nothing, as the French say, and a few moments later I was on level ground on an open space with a pier stretching seaward in front of me, and piled-up rocks of nitrate backed by the corrugated iron walls of bodegas rising on each side." "The roadstead is a good one, as implied by the name Caleta Buena, and there are few days on which nitrate cannot be sent off to the ships, of which about fifty come during the year, though as many as ten have been anchored together in the busy season. Last year about 900,000 quintals were shipped, this being accomplished by launches numbering 25 to 30, holding about fifteen tons, and making about four trips a-day. They are moored alongside the pier running out about 400 feet, this being done by the gremio, an official guild of labourers, of whom there are three quadrillas, a gang of seven men each. My inspection over and this information gleaned, I took leave of my host, and perching on the step attached to the hinder end of a car was hauled up to the Alto"

It would not be possible, even for an expert, unless he spent several weeks in visiting them one after another, and taking copious notes of the characteristics of each, to give a description of the different oficinas in Tarapacá from actual inspection. In 1883 the number of oficinas on the Tamarugal, Huara, and Sal de Obispo Pampas was 166, of which 39 were working, and 96 were held by the State; but a comparison of the works as they were then and as they are now would exhibit considerable changes in ownership and arrangement.

I was not able to visit many of the oficinas on the Pampas at Tamarugal, and I am indebted to my more active companions for particulars of one of the great manufactories, the development of which has been attended by marked disturbance in the affairs of the Nitrate Kingdom at home.

The Rosario oficina, or, more properly speaking, the works and grounds formerly belonging to Messrs. Gildemeister & Company, of Iquique, consisting of the maquinas of Rosario De Huara, San Juan, and Argentina, became the property of a company with a capital of £1,250,000, in April, 1889. Mr. Gildemeister took in part-payment of the purchase money 40,000 shares. Mr. Gallagher estimated that these *maquinas* would yield 30 millions of quintals of nitrate. There is a considerable percentage of iodine* in the *caliche*. The property consists of 162 estacas, or about 1,000 acres (an estaca is 200 varas square, a vara being 33 English inches, so that an estaca is just equal to $7\frac{3}{8}$ English acres). I should here state that the estate of Primitiva originally consisted of 215 estacas. Abrack Quiroga, containing 105 estacas, was subsequently added, so that the Primitiva oficina now owns 320 estacas. Messrs. James Inglis & Co., who sold it for £40,000, purchased it from the Chilian Government for 30,000 soles† in certificates not very long before, a striking proof of the rise in value of *caliche* ground. My informant, who inspected Rosario in July, says, he was much struck by the size and the neatness of the oficina. It may not interest shareholders at home very much to know that a manager's house is exceedingly comfortable; but a visitor on the Pampas may well be excused for taking note of the fact, and it certainly contributes to the successful working of

* As to "Iodine" see Appendix.   † The sole is worth about 3s.

an establishment to have the staff well lodged. Mr Vizetelly was particularly impressed by the extent and variety of articles in the pulperia, by the neatness of the workmen's houses, the airiness and order of stables, and the accommodation for the workmen. The machinery was of the best, and amongst the improvements which were noted was the method of boiling the *caliche* in covered tanks, which were fed by cars with shifting bottoms, opening over the tanks and precipitating the *caliche* through trap-doors, thus obviating the possibility of the frightful accidents which occur from men falling into the boiling liquid, of which several instances occurred while I was on the Pampas. Another improvement is in the saving of *agua vieja*, which is drained when the Nitrate is removed from the *batea* into a gutter to a sloping platform at the base, instead of being thrown out of the *bateas* on the *cancha* The establishment is on an enormous scale, with admirable equipment. Mr Vizetelly estimated the plant of Rosario as capable of turning out 200,000 quintals a month, which agrees with Mr Gallagher's report. The Nitrate can be carried by the branch line which runs into the oficina in connection with the main line of the Nitrate Railway Company, freight being paid, according to the terms imposed by Government, only on a maximum distance of forty miles, and put on board vessels in the port of Iquique, sixty-six miles distant. The Nitrate could also, in case of need, be sent to Pisagua, fifty miles distant. The ground is well adapted for working it, and the oficina has an abundant water supply conducted by piping, filled by powerful pumps, with suitable engines and boiler power, from two wells on the Pampas, three or four miles distant. In order to economise fuel, it was intended to put up a windmill to utilise, for pumps and machinery, the powerful breezes which sweep across the Pampas in the daytime. The oficina is fitted with the electric light.

The oficinas of San Juan and Argentina belonging to the same Company contain 287 estacas said to be about half-worked. There are 270,000 tons of Nitrate in sight at Argentina, and 100,000 tons at San Juan. Iodine is unusually abundant in the *caliche*. There is great difference of opinion, or rather, there is much want of unanimity respecting the cost of production, and I would rather not venture upon the field where so many experts agree to differ. It is obvious, that when there is a narrow margin of profit, the restriction of production bears heavily on the manufacturer. A few centavos per quintal make the difference between profit and loss. One authority stated that at a certain oficina Nitrate of Soda could be placed on the drying floor for 40 centavos, which would make $1 85 the price per quintal shipped for exportation. Another maker declared that the figures were absurd. It would appear certainly that there is a wide range in the cost of manufacture.

Ramirez, belonging to the Liverpool Nitrate Company, which I visited twice, was at one time the largest nitrate-producing establishment in Chile. It was constructed by Mr R Harvey, a gentleman who served the Governments of Peru and Chile as engineer with equal credit to himself and benefit to them, and who has returned to his native country in the prime of life to enjoy the fruits of his ability and industry. In an account, read before the Institution of Civil Engineers, of which Mr. Harvey is member, in 1885 he described the plant.

" Six steel boilers, 30 feet long by 6 feet 6 inches, double flues, with six Galloway tubes, constructed by Messrs. R.

Daglish and Co, of St Helen's. Twelve boiling-tanks with steel condensing tubes, ninety crystallizing-tanks, two feeding-tanks, a five-compartment washing-tank, as well as three circular tanks, 25 feet in diameter by 12 feet high, from the works of Messrs. Preston, Fawcett, and Co. The locomotives and rolling-stock, with a length of 2½ miles of portable railway, as well as two semi-portable engines for the wells, by Messrs. John Fowler and Co., of Leeds, the engines, pumps, machines-tools, &c., by Messrs. Tangye Brothers. And three crushing-machines by Messrs North, Humphrey, and Dickinson, of the Tarapacá Foundry, Iquique.

"The boiler, flues, and setting, constructed on Livet's system, are built in pairs, with a chimney 42 feet high by 5 feet in diameter, of iron, having a base of 9 feet for each pair of boilers.

"Ninety crystallizing-tanks, or precipitating-tanks, 16 feet by 16 feet by 3 feet deep on one side, sloping to 2 feet 9 inches on the other, in order to thoroughly drain the precipitate.

"The boiling is effected by the well-known Shanks' lixiviating system, introduced in nitrate manufacture by Mr. J T. Humberstone, causing a continual circulation of the lighter liquid to the other boiling tanks by following the denser and heavier solution. As soon as the solution, which has now become caldo, stands at 110° by Twaddell's hydrometer, it is allowed to settle for a short time and is then drawn off into the first canal, from which it runs into the crystallizing-tanks by means of other canals. The caldo is run off at a temperature of 240° Fahrenheit.

"The 'ripio,' or refuse, in the boiling-tanks is then washed by well water and the washings are run off into the washing-tank, taking in solution nearly all the nitrate of soda which may remain in the refuse. The washings are pumped up by a centrifugal pump, and used over again in the next boiling tank. When all the washings have run off, the doors at the bottom of the boiling-tank are opened, and the refuse falls into cars placed beneath, and is drawn away and dumped on the refuse heap."

It may be readily imagined that such an establishment costs money. Ramirez was set up for £110,000. It was designed to produce from 6,000 to 6,500 tons of nitrate a month. It worked an area of 6 square miles 300 estacas, to which 212 estacas were added. The caliche is very rich in nitrate of soda and in iodine.

I have given some account of the Nitrate Railway from Iquique to Primitiva, and I have tried to give an idea of the salitreras and oficinas on the way to and in the vicinity of my headquarters on the Pampas.

At Primitiva the nitrate "divide," as Americans would style it, is determined. The nitrate of soda produced at the great oficina, which was making 10,000 quintals daily when I left, is, as occasion arises, sent north to Pisagua, and west to Iquique. Before I left Primitiva for Iquique we made an excursion with Colonel North northwards, over new ground, and started to visit the country between the Central Station and the Jaz-Pampa. The Progreso, Mercedes, Amelia, Aurora, Salvadora, Democracia, Puntunchara (London Nitrate Company), Rosario, &c, communicate with the Negreiros Station, 5 miles beyond Primitiva and 76½ from Iquique, at which we halted for a few minutes on our way. The factories are scattered liberally over the Pampas. I have seen nothing in any part of the world so monotonous in colour and effect as this, the area of the greatest development of prosperous industry, of which so little is known in England. The Black Country—the iron and coal districts about Glasgow—the Biscayan mining fields—the Welsh collieries—the Bog of Allen—these are gorgeously hued, bright and cheerful to the eye, compared to the Tamarugal Pampas. But the latter enjoy perpetual sunshine, the favour of heaven, which is denied to the former. The oficinas, the corrugated surface of the land, the heaps of *ripio*, and *costra*, the ruins of nitrate walls, the nitrate makers' huts, the *adobe* walls, furnaces, pots and pans, are so like only a native can tell one property or place from another. Carolina transports its nitrate over the hills to the edge of the plateau over the sea, whence it is conveyed by steep zigzags to the beach, and shipped direct at Junin. At Santa Catalina, about 10 miles from Negieiros, Reducto, Concepçion, Agua de Bearnes, Camiña, Angela, and La Patria, find carriage seawards. San Francisco, San Patricio, La Union, and Santa, are connected with the main stream of traffic at Dolores Station, 91 miles from Iquique. The wells there supply Zapiga, Nivel, Cuesta del Arsenal and the railroad with water daily. At Zapiga Station, 3 miles, which serves Sacramento, San José, Cruz Compania, Matamunqui, and San Antonio, is a depôt for traffic.

The line beyond Zapiga enters a very remarkable ravine —not unlike that leading up from the Tchernaya Valley to the plateau at Inkerman—doubtless the bed of a river departed. On the edge of this ravine is the oficina of La Paccha, served by an offshoot from the main line. We drew up at the station of Jaz-Pampa, close to which are the works of the great oficina, 101 miles from Iquique. The *maquina*, magazines, and stores in the ravine are in communication with the nitrate fields by a railway to the

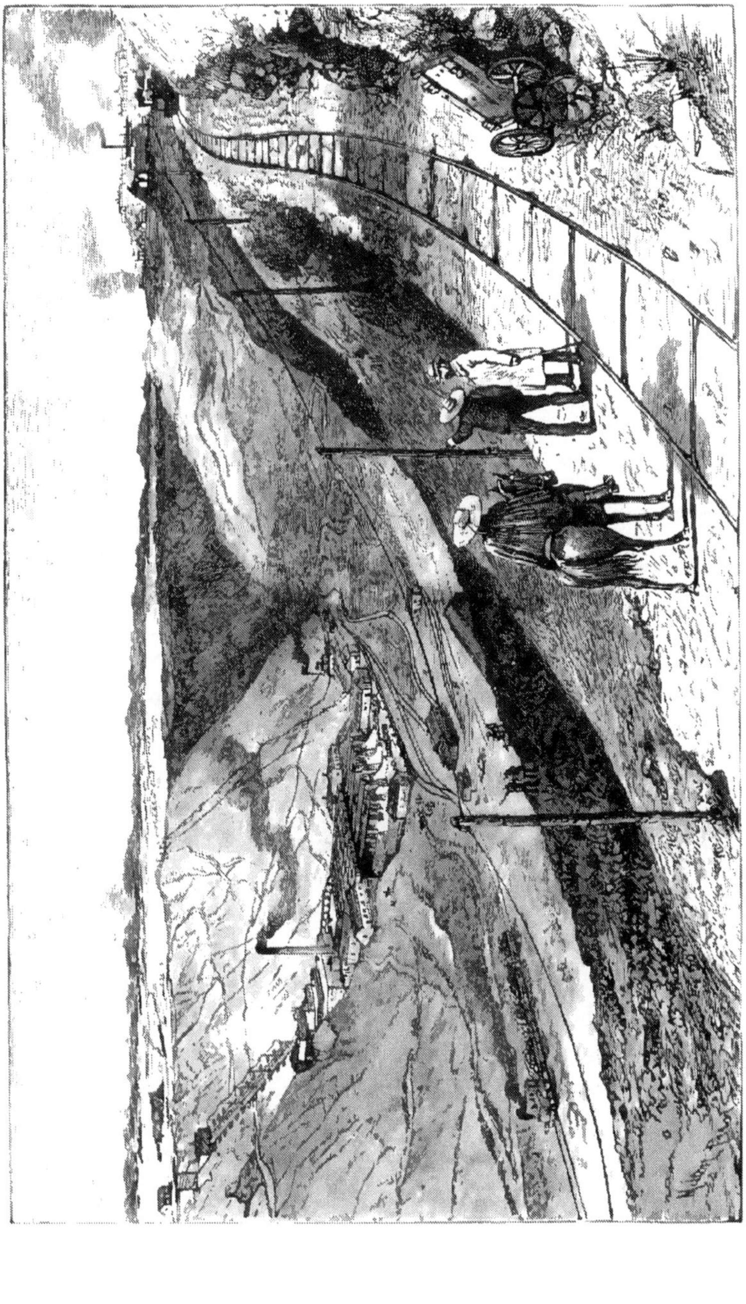

summit, and long shoots carry the *caliche* down to the tanks below in the valley.

The house of the administrator of Jaz-Pampa, Mr. Comber, crowns the steep slope; La Paccha is visible a short distance ahead on the opposite side of the ravine.

La Paccha.

The commodious dwelling of the administrator enjoys a view that few residences on the Pampa can boast—the *quebrada*, the line of railway, the station, workmen's huts, and the oficina, of which a good idea is given in the illustration. The word "jaz" means divided. The ravine that here "splits" the pampa affords unwonted facility for working the *maquina*, and for the disposal of the *ripio*. It is now provided with abundant water.

The nitrate ground attached to Jaz-Pampa consists of 108 estacas, of which about 25 estacas have been worked. The *caliche* is of uniformly high quality, and unusual thickness of stratum, some of it lying deeply below the surface. The amount of *caliche* still unextracted is estimated at 6,000,000 quintals. The plant of the officina of Jaz-Pampa comprises a large Blake crusher, eight boiling tanks, measuring 18 feet long, 7 wide and 9 deep; six settling tanks, 12 feet long, 6 wide and 5 deep; 32 bateas, 18 feet square, and sloping from $2\frac{1}{2}$ to 3 feet in depth, and three Lancashire and one Cornish boilers. The grounds attached to the La Paccha oficina have an area of 256 estacas, of which 100 contain caliche of an average thickness of 33 inches, capable of yielding 200,000 quintals of nitrate per estaca. The *maquina* is constructed to turn out 120,000 quintals per month. The *caliche* is conveyed from the *calicheras* to the edge of the ravine by a portable railway, with cars and locomotives by Fowler, the grade nowhere exceeding $2\frac{1}{2}$ per cent. The crushers are below. From each pair of crushers a long iron shoot runs down to the boiling tanks. The boiling tanks, fitted with patent traps for the removal of the *ripio*, twelve in number, measure 24 feet in length, 7 in width, and 9 in depth. There are eight settling tanks, 12 feet long, 7 feet broad, and 5 feet deep, and 60 bateas, 18 feet square, and sloping from $2\frac{1}{2}$ feet to 3 feet in depth. There are four boilers measuring 28 feet in length and $7\frac{1}{2}$ feet in diameter, and fitted with 30 Galloway tubes. The plant includes two boiler tanks, 40 feet long, 12 wide and 4 deep; five deposits for water, *agua vieja*, &c.; three feed tanks, two *agua vieja* wells, two deep well pumps, worked by a separate engine, and the boilers, an engine, with dynamos for the electric light, and an iodine house. The offices, stores, workshops, pulperia, and 200 corrugated iron huts for the workmen, &c., are new and of the most modern design. The nitrate at Jaz Pampa and La Paccha runs to 96 per cent., the legal standard being 95 per cent. Should the nitrate fall below that standard the seller must make good the loss to the purchaser. Nitrate of soda loses from 2 to 4 per cent. in weight on the voyage to Europe.

It is not my fault—I hope, at least, it is not—if the mechanism of portions of the nitrate kingdom proves to be of small interest to my readers, who wish to have particulars of oficinas I did not see. I have been obliged to write of *caliche*, *agua vieja*, and *caldo*, of *batcas* and *canchas*, because the business for which I went so far afield was to give some account of the industry in the Pampas. There is, in these later days, since I went out to Chile, not only a great fall in the value of nitrate shares but a great schism among nitrate makers, and it seems to be matter of regret that the wise policy which formerly directed the manufacturing interest in the Pampas, of which an account will be found in the chapter on what I term "Nitrate Legislation," has been abandoned. It would be a mistake to take a tabular statement of the quintallage, or tonnage, of oficinas as an actual index of value. An oficina in the last gasp, working on its only estaca of *caliche*, may give an enormous output ere it dies. But, as a general rule, the export tables, ranging over a certain number of years, afford a fair idea of the productive power of the nitrate oficinas. Whilst I was on the Pampas I never saw a Chilian nitrate work. I saw the ruins of many of the native failures

I am aware that there are many Chilian oficinas, but I do not think that any of them are in the first rank.* As

---

* I was told that the Chilian maquinas altogether produced only about one-third of the nitrate of soda exported to Europe yet the endeavour of the Government to place in the hands of Chilian manufacturers a substantial share of the nitrate-making business has not been successful. It is at Valparaiso that the trade is regulated in accordance with orders from Europe. The nitrate fleet for Iquique and Pisagua, &c., is generally dispatched from Valparaiso, and the destination of the cargoes is determined by commissions from the United States, the United Kingdom, Germany, France, &c. The majority of the vessels engaged in the trade are under the British flag, but by far the greater part of the tonnage shipped goes to foreign ports.

I was among the weaker vessels who were obliged to remain down below at Iquique when Colonel North ascended once more to the Pampas, leading with him five of our party to meet Mr. Humberstone and Mr. Vizetelly at the Central Station, whence they commenced their expedition, to explore the great nitrate plains called "Las Lagunas." There was much interest attached to the region which they were about to visit. Colonel North had purchased from a Chilian gentleman a large area of the Lagunas country, but the competency of the seller to dispose of the property was challenged by the authorities, and legal issues were raised by the Government which had not been finally decided when we left Chile.* Questions of title were under consideration in the courts of law, and the Chilian Government was supposed to be lending its weight to the opposition which had been aroused in the country to the acquisition by foreigners of the sources of wealth lying ready to be opened up in the new Nitrate El Dorado. The map, though on a very small scale, will show the relation of "Las Lagunas" to what may be called the Central Nitrate Fields.

* Since decided, I hear, in Colonel North's favour

From the Central Station the special train proceeded to La Noria, passed it without stopping, and went on to Peruana, an oficina belonging to the Colorado Company, which stands in the midst of caliche grounds especially rich in iodine. The oficinas on this part of the Pampas are those of Sacramento, San Fernando, San Juan de Gildemeister, Nueva Soledad, Solferino, Argentina and Esmeralda. At the last named a short halt was made by the party to lunch with Mr. Jewell, the manager, and to inspect the machinery used there in the processes of nitrate and iodine manufacture.

Continuing the journey by rail, and passing San Antonio, Solferino and Argentina, the train drew up at the oficina of San Pablo, where the party dined and remained for the night. There they bade good-bye for a time to the Nitrate Railway. Starting early in the morning they struck a track running in a south-easterly direction over the salt plain towards the mineral region of Challa-colla. They had a long day's journey on horseback and on wheels before they fairly entered on the road—the word is quite conventional—for the "Lagunas." Before them stretched the salt plain, "the dull brown surface of which, flecked with dirty white patches, suggested a choppy sea suddenly solidified" On the margin of this sea to the eastward, lines of vegetation and of trees were visible, marking the oases of Canchones and Pica, up to the foot of the Andes, which close the view in this direction. To the westward was a low range of brown hills. Travelling across this country was not very pleasant. One of the party compared his sensation as he sat in his carriage to that of being driven diagonally across a freshly-ploughed field, to which another added, "after a hard frost." Nor did a change from the carriage to the saddle bring much comfort to the travellers. To keep in the track was to be smothered by blinding dust from the carriages, whilst outside the track the shell-like surface of the ground broke under the hoofs of the horses into dust equally dense and disagreeable. These highly salted clouds from wheel and hoof were most irritating to the skin and the lips, and trying to the temper, and it was a relief to the travellers to halt near a hill called Cerro Pintado, and taking its name from a number of hieroglyphics, cut deeply into its surface at some period long prior to the Spanish conquest, but still as fresh in outline as though only traced a few days back. These symbols of Peruvian monarchy are locally spoken of as "Inca marks." It is difficult now to understand what interest the Incas could have subserved in asserting their dominion over this outspread crust of salt.

The route followed up to this point was immediately parallel to the contemplated extension of the Nitrate Railway to Lagunas, as traced from San Pablo to Cerro Pintado, where it will tap the borax region. As soon as the Tarapacá grounds, owing to exhaustion of *caliche*, are unable to meet the demand for nitrate of soda which increases year by year, the "Lagunas" district must be opened up, and it is in view of that result that the Nitrate Railway Company have applied for power to extend their system to the district.* Permission for this extension has been formally promised by the President, and only awaits confirmation by the Chilian Legislature.

Starting from the immediate vicinity of San Pablo the railway will run for about eighteen miles in a south-easterly direction, skirting the range of hills of which the Cerro Pintado forms part. Beyond this range it will bear round sharply to the south-west and continue in that

* This permission has since been given to the Company.

direction for nearly the same distance, as far as the nitrate grounds of Alianza, and thence onward almost due south through those of Buenaventura to "Lagunas," tapping what is held by many experts to be the richest caliche-bearing region in the province of Tarapacá, though up to the present the field has been practically unworkable, owing to the cost and difficulty of transport. The line has a total length of about fifty miles, the whole of which has been surveyed and staked out. There is also a probability of a branch line being continued from the vicinity of Cerro Pintado to Cerro Gordo, where there are important works for the reduction of the silver ore which is brought down from the extensive mineral-producing region lying to the west amongst the lower hills of the Andes.

The route followed by the party from Cerro Pintado to Cerro Gordo was nearly that of this suggested branch line, and their course still lay across the salt plain, the surface of which was now broken here and there by tracts of loose sand. However, signs were not lacking that these thirsty wastes were in some measure inhabited. Near Cerro Gordo, there were some native huts and baking ovens, and a few goats visible, and now and then the travellers met an ox-cart, a flock of sheep, or a few mounted peons. At Cerro Gordo, they found hospitable entertainment at the house of Señor Martinez, the owner of works for the reduction of silver ore. The refining works are placed in a small fortress surrounded by a strong outer wall and a ditch. Hostile Indians have disappeared, but they have found successors among the half castes, and if a stranger is travelling in the outlying parts of the Pampas it is necessary for him to take precautions for the safety of his property and person. Robberies with violence — even murder — are by no means unknown in this wild region, but ere long the Railway will render it as safe as the coast.

From the Cerro Gordo, the party started early next morning on horseback, and descending the steep hill to a plain like that over which they had journeyed the day before, save that the ground was somewhat more broken and undulating, and that it actually rejoiced in the possession of a well of water not altogether salt, struck out for "Las Lagunas." Some distance out on their right of the plain a range of low hills hid the nitrate grounds of Buenaventura, the property of a British syndicate, from view. After quick riding for four or five hours in a south-westerly direction, the cavalcade reached a stretch of rising ground and the travellers joyfully recognised a change in the character of the soil and scenery. The almost lakelike aspect of the plain gave way to marked undulations, and the colour of the surface was darker. They were in the border land which separates the Cerro Gordo district from the great Salinas they were rapidly approaching Towards "Lagunas" itself, in front of them, there was a gentle rise, which initiated a succession of promising slopes strewn with those angular fragments of dark-coloured porphyritic stone which are considered to be indications, all but infallible, of *caliche.* In the centre of one of the larger hollows bounded by these slopes, a gleam of white caught the eyes of the horsemen and its wide sheen marked the position of the dried-up salt lake or lagoon, whence the property derives its name For miles farther than the keenest eye could reach from the highest point of the bank or shore lay spread out before them the cream of the nitrate fields of Tarapacá.

The area of the "Lagunas" estate is estimated at close on a thousand estacas, or something like seven thousand acres. Though at least seven hours were devoted by the horsemen to riding over the region, the extent of it was beyond their powers of investigation, but far and near they could see the signs universally recognised as those of a rich nitrate-bearing country. It had, already, been thoroughly tested at close and regular intervals. The party passed shaft after shaft, sunk with this intent, at intervals of a hundred yards or so over the whole of the area on the slopes, and at each they could judge of the richness and quantity of the *caliche* which lay below the thin crust of *chuca* crumbling under the horses' feet. These exploitations or *tiros* revealed deposits of *caliche* of good quality, and sometimes eight or nine feet thick. Where some mines had been fired experimentally huge white masses like alabaster, varied now and then with similar blocks tinted with blue, regarded by some experts as the evidence of abundant iodine, were heaped up round the hole. Passing slope after slope exploited in this manner, the party halted at last at a house of corrugated iron, intended for the manager and for the *pulperia*, a smithy, a well and pump, a small condenser with furnace and chimney, and some huts of rough stones for the men— the small establishment which marks the site of what at some future day will be no doubt the "Lagunas's" equivalent for Primitiva. It served as a resting-place, and also as a restaurant for the travellers, a plentiful meal having been prepared from provisions sent on in advance. A tall black shaft, visible from their resting place, showed where a *maquina* had once been at work in the nitrate fields of Lagunas, but the scene of its operations was a speck in the vast area of *caliche* ground stretching around it. It had, nevertheless, though commercially a failure, turned out a certain quantity of nitrate, but even the thickness and richness of the *caliche* could not counterbalance the cost and difficulties of transport. These difficulties will vanish with the carrying out of the contemplated railway extension.

As regards the amount of raw material on the Lagunas, experts, who have based their opinion on a careful examination of the depth and quality revealed by the series of exploratory *tiros* already mentioned, estimate it as capable of supplying 200,000,000 qtals. of nitrate at the lowest. The tracing of the railway line from the little seaport of Patillos laid bare an unbroken stratum of solid *caliche*. The abundance and depth of the mineral may be further estimated by the fact, that the nitrate manufacturers of the party could not find ground from which it would not be absolutely necessary to clear out the nitrate of soda before an area of sufficient size could be obtained for the foundation of an oficina.

It was long past nightfall before the weary visitors straggled back to Cerro Gordo, where they passed the night. On the following morning they set out in a north-easterly direction for Pica, a little town built in a green oasis at the foot of the Andes, to inspect the Waterworks established there to supply the Nitrate Railway and the town of Iquique. At Pica a number of springs, both hot and cold, gush forth from the rocks, but, after serving to irrigate the gardens and orchards with which the town is surrounded, the water sinks out of sight in the broad stretch of sand extending for several miles to the westward. The Tarapacá Waterworks have been constructed with a view to check this waste of the precious fluid and to turn it into gold. The property in several of the most important springs of Pica has been acquired, and reservoirs have been erected by the Company to receive the waters.

From these reservoirs one line of pipes had already been laid across the desert to the station at Pozo Almonte, and at the date of this visit it was supplying the bulk of the water used on the railway, whilst a second line, destined to supply Iquique, was making good progress. After inspecting the waterworks and bathing *al fresco* in the hot springs, the party wound up the day with an improvised ball at the house of one of the residents, some of them venturing for the first time in their lives to attempt the national dance known as the *samacuecca*. The British community call the dance—for short—" the Quaker." Probably the performance, graceful as it is, would not find favour in the eyes of the Society of Friends, for when the cavalier and the lady, who dance to the clack of castanets, the cadenced handclapping of the spectators around them, and the twankling of the guitar, allow their "woven paces" and the dalliance of their kerchiefs free expression, the *motif* underlying the *pas de deux* might appear to be decidedly carnal. The next morning saw them again in the saddle, and another hard day's riding brought them, shortly before sunset, to Pozo Almonte, whence the majority of the party took train for Iquique, where we were now all assembled, and where we remained till we finally embarked for Panama on our return to Europe.

CHAPTER XVI.

THE NITRATE RAILWAY.

Ignorance and Bliss—*Raison d'être* of the Railway—Early Concessions and Forfeitures—Monopolies—New Companies and Loans—Lawsuits—Mortgages—The War—The Nitrate Railway Company of 1882—Mortgages—The New Loan—"Ikiki"—The Termini—The Decree against the Railway—The Appeal—The Decision of the Law Court—The President's Action—Diplomatic Interference

As I was trudging over a field at a covertside to lunch last year, a lady, who takes a living interest in all the topics of the day, the delight of all who know her, and a favourite child of Time himself, asked me, " What do you think of the Nitrate Railway? I hope you have got a good many shares in it? Tell me all you know about it, please." Up to that moment I had not even heard the name, nor had I formed the smallest conception of the nature of the thing itself. A Nitrate Railway! What could it mean? The only nitrate I was familiar with was the "villainous saltpetre," and so I answered according to my knowledge, and I was regarded with an incredulous look. "You are just like A ! he will not tell me anything either." The subject being dismissed from my mind, I remained for many months perfectly ignorant and incurious with regard to "the Nitrate Railway." It was not indeed until I was very near the sphere of its operations that I began to have some knowledge of the nature of the enterprise itself. When I arrived at the capital of Tarapacá, I began to understand the situation. Up on the Pampas there were great industrial factories where thousands of men, women, and children were employed in making a substance for which there was no use on the Pampas themselves, and on these Pampas there was neither water, nor vegetable nor animal life. So the Nitrate Railway which I saw climbing up the hill at Iquique, and which ran northwards through the Pampas till it found its terminus in that direction at Pisagua, was intended to supply the wants of the population so strangely and artificially collected on the saline deserts, and to carry all the wealth-producing results of their labours to the sea.

I would not recommend any of my readers who are in search of entertaining reading to continue the perusal of the pages which relate to the finances of the Company and working of the railway.* I feel I am unable to render a description of railway-stations, works, plant, &c., interesting, but the artist's labours will help better than any words of mine to give an idea of their outward form at all events.

The *raison d'être* of the Nitrate Railway was the existence of the nitrate fields or Salinas of Tarapacá. I was somewhat surprised to find that this unknown undertaking had been a long time in the air before it was on the land. Indeed, it was a revelation to the strangers who were within the gates of the Nitrate Kingdom for the first time in 1889 to learn that, so far back as 1860, the Peruvian Government had given a concession to two Chilians or Peruvians, José Maria Costas and Frederico Pezet, to make a line from Iquique to the Nitrate Pampas at La Noria. The concessionaires forfeited their rights in 1864, because they had not begun their work. But the Peruvian Government granted another concession in that year to gentlemen

* See Appendix.

named José Pickering and Manuel Orihuela, who, however, forfeited the concession four years afterwards for non-performance of the conditions. The railway had been laid, but it had not been worked They also obtained a concession for a railway from Pisagua to Sal de Obispo, but both of them were forfeited.

The following month in the same year, 1868, the Peruvian Government, which seems to have been very willing and amiable in the matter of concessions, granted to the Señores Montero a concession for twenty-five years for the exclusive control and profits of the Railway from the time of its opening for traffic and the ownership for forty years more, but it was to become the property of the Republic of Peru at the end of sixty-five years. It was to be free from taxation and from all duties on the material used in making and working and maintaining it for that time. A maximum rate was fixed for the carriage of freight ($1\frac{1}{2}$ ct. per quintal), the right to construct a pier at Iquique was thrown in, as well as a preferential right for making all similar works in Tarapacá. This concession was followed next year by another to the same gentlemen for the making of the Pisagua Railway under similar conditions in all respects as to time, taxation, construction of piers, &c. Two years afterwards Montero Brothers were granted, under existing concessions, the privilege of making branch lines from the district of La Noria to various points in the province and for the prolongation of their line to Bolivia. The privilege was exclusive. For twenty-five years no other railway of any sort or description could be constructed from the coast to any nitrate grounds between the coast and the frontier. That exclusive privilege was to last for twenty-five years, and the rights of ownership were to endure for ninety-nine years from the date of the opening of the railway. It was originally provided that the branch lines were to be finished within a year, and the line to the Bolivian frontier within four; but in 1872 the term was extended for thirty months. The works were pushed on with more activity than knowledge, and when the railway was at last in function it would have been a very hazardous thing for an Accidental Insurance Society to have accepted the money of passengers. If all one heard was true, goods and passenger trains now and then came thundering down the mountain side, dashing into the sea; and experts always had revolvers, and opened fire on the driver the moment the train ran off the line. The remains of the carriages were incremated, so to speak, as the readiest way of getting rid of them.

In June, 1872, Messrs Thomson, Bonar & Co. effected a mortgage for the sum of £1,000,000 sterling on the railway, by deed executed in favour of Weguelin & Gessler as trustees for the bondholders, to be redeemable by half-yearly drawings, bearing interest at seven per cent. per annum. In 1873 the Anglo-Peruvian Bank conducted another loan of £450,000 on the security of an agreement that a company should be formed to purchase and work the line, and in the following year a company with a capital of £1,200,000 was formed, and assumed possession of the railway. It was styled the National Nitrate Company's Railways of Peru, but it was never registered as an English company; and though there were directors in London, the working committee was in Lima. The loan of £1,000,000 was not forthcoming, and the trustees for the bondholders obtained from the London directors an order to place the railway in the possession of their representative, which was agreed to by the Lima Committee.

Montero Brothers, objecting to the arrangements which

were made, commenced legal proceedings to dissolve the company; and were so far successful, that they obtained a decision for the appointment of a receiver, but the lawsuit in which the Anglo-Peruvian Bank and the trustees for the bondholders were parties was settled out of court, and agreements ratified in London on the 22nd July and 28th August, 1878. The first agreement regulated the issue of the second mortgage loan, the amount of which was fixed at £850,000, the subscribers to the loan of £450,000 in 1873 receiving bonds for £600,000, and Montero Brothers bonds for £250,000. The second agreement provided security as to also the first for the future payment of the interest and of the redemption, and under the arrangements which were finally made the railways were delivered in February, 1879, to the National Nitrate Railways Company of Peru.

Very soon afterwards a war, the great solvent of agreements as well as of treaties, broke out. Pisagua was bombarded and laid in ruins. The Chilian flag floated over the whole province of Tarapacá, ports and pampas, ere the year closed, and the Chilians began to work on the railway for their own purposes. But in June, 1881, they handed the line over to the National Nitrate Company of Peru. The dislocation and confusion which followed the war precluded any attempt to develop the enterprise till August, 1882, when a company was formed in London with a capital of £1,200,000, and a loan of £1,100,000 at six per cent. interest was sent on the market by Messrs. Huth & Co. The new Nitrate Railway Company by mortgage deed a few days afterwards provided for the payment of the unredeemed capital of the mortgage of 1872, and for the substitution of the new mortgage as a first charge on the railway, the second mortgage of £850,000 coming next with certain variations in the arrangements for redemption. In 1888 the portions of the two loans which had not then been redeemed were paid off, and a new loan of £2,000,000 was issued at 5 per cent., which was the only mortgage on the railway of which the directors shortly afterwards issued deferred shares for £180,000, thus completing the financial history of the line, which is now engaged in active work at assured profits under the excellent management of Mr. Rowland at Iquique and of Mr. Clark at Pisagua. The map will give a better idea of the railway as regards its course, stations, and branches than any verbal description of mine.

I have already said a few words of the magnitude of the works at Iquique, a place of which I honestly confess I had never heard until I was informed that I must give it as the address for my letters. I am not so much ashamed of my ignorance now that I know it is shared by so many much better informed people. A naval friend of mine acknowledged that he was considerably distressed when he received an order during the war to look into the port of (what he thought must be called) "Ikiki." Something I think has slipped in in my earlier account of first impressions about a resemblance to Crewe. It is allowable to compare small things to great, and, with a due regard to proportion, the comparison of the Nitrate Railway Terminus on the Pacific is not altogether unjustifiable. There is a passenger station 170 feet long, provided with booking offices and all sorts of appliances, offices for baggage and booking and despatch of goods, vestibules for first and second class passengers, waiting-rooms, offices for the station master, for the telegraph inspectors, for documents, lamps, &c., roofed with galvanized iron, solidly constructed with broad verandahs.

Another great building of similar size contains apartments for the general manager, staff, accountants, and drawing offices, engineers' offices, telegraphs, &c. There are large goods platforms for the jute bags going up to and the nitrate bags coming down from the pampas. Beyond there is a workshop 277 feet by 104 feet, provided with Stobardt & Pitt's travelling cranes for lifting engines, in which eight engines can be repaired at a time. The whole of the repairs is executed here, the engines, provided by Fowler & Fairlie, being of course sent from England. The boiler shop, 120 feet by 40 feet, contains boiler-plate roller, punching, and shearing machines, drilling machine, and three furnaces. The smiths' shop, 95 feet by 56 feet, has twelve fires, a furnace for tempering springs, a steam hammer, and overhead crane running the whole length of the shop. In the next machine shop, 132 feet by 46 feet, there are 24 machines, driven by a 34 horse-power horizontal engine, supplied with steam from two single furnace boilers 30 feet long by 6 feet wide. The round house contains 9 pits, each 50 feet long, all leading to one turn-table 45 feet in diameter. Then come the tire heating furnace, hydraulic wheel presses, carpenters' shop, measuring 180 feet by 72 feet, with a 10 horse-power horizontal engine working the patent circular saw, band-saw, and mortising machine. The running shed, 150 feet long by 73 feet, is provided with 4 pits for the action of the pumps, and there are 12 hydrants for filling tanks and boilers. Outside there are two coaling stages, 140 feet by 16 feet, and with 8 feet water alongside. The Pisagua terminus is nearly as well equipped as that at Iquique, and of the other stations on the line, of which I have made some mention in the chapter describing the journey from Iquique to the Pampas.

Whilst these sheets are in the press there is a question of the highest importance in suspense; it may be, perhaps, decided at this moment, but if the decision which the President and the Council of State announced last year with respect to the annulment of the privileges of the Nitrate Railways Company be carried into effect, an unfavourable impression with regard to the equity, in the best sense of the word, of the Government of Chile, in its dealings with vested interests, may be created among the capitalists of Europe.*

Briefly stated, the case stands thus. In 1888 the Government issued a decree declaring that the Nitrate Railway Company had forfeited its rights and privileges, which had been given by the Government of Peru and acknowledged by Chile, under the concession of 1871 to Montero Bros. That concession provided for the construction of a railway from Iquique to Pisagua (on conditions set forth elsewhere), and for an extension of the line to the frontier of Bolivia. The rights as well as the privileges and monopolies were transferred, with the consent of the Chilian Government, for the first part of the concession, to the Railway Company which has been formed to carry out the work from Iquique to Pisagua. The part of the concession which related to the making of the railway to Bolivia was not acquired by the company, but remained the property of the brothers Montero. They did not make the railway to Bolivia Whereupon the Chilian Government decreed that the privileges of the Nitrate Railway Company lapsed, and indicated that they were prepared to grant concessions to nitrate oficinas for making other railways in Tarapacá. The Company appealed to the Supreme Court of Chile.

---

* In the Appendix there will be found a summary of the concessions of the Governments to the Nitrate Railway Companies.

Thereupon the Attorney-General lodged an objection to the appeal, alleging that the Courts of Law were not competent to deal with the issue, inasmuch as the President, as head of the Executive, regarded the declaration of forfeiture as an administrative act, beyond their jurisdiction. The Railway Company were bound by the terms of their charter to refer questions in dispute between them and the Government to the Courts of Law of Chile. The Supreme Court decided that they were competent to deal with the question of contract and the question of right. But the President, supported by the Council of State, overriding both the report of a committee of the Senate and the judgment of the Supreme Court, insisted on the absolute right of the President to annul the privileges of the railway.

As the President and his Government refused to admit the competency of their own Law Courts, the Company was obliged to invoke the assistance of the home Government which, no doubt, with all due regard to the dignity and susceptibilities of Chile, authorised the British representative at Santiago to place before the Chilian Government the view which it took of a matter affecting five millions sterling of English capital, embarked in a legitimate and beneficial enterprise in the province of Tarapacá. Nevertheless, a concession has been granted to one company* to make a railway from its oficina to a port on the coast.

* The Agua Santa

CHAPTER XVII.

VISIT TO PISAGUA—RETURN TO IQUIQUE.

Seals, Sea Lions, Pelicans, Sharks, and Swordfish—Caleta Buena—Junin—The Capture of Pisagua—The Railway Station—A Train for the Pampas—An Englishman's Experience of Peru—The Bolsa Men—Shipping the Nitrate—The Mussel Divers—The Nitrate Scales—The Bodega—Return to Iquique—Farewell Visits—The Intendente—General Baquedano—Don Gonzalo Bulnes—"Adelante!"—Last Day at Iquique.

We had been a month in Iquique, and as the legal and other difficulties which had arisen in connection with the title and acquisition of mineral rights in Las Lagunas did not present any prospect of immediate adjustment, and Colonel North's interests would always find a most efficient advocate and guardian in Mr. Dawson, we were thinking of home at last, and as the moment of our departure from Chile drew near, my regret at the unavoidable impediments which had arisen to a longer stay and more extensive exploration in the country increased. Colonel North intended to return to Santiago, and embarking at Valparaiso to proceed homewards, with some of his friends, by the Straits of Magellan. Others, amongst whom were my wife and I, decided on continuing our journey northward to Panama, and to take there the most favourable opportunity that presented itself of journeying to Europe.

Ocean itineraries and local steamer tables were anxiously consulted. Some were inclined to favour the idea of taking the American steamer at Panama, and coasting for three weeks along the western shore of Central America and Mexico to San Francisco, where several routes to Atlantic ports were open to them. Others were disposed to take the steamer at Aspinwall for New Orleans. But there rose up the spectre of quarantine in the Mississippi. Another route homewards, if the connections, which were also harassed, however, by quarantine contingencies, were good, presented itself *vid* the French steamers for Havre and Bordeaux, or by the Royal West India Mail packets. The line of American steamers in connection with the Panama Railway between Aspinwall and New York appeared to offer, on the whole, the shortest and most convenient access to the Atlantic lines. Eventually Colonel North renounced the idea of returning to Santiago, and determined to travel with us to Panama.

I had not been able to complete the circuit of the Nitrate Railway or to visit all the oficinas along its course, because on the evening of the day of our excursion to Jaz-Pampa I had to return to Primitiva and thence to descend to Iquique, instead of continuing my journey to the Northern terminus of the line. Before our final departure from Iquique the Colonel decided on making a marine excursion to Pisagua, and on June 3rd we embarked on our expedition, which gave me a good opportunity of visiting the other end of the Nitrate Railway, on board the *Maria Luisa*, one of the water boats which the Tarapacá Company employs for the service of the towns along the coast. She is not particularly fast, say seven knots an hour, but proved to be easy and comfortable. The sea was smooth, and we kept so close inshore that we disturbed the seals and sea-lions on the reefs or playing about in the sea in such numbers, that their round heads were to be seen bobbing up and down in all directions in front of our bow and on our broadside. Myriads of pelicans were visible, steering their course in long lines or in dense columns, on the wing, bent on some predatory enterprise, or settled down, island-like, on their fishing grounds.

Whenever there was a shoal of fish near the surface the pelicans ascended to the height apparently of a hundred feet or thereabouts, and from time to time one of them plunged like a meteorite into the sea, splashing up the water, and rising with a fish to be pouched in his bill. The fins of sharks and swordfish rising above the smooth swell showed that the fish had other enemies in their own element close at hand. To these were added shoals of porpoises and dolphins around the steamer.

There were extensive patches of white on the ledges of rocks at the foot of the monotonous greyish-red mountainside which forms the western slope of the Andes along the coast. It looked as though an army of whitewashers had been busily at work. They were due to beds of guano. The deposits are protected as far as possible from private depredation by the Coastguards; but the Indians are acquainted with the value of the material, and carry it when they can into the interior to fertilise the land.

As there was plenty of what might be considered objects for sport to be seen, an old Winchester rifle was produced from below, but I confess I was not sorry when efforts to mend the broken spring of the weapon, and get it into shooting order, proved unsuccessful. There were very few objects of interest to attract attention on shore; and the seals, sharks, swordfish, and pelicans exclusively occupied our attention. It was a pleasure, after some hours' steaming, to have the little bay, the small hamlet, and the storehouses of Cáleta Buena to look at. Three barques were at anchor taking in cargoes of nitrate, which are carried from

Agua Santa, the oficina of Campbell, Ontram & Co., twenty-four miles away, in carts to the Receiving-house at the top of the cliff. From the Receiving-house the nitrate bags are conveyed in waggons down a tramway in three sections of 700 feet each. The descent and ascent is very ingeniously regulated, but accidents have sometimes occurred. Captain Castle says:

"The port of Caleta Buena deserves some mention. It is situated a little to the south of Mejillones Bay; a great deal of the foreshore has been recovered from the sea at considerable labour and expense. Along this sea frontage runs a tram line, facing the tram line are large bodegas, constructed of galvanised iron; to the northward of the pier are the dwellings of the Administrador and Aduana, the Pulperia, peons' cottages, bowling alleys, billiard-room, and workshops; on the extreme right, the water maquina. The flag of Chile floats over all the principal buildings.

"Notwithstanding the facilities that this port affords, it must not be forgotten that it was only opened, by permission of the Government, at a time when the Nitrate Railway Company were unable, from want of rolling stock, to meet the requirements of the nitrate makers, and it may be that since such an enormous sum has been laid out on the incline railway and port by Campbell, Ontram, and Co. (700,000 dollars), some concession should be made to them either by the Government or by the Nitrate Railway Company."

After the steamer had passed a small town called Mejillones, on the bay of that name, another of the small nitrate ports called Junin came in sight. A road in zigzag runs from the beach to the summit of the mountain to the nitrate oficina. Mr. Comber, of Jaz-Pampa, is under a contract to deliver 3,800 quintals of nitrate every month to this port for shipment. We passed Caleta Buena and Junin without stopping or signalling, and the most careful scrutiny of the coast for the rest of the day revealed no object of interest to look at, or to beguile the tedium of a monotonous voyage, but we were near the end of our journey as the sun, ere it set in the sea, was lighting up the mountain tops to the East.

At 5.30 P M. the *Maria Luisa* anchored off Pisagua. It is an Iquique in miniature; there were the trains ascending and descending the mountain-side and the port between the Pampas, exactly in the same manner, the bodegas, the railway station, the houses, &c., all shrouded in the shadow of the mountain. There were twenty-five or thirty ships of large size anchored in the roadstead. The Railway Station, storehouses, and magazines gave an air of importance to the place which was not altogether sustained by nearer inspection, but as the inhabitants atone for the want of colour in their surroundings by painting their houses red, yellow, blue, orange, &c., Pisagua, illuminated by the rays of the sun declining in a bank of orange-tinted clouds, looked quite pretty and *coquet* from the sea It is the most northern port of the Nitrate Kingdom The surf was running high very near the little pier where the Pisaguans were assembled to watch our arrival. A number of boats at once came off with Colonel North's friends. We had to land, but it was not so easy to reach the quay dryshod, notwithstanding the skill of the boatman; and probably some of the natives were not altogether displeased, when the efforts of the strangers to get up the steps before the water wet their feet, were occasionally unsuccessful My wife, myself, and some others of the party took up our quarters in Mr. Clarke's comfortable residence at the Railway Station, where Mrs. Clarke gave us all a most kindly reception.

I could not help thinking it was rather bold (tidal waves and earthquakes to wit) of our excellent host to trust his family and himself to a two-storeyed house, with the sea at its base and a mass of rock rising behind it, a spur from the imminent Andes. It is touching to see how the traditions of the English household assert themselves under adverse circumstances. There is in every English house on the coast the home drawing-room with mirrors, easy chairs, sofas, tables covered with albums, the piano, the inevitable photograph stand, the last assortment of books, illustrated papers, magazines, flowers in vases, caged birds in the verandah. Mr. Clarke's residence had not much room to spare. The reception and sleeping rooms were on the first floor; down below is the courtyard. In the courtyard there is a little well, round which pigeons, ducks, and poultry, useful adjuncts to the table—suffering much from the depredations of enormous rats—collect for bathing and drinking; there were plants in boxes, creepers carefully tended up the lattice-work, and small plants to lend their green to the place, and a sleek llama with a soft black curling coat, stalked about the enclosure inviting the children to come and play with it. I hope that neither tidal wave nor earthquake will ever visit that hospitable house. At night the sea breaking against the foundations of the house disturbed my rest, and I could not help thinking that it would be better if we were a little higher up the hill-side.

There is plenty to see at Pisagua. I am not speaking of the plants or of ferns, strange enough in composition and distribution, of the geological formations, of the railway clambering boldly to the sky line with its trains of passengers, provisions and materials, up a mountain which looks as steep as the side of a house, and vanishing on the Pampas beyond, nor of the trains coming down in well-ordered procession, laden with cargoes of nitrate sacks, nor of the activity and bustle in the Railway Terminus, where customs officers are weighing and officials are testing the nitrate bags accumulated in huge blocks by the wharves in readiness for shipment. I am alluding to the town itself.

The street of Pisagua, consisting of wooden houses, follows the line of the shore. Stores full of ready-made clothes, ironmongery, agricultural implements, refreshment saloons, two banks, merchants' offices, and bodegas lie at the foot of the mountains, which rise, almost from the street, behind a chain of scarped hills of 500 or 600 feet high. A railway runs from the Custom House pier to the Station, *à l'Americaine*, through the street. The names over the shops are German, Italian, English. The Chilians say that these hills were trenched and defended by Bolivian riflemen; that batteries, *à fleur d'eau*, garrisoned by a brigade of Peruvian artillery, commanded the port, and that 1,200 Bolivians were in position behind their earthworks when the Chilian flotilla of nineteen men-of-war and transports, with an expeditionary army from Antofagasta, elated by the victory off Angamos and the capture of the *Huascar*, appeared before it on 2nd November, 1879. The Chilian men-of-war silenced the batteries in an hour. The Peruvian artillerists bolted from their guns. The Chilians, landing in detachments, were held in check under the fire of the enemy in the houses, hid behind nitrate bags and up the hill-sides, till the fleet once more swept the shore and drove the allies from their shelter; but the Chilians did not succeed finally in occupying the town and the heights till the combat had lasted five hours. I am inclined to think that with troops of greater tenacity to face them they would have paid dearly for the attempt to take Pisagua. The shore batteries were obviously badly armed and were probably worse manned. Meantime the Chilian General-in-Chief had disembarked a corps of Chilians at Junin without resistance, and was marching along the coast. Villamil and Granier, the generals of Bolivia, and the Peruvian chief, Buendia, with the view of concentrating all their forces at Tarapacá, fled with their broken bands towards Dolores, whence they were driven soon after. The Chilians lost in killed and wounded 350 men out of the 2,000 who landed; but they secured the railways, stores, magazines, distilling apparatus, and a base of operations, which they lost no time in utilising.

After I had taken a look at the position in the early morning, I strolled down the street, and then turned back to the railway terminus. There was a train starting at seven o'clock for the Pampas, filled with men, women, and children, mostly Chilenos, third-class passengers, whose fares are regulated at five cents a mile—the dollar just now is worth 2s. 3d.—so that the fares are a little more I think than those of the parliamentary trains at home. Such a variety of headdresses, indeed of dress and physiognomy, I never saw before; long-faced, large-nosed, straight-haired Bolivians, barring the full beards and whiskers of the Asiatic, quite Afghan in type; Indians with wire-like tresses, broad cheeks, square and firm-set jaws, piercing small black eyes; Chilenos, like Basques or Biscayans, who might have been just landed from the northern ports of Spain—chattering, laughing, and gesticulating, all smoking, all with bundles — some fair-haired Germans, here and there a negro or a mulatto, probably of Peru

Bolsa Men and Boisas, Pisagua.

[To face page 236.

As I was watching the departure of the motley multitude, I made the acquaintance of an English gentleman, connected with the place, and in the course of a conversation all too short I learned a good deal about Peru. He had settled down on the banks of a tributary of the Amazon, a paradise for the naturalist and the sportsman; he had laid out his fortune, and after years of struggle he had abandoned his hacienda in disgust, and left it to anyone who chose to come in and take possession. "I get letters from tax-collectors and agents and officials of all kinds," he said, "but I never open them when I see the postmark, for I know what they are about. There is no law. There is no labour to be had. The taxes are enormous. It is a hopeless country." He had but a very bad opinion indeed of the future of Peru. The future might either mean a revolution, which would rather make what was bad still worse, or it might mean a protectorate which could, he thought, only end in the destruction as a self-governing state of the Republic.

From the Station I walked to the beach, close to the railway, where the surf was breaking on the rocks, and the *bolsa* men were loading the lighters with nitrate, an operation exceedingly well-managed and very interesting to look at. The lighters cannot approach the shore owing to the surf, and they can only lie at the pier when it is very smooth indeed, and that very seldom happens on this Pacific coast. So the nitrate bags are carried from the wharf by the *bolsa* men off to the lighters, which lie outside the line of breakers. "Practice makes perfect." The *bolsa* is simply a couple of large bladders, which are made from the skins of the sea-lions, which are dressed and trimmed by the Chilians along the coast, the extremities being closed and sewn up in the form of a bolster with sharp ends, or something like enormous cigars; they naturally need no water-proofing, and they are exceedingly light and durable. Two of these are fastened together with a platform on the top, very like the double ship which ran between Dover and Calais; they are blown out artificially, and it is astonishing to see how cleverly a Chilian will distend the cylinders by his breath. I have been exercised by the name of the man who does this work; he is called a *cachuchero*; now a *cachucha* is "a sort of cap," "a national dance," or "an air to accompany it," and unless the *bolsa* man is supposed to dance on the waves, there seems to me no reason for his being called *cachuchero*. Whatever the reason of his name, the fellow is adroit, strong and skilful in his trade.

The sea has cut out the softer part of the rocks and formed little docks just large enough for a *bolsa* to float in. The nitrate bags are stowed in tiers on the beach, under neat sheds belonging to the railway, beyond the reach of the surf. Now here is a *bolsa* in the *caleta*, its harbour, so to speak. The boatman is on the shingle, and is steadying his craft. A roller has just passed away seaward. Five men, stripped to the waist, with trousers tucked up above the knee, each with a bag of nitrate on his back, are ready. They run one after the other, place their load on the platform of the *bolsa*, then as the next roller comes in the boatman jumps on the *bolsa* and seizes his oar. The *bolsa* is carried out by the reflux, and, floating lightly over the surf, is dexterously propelled by the boatman, or *bolsa* man, till he comes alongside the lighter. The latter is loaded, and is brought alongside the ship by the crew, where the cargo is transferred into the hold with such rapidity that twenty-five tons of nitrate, the usual freight of the larger lighters, is hoisted on deck in less than half-an-hour. Great care must be taken in placing the nitrate on the platform of the *bolsa*, putting it in the lighter, and carrying it to the ship ; for the wetting of nitrate means heavy loss. The bags are put away below by a stevedore, who is paid 7 dols. for 1,000 quintals, each quintal being 100½ pounds. A strong man can stow 3,000 quintals a day.

Any one who doubts whether men can get up muscle upon beans, has only to look at these nitrate carriers. From early morning they work for about four hours, carrying bags of nitrate weighing from 300 to 310 pounds all over, then they have a meal—a large one—of peroto. At twelve o'clock they begin once more. They leave off in three hours, the six-and-a-half hours' work being quite as much as they do in the day. They belong to a trades' union, or Gremio, to which a charter was given by the Government of Peru, just before Tarapacá was annexed. They form a public company, with a commandant, overseers, clerk and labourers; they have their school, their account in the National Bank, and their reserve fund. The men's wages are fixed by the Gremio ; the variable exchange affects the value, but it may be put down roughly that they get from ten to eleven shillings a day, or less than two shillings an hour for their working time.

Not very far from this scene there was an exhibition of another kind. Close in shore boats are passing to and fro. One of them stops. A man appears with a small net over his shoulders, at the bow; in his hands, which he holds over his head, he has a stone. He dives, and is lost to view for half a minute. Then he rises, clambers into the boat and empties his net; he is diving for mussels ! The water is so clear that he can see them at the bottom. Sometimes a weighted basket is let down from the boat by a rope, into which the diver puts the shellfish ; he gives the rope a tug, and he comes up to take breath. Sometimes he rises by the aid of his feet alone, holding the mussels pressed against his chest.

At the south end of the Bay there is a reef, on which the sea, breaking continuously, spreads out a milk-white expanse of foam, and in the midst of this you see, in the sun, shining, sleek, black creatures gambolling in pursuit of their prey. These are sea-lions, or large seals, which abound along the coast; they are protected by the port authorities, as a couple of my companions found to their cost on one occasion, when they made a shooting excursion from the vessel.

I paused outside the storehouse at the station to look at the operation of sampling the nitrate. The Custom House officer, the agents of the nitrate sellers and buyers, notebooks and ink-horn in hand, in front of a pair of scales, constitute a little court. The porters place on the scale five bags of nitrate, which are accurately weighed. Then a sample of the nitrate was taken from each bag and placed in a box, which was locked up till the quality can be tested and analysed. The standard of nitrate of soda is 95 per cent., and if nitrate of an inferior quality is sold, the oficina has to pay the purchaser in proportion to the deterioration below the standard. This is ascertained at Valparaiso by the chemists appointed for the purpose, and there is an arbitrator, also an official, whose judgment is final in case of dispute.

There are at this moment twenty-seven vessels in the harbour, riding with their bows pointing south towards the swell and the wind, which at this time of the year comes generally from Cape Horn. There are some ten or twelve barques, the rest being three-masted schooners and brigs. Lighters are alongside most of them, and a line of these large and well-appointed carriers is moored close inshore.

I spent a couple of hours very pleasantly watching the *bolsa* men, the trains departing, inspecting the shops and the people in the street, marking the ravages of earthquakes, a newly-built wall overthrown a couple of days ago, and then I think I had exhausted all the sights of Pisagua. When I got back to Mr. Clarke's breakfast was ready, and an hour after my return we were on our way to the steamer and embarked in the shore boats to return to Iquique. Our departure from Pisagua, which was fixed for ten o'clock, was not effected, however, till a quarter past twelve o'clock. There were so many friends coming off to say good-bye, and to take a last look and a cocktail—(not by any means the last—it is always the time to take one along the coast; of it as of the Royal Prerogative it may be said, "*Nullum tempus occurrit*")—that the time passed quickly, and the steamer did not leave till noon. The wind from the south, which favoured us on our way north, was naturally against us on our return to Iquique. The *Maria Luisa* made a hard fight against the head sea, and was greatly agitated in the combat, so that the ladies, after a struggle on deck, took refuge from the war of waters in their cabin. The appropriate water-boat, however, took us safely, if slowly, back to Iquique. It was late at night when we arrived, however, and the landing was not pleasant in the dark, but "all's well that ends well."

CHAPTER XVIII.

EARTHQUAKES

Shocks at Iquique, on the Pampas, at Santiago—Effects of the Temblor—The Noise—The Effect—The Giant's Kick—The Tidal Wave—Make for the Open—The Mountains of Refuge—The Indian Woman and Child—H M S *Caroline*—Pisagua—An Earthquake Register—Darwin's Remarks—The Moral Effects

WHILST we were at sea, on our way to Pisagua, there were several *temblors* at Iquique

I may as well introduce in this connection all I have to say from my personal knowledge respecting these visitations. There were no shocks at Coronel, Valparaiso, Viña del Mar, or Cauquenes whilst we were in residence, but they are not by any means unknown at those places Valparaiso has been twice destroyed by earthquakes, and I have spoken already of the ruin of Concepçion in 1822 and 1835. From Valparaiso up to Arica the coast is much harassed. Arica, Callao, Quito, &c., are frequently visited, and the towns on the seaboard of Ecuador have, from time to time, suffered severely. The merry month of May seems to be a very favourite time for bad shocks—some of the most severe earthquakes recorded have happened in it.

I unfortunately lost the memorandum-book in which I recorded my earthquake experiences at Iquique and on the Pampas, but I am sure that during the latter part of the time we were on the coast, between the former town and Pisagua, we had two shocks a week.

None of the *temblors* which occurred during our stay in Chile were severe. The slightest was, however, sufficient to arouse us to a condition of vivid expectancy and rapt attention. When once we felt the earth shaking and heard the doors and windows clattering, peace of mind was at an end till motion and noise ceased. Our first experience was at Santiago. They were more frequent soon after our arrival at Iquique, but one or two were so slight that we would have doubted if the vibration was not due to some passing waggon, but for the evidence of other people. I say "we," as my wife, the companion of my solicitude, was generally the first to detect the advent of the earth wave.

The favourite time for the commotion was just at the end of our first sleep. Sometimes there would be a shake in the night, but generally the quakes began seriously about seven o'clock in the morning. Sometimes a strange noise would precede the shake—a sound like the roar of the sea, or of a distant railway train. Only there was in it a subterranean element also—as if the train were in a tunnel—and then doors and windows shook, and crockery and glass clattered, the clothes hung up on the walls waved to and fro, the bed was shaken, and it seemed as if some one beneath were kicking it violently. Then after a few seconds, during which we watched and listened in rapt attention, the tumult subsided, and there was at once a glow of an inward satisfaction, and audible expression of it on our part, that it was all over. However, that feeling of thankfulness was sharply dissipated on several occasions by the speedy recurrence of the shock. No one knows when and where and how an earthquake is going to end.

One morning we had to endure three shakes at intervals

of some minutes; and I am bound to say that familiarity in our case did not breed contempt or indifference. Nor are the people, to the manner of earthquakes born, at all more callous than strangers. Indeed it may be true that they are more nervous. They have seen—many of them—the ruin wrought by these dreadful agencies; they have heard from their elders of the destruction of cities by earthquakes—of widespread wrack and ruin by the dreaded tidal-waves along the coast—of whole towns overwhelmed, with their inhabitants, by the sea. The visitor is shown the remains of the mischief worked in a few seconds by the earthquake of such a year—the marks which indicate the course and extent of such and such a wave are pointed out to him, and the story is illustrated by narratives of hair-breadth escapes and dreadful adventure. The effect of these experiences on the minds of the inhabitants is evinced by the readiness with which they receive as authentic vague, and often exaggerated, reports of the destructive results of earthquakes along the coast.

When there is a severe shock, the inhabitants of coast-towns, like Iquique, generally make for the open—then their eyes instinctively turn seawards—they are warned to look for the dreaded wave, of which the first token is the sudden retreat of the water on the shore. The sea retires as if it were sucked, or drawn, back by an unseen agency, and then it gathers to form the advance guard of the irresistible column of the tidal wave which rolls on like a green hillside till it reaches the reefs in thunder crested with foam, sweeps over the beach for great distances inland, and high up on shore, overwhelms everything within its ruinous range. The recession of the sea is attributed to an upheaval of the land temporarily, or to the influence of the distant wave which is forming for its irruption, after the manner in which the water retires from a beach when a steamer is passing. That is Darwin's illustration But there is no satisfactory explanation of the *modus operandi* in the creation of the wave itself, as far as I know. There is only one agreeable circumstance—rather let me say everything about these tidal-waves is disagreeable, with one exception —there is an interval between the earthquake and the genesis of the wave—it may be half an hour or more. Therefore, although men's minds—and women's—are not in peace after the shock, and their eyes are fixed on the ocean for many minutes, they have time to escape towards the rising ground if it be in the daytime. The lines of retreat and the heights to seek for refuge near each town are well known and designated beforehand. I confess it was not a line of retreat I was at all anxious to follow when it was shown to me at Iquique.

Several notices of earthquakes are briefly entered in my scribbling journal in March, April, May, and June—some on the coast, some at Santiago, one or two on the Pampas, and a considerable number at Iquique, but no details are given. The smaller demonstrations have a great family resemblance to each other. It is believed that the bodies often found in mines, &c., on the coast, are those of people who were swallowed up in these convulsions. Very recently two men who were journeying to Iquique found, in a hollow in the ground, the mummified corpse of an Indian woman with a child in her arms which she was feeding when they were instantaneously killed either by lightning or by an earthquake. They had remained for hundreds of years there, and people who saw the remains at Señor Zuberia's office thought they could recognise an expression of terror still haunting the woman's face. In my diary I find entries like these:—

"*March* 31*st*. (Sunday.) At 6.30 awoke by a rattling noise—like stage thunder—and sitting up, I was informed by my wife, with an air of conviction, 'That was an earthquake!' It was the shake, not the noise, which had aroused me. The dresses hung up on the hooks on the walls were still waving, although the 'quake' was at rest" (This was at Santiago.)

"*April* 3*rd*—A *temblor* on the coast reported. Some say it was felt here this morning" (Santiago.) "A Chilian gentleman told me he was certain we had many earthquakes in England which were not noticed. Here they are so interesting that every one is put in the papers, and every one is obliged to know and talk of it."

Our earthquake records became frequent after our arrival at Iquique, and there were several *temblor* manifestations on the Pampas, but there was a comparative indifference to earthquakes up there, as there was no fear of a "tidal wave"—the name which is given for want of a better to those fearful invasions of the ocean.

"*May* 15*th*.—We were to start early for the oficinas." (This was at Primitiva.) "I was thinking of turning out for my bath about 6 30 A.M. when I heard the rumble and 'growl' which I now recognise as the flourish of drums and trumpets of '*el rey Temblor*,' and in a few seconds there was a touch of his majesty's hand and a kick of his foot which shook the earth and the house So I was up in good time for early breakfast and for the special train, which started at 8.30 to make a run to Jaz-Pampa and La Paccha, visiting several oficinas in the way."

"*June* 2*nd*. (Second Sunday after Ascension.)—Such a shaking this morning! As I was getting up, at 7.35, there was first the usual underground 'growl,' then in a second or two, rattle! rattle! rattle! went the doors and windows in our room, and the outer verandah shook visibly. It was only for a moment. 'That was a good one!' quoth my wife, with the air of a connoisseur in these things, a little pale all the same. (It is her general remark now, *pour encourager l'autre*.) The words were not well out of her mouth when the rattle was at work again louder and stronger, and this time a giant below gave a kick to the floor that shook the bed and transmitted the blow to our bodies very forcibly! Then that commotion ceased, and we pulled ourselves together again. In a minute more there was a third shock, much more prolonged, but not so violent. I went on the leads, and looked out on the port. There was the usual surf on the rocks, and the vessels in the roads were rolling, as is their custom—nothing more. The earthquake was mentioned casually among my friends. Different impressions concerning the shake—some thought it slight; others confessed they thought it was quite strong enough. . . . The ladies, with the exception of my wife, who is bad at boating and ladder-climbing, went on board H.M.S. *Caroline*, Sir W. Wiseman, to tea in the afternoon. They were told by the officers that the shock had been plainly felt in the ship. At 4 20 P.M., as my wife and I were sitting on the balcony, there was another quake. Four in a day is more than sufficient! It is very astonishing how soon people, acting on the Duke of Wellington's maxim: 'Never be afraid of a danger when it's over,' recover when the quake is really quiet"

"Left Iquique for Pisagua in the North 'water-boat,' *Maria Luisa*, with the Colonel, the ladies, and some others of our party; Mrs. Russell remained behind. Arrived before sunset. Many friends at the landing to welcome

N——, who began his career at Pisagua. Heard there had been a severe shake here yesterday, and on our way to Mr. Clarke's house, saw a wall which had been thrown down by the side of the street. It is probable that the shock ran all along the coast for many hundreds of miles.

"*June 3rd.*—It is reported from Arica that there were twenty-one shocks there yesterday, so we have no right to complain of our perturbation. It is a pity some system of accurate observation and record is not adopted by the Government. There are Chilian and American telegraph stations in all the towns, and if proper registers were kept at them, of time when, duration, and the like, a deal of valuable, or at any rate interesting, information would be accumulated."

That same night there was, as we heard afterwards, another considerable shock at Iquique at 3.30 A.M., but we had no further personal experience of earthquakes that I can remember.

I had felt in other lands the truly awful and unnerving sensation—the fearful apprehension of a greater wrath to come—of which Darwin has given such an accurate analysis in his account of the shock he experienced at Valdivia in 1835:—

"A bad earthquake at once destroys our oldest associations; the earth, the very emblem of solidity, has moved beneath our feet like a thin crust over a fluid; one second of time has created in the mind a strange sense of insecurity, which hours of reflection would not have produced. In the forest, as a breeze moved a tree, I felt only the earth tremble, but saw no other effect. Captain Fitzroy and some officers were at the town during the shock, and there the scene was more striking; for although the houses, from being built of wood, did not fall, they were violently shaken, and the boards creaked and rattled together. The people rushed out of doors in the greatest alarm. It is these accompaniments that create that perfect horror of earthquakes, experienced by all who have thus seen, as well as felt, their effects. Within the forest it was a deeply interesting, but by no means an awe-exciting phenomenon. The tides were curiously affected. The great shock took place at the time of low water; and an old woman who was on the beach told me that the water flowed very quickly, but not in great waves, to high-water mark, and then as quickly returned to its proper level; this was also evident by the line of wet sand. This same kind of quick but quiet movement in the tide happened a few years since at Chiloe, during a slight earthquake, and created much causeless alarm. In the course of the evening there were many weaker shocks, which seemed to produce in the harbour the most complicated currents, and some of great strength. . . . Earthquakes alone are sufficient to destroy the prosperity of any country. If beneath England the now inert subterranean forces should exert those powers, which most assuredly in former geological ages they have exerted, how completely would the entire condition of the country be changed! What would become of the lofty houses, thickly packed cities, great manufactories, the beautiful public and private edifices? If the new period of disturbances were first to commence by some great earthquake in the dead of night, how terrific would be the carnage! England would at once be bankrupt; all papers, records, and accounts would from that moment be lost. Government being unable to collect the taxes, and failing to maintain its authority, the hand of violence and rapine would remain uncontrolled. In every large town famine would go forth, pestilence and death following in its train."

Some of the incidents which the great naturalist has sketched with a master hand have occurred on the Pacific Coast, but Darwin appears to have exaggerated the consequences of earthquakes in the dictum that they "alone are sufficient to destroy the prosperity of any country." They have not by any means effected the ruin of Central American and South American States, which have been cruelly vexed by the severest manifestations of their irresistible power, nor can it be admitted that England would at once be made bankrupt by an earthquake or by a series of them, though it is quite possible that the result of a series of shocks in our great cities would be of an appalling and fearful character. It is held by some Egyptologues that the Temples at Karnak were laid in ruins by earthquakes, but the force which laid pylon, pillar, and obelisk prostrate would suffice to destroy the grandest works in London without the consequences imagined by Darwin to be necessary. Still let us hope and pray that the subterranean forces of which he speaks may be content to remain inert as they have been so long content to do after they rested from their labours.

Fortunately for our own poor nerves and my legs we had no occasion to fly from tidal wave, or to escape from falling houses, but it was not pleasant to be told at first that it was just as well not to close the bedroom door, lest a shock should jam it and prevent our opening it if the house were falling.

On our return from the Pampas to Iquique I put in shape some notes I made during my visit to Chile. Those which relate to the Nitrate of Soda oficinas have been worked out in the previous pages, which my readers have seen. The observations and reflections relating to the policy of the Republic and its relations to the outer world, which suggested themselves to me in the course of my visit, will be found recorded in chapters of a general character, and I can answer for their having been written in a spirit of entire friendliness and under the influence of a sincere regard for the fine qualities of the Chilian people.

CHAPTER XIX.

OUR LAST DAYS IN CHILE.

The Intendente—The Power of the Intendente—The Press—Gonzalo Bulnes —General Baquedano—Colonel Bulnes—Law and Lawyers—The Chilians —The Immigrants from Europe—Chile for the Chilians—" Viva Chile"— Preparations for the Voyage home—Last Night in Iquique—A Moonlight " Adelante!"—Our Last Day—Adieux

LONG as we have been in Chile, we have had little intercourse with the ruling powers; but now we were about to return to Europe, and therefore before we left Iquique a formal call was made on the Intendente, who received Colonel North and the members of the party, *en petite comité*, with his wife and children. Champagne—exceedingly sweet—which it was obligatory at all events to taste, was handed round, and after an interchange of civil inquiries and answers on both sides, we bowed and shook hands and retired. The visit was returned by the Intendente and his wife in due course. The gentlemen who fill the post of Intendente are generally politicians belonging, it is needless to say, to the party in power—very often lawyers not in great practice, and as their office is only held for a term—I think of five years—it is not the practice of Intendentes generally to dissipate their income in prodigal living or profuse hospitality.

Apropos of the power of the Intendente, it would seem that it is not to be lightly questioned in the public press, at all events. On my return one day from a round of visits

I was informed that the editor of a paper of high character who had just been released from prison for some ill-considered observations on the conduct of the powers that be, was about to be subjected to penal consequences for publishing documents in his paper of an official character, said to have been improperly obtained; but there was, it was stated, no legal evidence of the fact. The editor left Iquique to avoid further annoyance. There is, however, considerable licence allowed to the expression of abstract opinion and to political discussion in the press, and there was, for example, one paper in Iquique which might be said to advocate a re-vindication of the territory of Tarapacá and Arica by Peru à la Alsace-Lorraine. Señor Zegers, formerly secretary of General Iglesias, ex-President of Peru, is the editor of *Il Progreso*, a paper which he conducts with sprightliness and ability; and he manages, without offence to Chilian susceptibilities, to imply that he is attached to Peru, and regrets her overthrow in the last war.

In the absence of the Intendente his post, when we first arrived at Iquique, was filled by the accomplished Don Gonzalo Bulnes (son of the distinguished General and President), who has written an exceedingly complete history of the Chilian Liberating Expedition, which his father led to Peru. It was Señor Bulnes who originated the *déjeuner* at Cavancha to General Baquedano and his companions before they sailed to Europe as members of the military commission constituted by the President and the Government of Chile to report upon the military establishments of the great Powers, to which Colonel North and I were invited. It was interesting to meet one who had led the Chilian Army in the victorious campaign which put an end to the war with Peru by placing Lima in the power of the conquerors and the country in possession of their armies. A very modest man — saying little, and desirous of silence rather than of speech, Baquedano is not imposing in appearance or in manner, but he is respected by his countrymen and he is said to be free from the ambition which in South American Republics often makes successful soldiers dangerous citizens. Colonel Bulnes, one of his companions, bears a high reputation; but I doubt if many of the military gentlemen they will meet in Europe have paid attention to the details of the singularly successful and well-designed aggressive operations which assured the predominance of Chile on the Western shore of the South American Continent.

It is not without reason that foreigners in Chile attribute to the natives an unusual love of litigation. In a country with a population far less than that of London, the number of lawyers is astonishing, and the daily papers in the cities contain long lists of causes in the courts, of which very many relate to disputes concerning property, mining rights, and commercial transactions. There is an elaborate system of criminal and civil jurisprudence, and a large establishment of judges.

Notwithstanding the impediments which undoubtedly exist to the establishment of intimate relations between the Chilians and the strangers within their gates, the latter, after a residence in the country, are generally attached to it, and if they cannot form close and warm friendships, establish many pleasant relations. Indeed, let us admit that in any country under the sun, foreign residents are necessarily not included in the intimacy which exists amongst the families of residents with whom they are brought into every-day intercourse by business associations. In Chile the restraint which is imposed by difference of race and speech is intensified by national peculiarities and sentiment. The people are of the Latin race, and they are Roman Catholics, not indeed of the strictest, but nevertheless they are by no means disposed to regard heretics with favour. The strangers come to the country poor; and they go away or remain amongst them rich. They take the lead in commercial enterprise; they practise as physicians, barristers, engineers; they establish prosperous banks, commercial houses, agencies; they work railroads, coal and copper mines, and control the markets. Their descendants — McIvers, McKennas, Edwards—occupy great positions in the Chilian world. The Chilian has more than one barrier to oppose to their progress, he has the constitution, the legislature, the clergy, the women—or let me say the ladies, who are not, however, always hostile—but he cannot check it, or at least, he has failed to do so up to the present. Over and above all his *impedimenta* he has a facility for litigation, a system of jurisprudence, and a fertility of legal invention, all of which he uses with singular ability to harass his enemies and rivals. Would it, however, be so very surprising if the people of Chile declared that they would get rid of all foreigners if they could? They have not done so, but the existence of a desire among certain classes to handicap immigrant capitalists and manufacturers is proved by the constant allusions in the press to the good time coming, when "Chile for the Chilians" will be more than a national aspiration—when it will be the statement of an accomplished fact. Fortunately the President and the oligarchy at the head of affairs are men of intelligence, as liberal as they are strong, and there is no probability that the Republic of Chile will forget what it owes in any way to foreign capital and enterprise, or that it will ever give the stranger reason to refrain from joining in the cry "Viva Chile!"

The short time which elapsed at Iquique after our arrival was devoted to much packing. We dined the evening subsequent to our return with Mr. and Mrs. Clarke, and met some interesting people, among whom there was one with personal experiences of the grievous wreck of the *Cotopaxi*, which will be talked of by the survivors " on the coast" for many a long day. We devoted June 6th to visiting our friends in Iquique, ending with a drive " by the sad sea wave "—which was tumbling in magnificent rollers on the beach— to Cavancha for the last time.

Our departure from Iquique was fixed for the 7th June, and our berths were engaged by telegraph at Valparaiso on board the *Cachapoal*, one of the Chilian Company's coast line, which was scheduled to arrive at Panama on June 20th. It was natural that our last night on shore should be made the occasion of a farewell banquet, but the travellers had to face a divided duty, for, unaware that Mr. Dawson claimed the greater number of her intended guests—among whom I was one—Mrs. Rowland had arranged a dinner for all the party, which taxed the resources of Iquique, and as we could not dine in two places at the same time, we were not united at one table.

Except at the clubs, and of ball nights, people go to bed early at Iquique. It was a very pleasant dinner, as it was wont to be at our hosts', but there was a dance to follow and a prospect of a late night. I was tired at the end of a long day, and so I set out to walk from Mr Dawson's to Mr. Rowland's, a few hundred yards off. It was bright moonlight. I was walking in the middle of the road, one side of the street being in the shade, when two men stepped out from a doorway in the dark a little in front and advanced as if to stop me I had nothing but a stick —a stout one—in my hand, but as they came near I halted and shook it at them, saying, in a loud voice, "*Adelante!*" Whereupon the fellows turned and fled, disappearing round the corner of the street to my great satisfaction! In an instant afterwards I heard the shrill whistle of a policeman, whom the steps of the fugitives had summoned to the spot, and who came up to see what manner of man I was; being satisfied, apparently, that I was not dangerous, he followed till he saw me turn in at Mr. Rowland's house. It seems I had inadvertently used a word of power in addressing the men in the street. I meant to say, "Stand back!"—instead of which I had invited the men to "Come on!" The invitation so disconcerted them that they adopted a course which was much more agreeable to me than if they had taken me at my word. My friends were greatly amused when I told them the story. I should mention that it is the habit of the police in Chilian cities to notify when a stranger enters a street at night by a whistle; he announces in like manner to his comrade when the stranger has passed As the conductors of the tramway carriages also clear the way by whistling, the early night at Santiago and other towns is made hideous by the ceaseless "siffleing."

FROM MY DIARY.

"*June 7th.*—Our last day at Iquique. The *Cachapoal* is in harbour. Everything—and that means very many things—is packed. A small force of stout Chilenos under the command of Frank, Colonel North's factotum, has been busy since 8 A.M. in carrying down cases, boxes, portmanteaux, ladies' dress baskets, and the *impedimenta* which so large a party, somehow or other, needs or accumulates, and heaping them in a huge pile in the courtyard, whence they were conveyed from the railway-pier by lighters to the steamer. A morning of hurried adieux. The forenoon was devoted to parting visits, and in the morning there was a large *levée* at the house of Mr. Rowland, under whose roof my wife and I had found a most comfortable, kindly home I breakfasted with the vice-consul, Mr. Buckland, to whom I have been indebted for many attentions and good offices. In a month acquaintance at Iquique rapidly ripens into friendship; and when we were about to leave friends whose kindness and hospitality we had experienced without stint during our stay we had every reason to feel regret, as it was probable we would not ever meet on this side of the grave.

"There was a great crowd at the Custom House pier to see Colonel North and his friends off, and the deck of the ship was thronged for hours by people who came from the Pampas to do honour to the strangers, of whom it was not likely they would see many, if any, again on the Pacific coast. The Captain, Captain Chase, an American who has been some time on the coast, did his best to accommodate the party, and succeeded The Colonel had, of course, to make a speech, and in alluding with emotion to the early friends he saw around him, and to the struggles in which they had shared long ago, he touched a chord which vibrated in every heart. On the aforesaid coast meetings and partings—and indeed the intervals between them— are very much devoted to libations, not immoderate but constant. The deck of the *Cachapoal* was a prolonged scene of affectionate and sorrowful leavetaking till it was time for those who were not bound northwards to go on shore."

At 1.30 P.M. the *Cachapoal* moved gently ahead, and the boats, crowded with ladies and gentlemen, which hung on to her sides, cast off, the flotilla bidding us good-bye with much waving of handkerchiefs and many loud cheers. And so we coasted northwards and bade adieu to Iquique for ever! There was the train travelling up the mountain-side in pursuit of the tiny smoke-puffing objects gaining the summit of the plateau—the surf-lined coast, the factory chimneys, the cathedral dome, the gasworks, the railway, the foundry, the bay and its tiers of ships rolling in the swell, the white houses of Cavancha in the distance *Vale! vale! longumque vale!*

CHAPTER XX.

FROM IQUIQUE TO PANAMA, ETC

Homeward Bound—The *Cachapoal*—Stowaways—The Paris Exhibition—
—Arica—Sad Anniversary—The Last of Chile *pro tem.*—Mollendo—
Chala—Cruelty to Animals—Millions of Pelicans—Pisco—Callao—Lima
—The War—Guayaquil—Panama—The Canal—Special to Colon and
New York—Fever—Departure for Europe

It was so late when we left Iquique to-day that it was nearly midnight when we anchored off Pisagua, where we touched in order to land some passengers

The *Cachapoal* was well laden with the usual living cargo. The pacotilleros, of whom I have already spoken, filled the waist of the ship ; they had an immense variety of specimens of the animal and vegetable kingdoms on board ; and there were also a considerable number of first-class passengers, many bound to Paris for the Exhibition.

It may be remarked, *en passant*, that the Chilians evinced a great interest in the Exhibition, and that crates and packing-cases were shipped for it at every port on the Pacific ; Chilians, Peruvians, and the Republics in the west vying with Mexico, Brazil, and the Argentine Republic in their efforts to make a good show under the Eiffel Tower.

The floating costermongers must have a struggle for life, notwithstanding that the market is brisk at every port for what they have to sell. They pay for everything they take on board, so much for a basket, a melon, or a bundle ; so much per head for goats, sheep, poultry.

Stowaways are more troublesome to the captains of the coasting ships than their passengers and cargo; it is scarcely possible for the most vigilant officers to prevent these fellows getting down below and hiding between decks, when the ships are taking in or discharging cargo. The ingenuity of the captains in punishing the delinquents, though it is exhibited in vain, is not always commendable. On one occasion five stowaways were secured with rope round the coating of a boiler; the unfortunate wretches, as they felt the heat on one side, pulled to get away from it. The effort brought those on the other side into closer contact; and so the struggle went on till it was thought they had had enough of it. Sometimes the unfortunates, in their devices to hide themselves, meet with terrible punishment. Four stowaways managed to get along by the shaft, and settled themselves down, as they thought very comfortably, in the space left for the rudder head astern. As long as the ship was at anchor they were safe, but it so happened, when the ship got under weigh, that the rudder was put to port or starboard, as the case might be, and three of them were crushed to death at once. "These Chilians are splendid material for soldiers," said one of my friends; "they don't care for pain, and they are not at all afraid of being killed."

Half-a-dozen of these "miserables" were discovered after we left one of the ports and were immediately given over to *peine forte et dure*. A captain is obliged to be severe. If he got a character for good-nature he would ruin his owners. These culprits were put in irons and treated to the lightest diet and plenty of water. It is desirable to land them in a condition which will impress itself on the minds of the population where they are put on shore; but it is not easy to produce the result. They are philosophers of a practical turn and take life and its ills very easily. When Mr. Spencer, who is active in the pursuit of knowledge and in the study of the manners and customs of the people, made the acquaintance of the "chain gang" a morning or two afterwards and presented them with some cigarettes, he established friendly relations with them at once, and they were as easy and free as so many Don Cesar de Bazans They were being carried for nothing from a place they wanted to leave, and the tobacco added to their simple fare filled the measure of their contentment.

DIARY.

June 8th.—I was awakened out of a sound sleep early this morning by the signal-gun, and the rattling of the cable through the hawse-hole in the port of Arica. We have arrived at "No Man's Land." We have left the Nitrate Kingdom behind us. The *Cuchapoal* was anchored under the Morro, which is the culminating point of a line of sandhills commanding the town towards the south and east, very much like the rock of Gibraltar. Arica is deserted. There was only one small store steamer at anchor, and not a sail in view. But on a wide plain spreading away to the foot of the eternal Cordilleras, above which towered in the distance two snowy crests, our eyes rested on—unaccustomed sight—"vegetation!" Further off cloud-like white specks, denoting a loftier range, were visible through the glass. Cultivation, clumps of trees and houses, cattle on the plains, and a bright belt of verdure marking the course of a river, were indeed new to our eyes. All the time we were in Iquique there was not a shower—not the slightest —but once indeed the camanchaca descended from the hills to the plain and fell like a drizzling Scotch mist on the roofs of the houses. Of Arica itself there is now but little left It has not yet recovered the shock of battle and

Pisagua Nitrate Railway Terminus.

To face page 261.

misery of defeat and hostile occupation. Yesterday, the date of the capture of the place, was a sad anniversary for its people. It was kept in sorrow and in tears by the Aricans. The Chilian flag waves over them, but they are, I was assured, Peruvians at heart, and intend to remain so.*

They did not intend to submit, but they had no officer fit to direct the defence. The crest of the Morro is fortified. I could count five embrasures, facing seawards, in the fortifications which the Peruvians constructed, supposing they would be attacked from that direction. They had breastworks inland from the eastward slope of the bluff, and there were also batteries or a battery lower down the hill. Three small redoubts could be made out through the glass north of the town. One of the passengers said that the Peruvians had nine rifled guns on the Morro, three on the work below it, and two in a redoubt—varying in calibre from one hundred and fifty to three hundred pounders. There was also a floating battery covering the town seawards. All these works were connected by electric wires. The forts, moreover, were mined with dynamite mines, which could be discharged from the central bastion. The garrison consisted of about two thousand men.

The Chilian general, Baquedano, using the railway from Tacna, gathered about five thousand men at Chucalata. The Peruvians appear to have behaved with astounding indifference to their own safety; no outposts—Arabi at Tel-el-Kebir. They had been summoned to surrender the day before—they could see the Chilians on the hills—and yet they allowed Baquedano without hindrance to push forward two thousand men under cover of night, to rush the forts and redoubts at daybreak. The old story over again—the garrison taken by surprise—the Chilians

* See note, Appendix.

inside the works before the Peruvians could believe their eyes—then a desperate rush out of the entrenchments for the Morro! When they got there it was indeed to be between the devil and the deep sea! The Peruvian officer in command, Bolognesi, and his second, Captain Moore, of the Navy, did their best to rally the panic-stricken crowd In vain. The Peruvians were driven headlong over the cliff into the sea. The white flag was hoisted! But at that moment the mines in the forts were fired. A cry rose from the Chilians, "Spare not!" There was a frightful massacre! Arica was set in flames, and Baquedano reported to Santiago that evening that "all the enemy were prisoners or slain."

It seems strange to-day to read of the doings of our own countrymen in these very seas in former times. Two hundred years ago, the delectable pirate or buccaneer, John Watling, who signalized his captaincy "by ordering the strict observance of the Sabbath in all his ships," "landing at a small island named Yqueque," on his way to attack Arica, plundered an Indian village of provisions. The people of Arica were then supplied with water from the river Amerines, eleven Spanish leagues north of "Yqueque." Watling examined one of the old Spaniards he had taken at Iquique concerning the force at Arica; and, "being offended at his answers, ordered him to be shot"— which was done The attack of Watling on Arica failed. Out of his ninety-two men the Spaniards killed and took twenty-eight, and the estimable Mr. Watling, though he practised the expedient of putting the prisoners he had taken in front of his own men, was repulsed disastrously, and he was found by the Spaniards among the slain on the beach.

Colonel North and most of his party went on shore to

lunch and see the place. It is from the river Azapa, and from the reservoirs on shore here, that the tanks of the water boats to supply Pisagua and Iquique, are filled.

The arrival of Colonel North, who was closely associated with the fortunes of the town in past days, produced a considerable sensation in Arica. The Peruvians, who came on board to welcome him, forgot their troubles for a time. They say that they hope for better days to come, and that they are real benefactors to Chile. Though they did not forgive their conquerors, they were fain to confess that the Intendente was a very just administrator, and that he was as good as any Chilian could be expected to be under the circumstances. Nevertheless, if the gentlemen who visited the ship were fair exponents of the popular will in Arica, there could be no doubt that the province will revert to Peru by the plebiscite which is to be taken in 1893.*

By the treaty with Peru, which was signed provisionally in June, 1883, the Province of Tarapacá was ceded to Chile, and Tacna and Arica were handed over to her administration for ten years, at the expiration of which the people were to decide by a plébiscite whether they would revert to the Republic of Peru or remain under the flag of Chile. The State to which they desire to adhere is to pay the other an indemnity of $10,000,000. The protocol was signed October 20, 1883, General Iglesias having been elected President of Peru and recognised by Chile, and two days later the Chilians evacuated Lima, and Iglesias entered the city and was installed as President.

The *Cachapoal* did not weigh till five o'clock at night. To wile away the time two of our friends went off with Frank in a shore boat to get a shot at the seals and sea lions disporting themselves in the surf off a rocky island

* But it is doubtful for all that. See Appendix

near at hand. A little adventure, which was amusing enough to those who saw it from the deck, ensued. The Captain of the Port, having observed the sportsmen land on the island, sent off a cutter which bore down on their boat and carried it off with Frank and the boatman to the town. There they were taken before the magistrate and fined pretty heavily, especially the boatman, who was told he ought to have known better. Meanwhile the sportsmen, having loosed off several rounds of musketry at the seals, and who had not observed the capture, thought they would return to the steamer. There was no boat to take them, and we watched them parading the beach, disconsolate, by the sad sea wave, wondering what had happened. All our boats were on shore with the Colonel and the passengers, &c., but after an hour's wandering on the rocks in the sun the sportsmen were released from captivity on the island to be conducted before the authorities and fined, as Frank and the boatman had been, for molesting creatures protected by the law.

June 9th.—Anchored off Mollendo, soon after dawn. A very heaven-forsaken looking spot, huts and sheds, one or two good houses—that is, by comparison—scattered over a coast line of beetling rocks, beaten by furious surf and backed by dreary sandhills. Flags were flying from consular offices in honour of the Sabbath day, which otherwise received no particular attention. Some adventurous people went off from the ship, and I saw them, tossing up and down in their boat, with serene satisfaction. They had little to report when they came back. The landing-place, formed by a reef in some degree sheltering a short jetty from the breakers, was not inviting to a lame man.

How strange in his ways is that deity called "Fortune." It happened that the chance visit of one of these very strangers saved an English lady, resident in the place, from utter ruin. Her husband, once worth £100,000, had lost it all in mining ventures; he was in Iquique looking for employment, and meantime a creditor had come down upon his house, and was about to dispossess his wife.—"*Deus ex machina!*"—A steamer looks in—a boat puts off from her—a friend steps on shore, walks up to see the wife of his former partner—hears the tale of distress—and at once gives the substantial relief which turns sorrow into joy! And so we proceed in the early afternoon.

June 10*th*.—There is no enchantment lent to the view of Chala, where the *Cachapoal* is at anchor this morning, by distance. The Peruvian flag is flying proudly from a wooden shanty, and here and there are clumps of trees inside the wooden palings surrounding detached houses. Sheds, bunks, bungalows, huddled together in the recesses of sandhills fenced in from the sea by rugged cliffs. Outlying bastions of rock fighting the surf; external barriers of reefs attacked by incessant rollers. The Custom House, with a much-troubled pier, faces the sea. Some five-and-forty miles away there were formerly great gold mines passing rich, but an earthquake destroyed the mines, burying three hundred miners, whose remains lie engulfed there to this day. The mines have been abandoned ever since, but I believe that Colonel North and some other gentlemen are going to work them again.

Herds of cattle, driven in from the Pampas by mounted men to the pier, where large flat-bottomed barges were holding on uneasily for their cargo, were shipped here for the north. The beasts are caught up, slung by the horns, lifted by the crane, and swung into the flats. They are packed as close as they can stand. Then the lighters are rowed alongside—the wretched animals, with wild staring eyes, lowing piteously, and trying to keep their legs in the swell. A hawser with a running noose is lowered into the flat; the noose is slipped with a dexterous hitch, over the horns of the nearest beast, with many a hard blow and kick, and volleys of terrible words; the donkey engine is set to work, the hawser tightens, and up comes the animal, which is lifted over the gunwale, with the whole weight of its body hanging from the insertion of the horns into the skull, and is dropped half lifeless on the deck. Barbarous! "*Ma che farè?*" asked an Italian.

After a delay of three or four hours, which we devoted to fishing with indifferent success, the *Cachapoal* weighed, and proceeded along the coast northwards. Low down on the hills were layers of camanchaca as regular as strata of masonry; above them the Andes, and distant snow peaks. At half-past four a huge column of dark-coloured smoke spurted out from a recess in the mountain chain, and spread out in the form of a mushroom with a slender stem above it. There was apparently a strong wind blowing, for the smoke was speedily drifted away over the sky-line. It was an outburst from some volcano. Half an hour later, we were rewarded for our watchfulness with the display of a similar phenomenon, but our skipper could not "locate" it.

June 11*th*.—The sea in front of us—*i.e.* towards the north —presented a marvellous appearance to-day; there were black patches on the water, looking like low islands—nay, like the solid earth itself—but they rose and fell on the heavy swell, and as the steamer approached, island after island shattered into fragments—each a pelican! Hundreds of thousands! Probably millions! They flew like great armies towards islands on our port bow, which they covered as with mantles of feathers. The Chincha Islands which yielded to Peru so many millions' worth of guano are further off. We were entering the Baccarones—a deep recess or gulf—not unlike the entrance to the Minch between Skye and the Scottish mainland—girt in on the west by rocks and islands About an hour before we reached Pisco, a cross with a sword on the right and some symbol on the left, deeply cut in the soil and outlined with stones or masonry, came into view on a sloping hill over the sea. There are legends connected with this cross. It is said that there are gold mines of extraordinary richness in the vicinity, but attempts to work them have always been frustrated by the sudden death of the miners, and now they are abandoned. Patches of snow-white stones were visible on the hill-sides all along the coast hereabouts.

Pisco, with an entourage of abundant vegetation, sugar, Indian-cornfields, and gardens, houses of many colours, on a plain backed by hills of moderate elevation, showed to advantage. A long pier stretches out from the town; two churches with towers, and domes, like mosques without minarets, give an air of importance to the place. Pisco gives its name to a spirit or liqueur, by no means to be despised, much in favour along the coast, and the district is famed for fruit, and for abundant and excellent grapes. We anchored in four fathoms at two miles' distance from the pier. The Peruvians made preparations to defend Pisco, but detachments of the Chilian troops were landed, one to the north and one to the south of the batteries, and turned the works. We amused ourselves for some hours by fishing from the vessel, not with much profit; the ladies, favourites of fortune, managed to catch some pretty roach-like fish, which proved to be indifferent eating. We left at half-past three in the afternoon. The rocks on the headlands of the coast are white from deposits of guano, but the great beds from which formerly fleets of ships carried the fertilizing cargoes to the Old World have been nearly exhausted. There is little life to be seen on shore; a train of mules was watched with the greatest interest; we have seen but three vessels at sea since we left Iquique.

June 11*th.*—We have now coasted four days northwards, never out of sight of land, generally not more than four or five miles from it, and rarely have we had at any time a clear view of the Andes; but the sea around us is always interesting, the infinity of sea birds and the multitudinous pelican betokening a wealth of fish beyond belief. Porpoises and bonitos play about in the midst of the swarming shoals which break the water. The sharp fins of the swordfish or the shark furnish bull's-eyes, not always hit, for the idle riflemen on board.

Wednesday 12*th.* — Screwing gently since midnight towards Callao, off which the *Cachapoal* came to a standstill at 7 A.M. There we lay for a couple of hours, till the port officer and harbour-master and the local health officials boarded us, and, after the usual formalities had been observed, allowed the ship to enter the docks. Since the war with Chile this once busy port has lost much of its importance. It is only on the spot that the traveller from a distant land can appreciate military operations of which he has read, retaining probably but a confused impression of them from telegrams and correspondents' letters. And for the first time I am now taking an impression of the events of the campaign of 1879-81.

There are still broad and deep traces of the war around Callao. The remains of the works constructed by the Peruvians to resist the enemy may be seen decaying and subsiding under the action of wind and rain, some leading to the enquiry suggested by the fly in amber. But the measures of the conquered are viewed generally through the spectacles of the conquerors.

After Arica was taken the Chilian fleet blockaded Callao. The Peruvians showed cunning as well as enterprise and courage in torpedo hostilities in which the Chilian cruiser *Loa* and the historic *Covadonga* were destroyed. The Chilians retaliated by bombarding Callao. But the situation might have lasted much longer had not Lynch's expedition, landing at Chimbote, marched inland, captured a great quantity of warlike stores at Supe, and then embarking landed again at Paita and there enforced the counsels of those who were anxious to persuade Peru to come to terms with her victorious enemy ere it was too late, by demonstrating her inability to resist invasion.

Without offering an opinion on the rights and the wrongs of the war between the Republics, I must express my regret that Peru did not recognise the impolicy and danger of rejecting the chance of compromise which was offered at the conference at Arica. Lynch had been wasting the coast, levying contributions, and destroying property, without a show of opposition, for two months, in expeditions which he conducted with singular energy, skill, and enterprise, and with uniform success. "Don Patricio," who was educated in the British or Anglo-Indian navy, and was a captain in the Chilian service, displayed extraordinary capacity as a military leader and as a civil administrator. He rightly considered that the most efficacious way of injuring an enemy was to destroy his material resources and to shake his moral courage. He was both humane and just, but he maintained order and discipline with an iron hand, and the memory of the gallant Irishman is held in respect all over Chile. Don Patricio Lynch was appointed Minister to Madrid—it was hinted to remove him from evidence—after the war, and died at sea on his way back from Spain after the war.

Chile had nearly 27,000 men at Tacna, Arica, Iquique, and Antofagasta, with a reserve of 10,000, so that Baquedano had more than 40,000 men ready to take the field the moment negotiations were broken off. In less than three weeks from the refusal of the allies to agree to terms Baquedano led an expedition to the coast of Peru, and landed two divisions with which he commenced his march towards Lima. The Peruvians had collected about 25,000 men for active service. It seems incredible that with such a force they should have allowed the Chilians to remain unmolested after their first landing at Curayaco, where they were exposed to an overwhelming force and could have been driven into the sea if attacked at once. Pierola relied upon forts and fortifications and the long line of trenches by which the commanding positions outside Lima were defended. And indeed it was with some reason he trusted in them, for it was not till after a long-continued and most desperate action at Chorrillos that the Chilians carried the works and became masters of the capital and of the Republic. Their loss was upwards of 3,300 killed and wounded. More than 5,000 Peruvians lay dead on the field and in the villages, and the Chilians took upwards of 2,000 prisoners and 120 guns.

When the news of this crushing disaster reached Lima, to convert the exultation aroused by lying telegrams from the field into dismay, a mob, composed of the villainy and rascality of a hybrid population, and of the soldiery who sought refuge from the battlefield in the city, arose for the work of plunder and murder, and revelled in both. The foreign residents in the capital and in Callao turned out to defend their lives and property, and showed a firm front to the gangs of plunderers, which no doubt averted great misfortunes. It is a curious proof of the force of what is called "nationality" that in such a supreme moment the friends of order grouped themselves as separate little corps as French, Spanish, Swiss, English, Americans, &c., and acted independently. Mr. Milne, acting with his own countrymen, told me he had the satisfaction of inflicting condign punishment on some of the robbers who were engaged in sacking the houses.

Callao, but a few years ago one of the most frequented ports in the world, is to-day a melancholy waste of waters. The wrecks of the ships, which the Peruvians sank rather than surrender them to the Chilians, lay stark and stiff inshore. The only vessels in harbour were a few coasting and ocean steamers, merchantmen, and a couple of small craft, which could scarcely be denominated vessels of war, flying the Peruvian flag. The magnificent docks, the work of the late Mr. Brassey, are almost untenanted, and the busiest thing about them is a seal, apparently an habitué and privileged denizen, as it swam and fished at the entrance, quite close to the steamer. We drove to the house of Mr. Milne, a representative Aberdonian, in one of the suburbs of Callao called Punta (the Point), and were luxuriously entertained at the hotel as a preliminary to a visit to the extensive and well-organized flour-mills owned by our host. Lord Donoughmore, rejoicing in the success of his negotiations, met us at Mr. Milne's house, and did his utmost to contribute to the interest and amusement to be derived from our visit for the short time we were in Peru. Lady Donoughmore, who had been living in a villa close to Mr. Milne's house in the shingly suburb, "by the sad sea wave," had gone home a short time before our arrival.

The outlying streets of Callao are not savoury or

picturesque, nor is the formation of the ground, however interesting to the geologist, attractive to the ordinary traveller. The sea beaches here are accounted "the most instructive" in the world, but it needs knowledge and personal investigation to derive benefit from a study of their peculiarities. On our way through the streets, which perhaps it would be as unfair to take as specimens of Callao, as it would be to estimate London from a drive through Whitechapel or Wapping, we disturbed at every three or four yards groups of the gallinazos, or horrible little vultures, which act as public scavengers, none of which we had seen in Chile

The evening of our arrival at Lima, where we put up at a most comfortable hotel—De France et d'Angleterre—was devoted to various excursions—to the Plaza de Armas where stands the Government House—to churches, of which most were shut, and to strolls about the streets and arcades. As one of the principal reasons which actuate Englishmen to go far abroad appears to be the business of arranging for a cricket-match, the preliminaries for a friendly encounter between the travellers in the *Cachapoal* and the British residents in Lima were arranged for the next day. I am not ashamed to admit that I think scratch cricket in one place is very like the same game in another. *Campos non animum mutant*, &c. So my wife and I set out with an intelligent Peruvian gentleman to inspect the churches, the Public Library, and the gardens which had been recently the scene of the Great Exhibition of this part of the world. At the Cathedral—I am not quite sure I am right in designating the massive building, where the bones of Pizarro were laid, by this name—our guide was refused permission, generally accorded, to view the relics of the conqueror, on the ground that the archbishop had locked them up and put the key in his pocket. The verger gave as a reason for this precautionary measure, that foreigners, particularly Americans, were in the habit of abstracting Pizarro's toe, and finger, bones, &c. There is reason to suspect that much of the "remains" on show never belonged to the "conquistador," the impress of whose finger in lieu of a signature on the contract he signed with his colleague for a division of power is still extant.

Our very brief stay at Lima enabled us to see just enough of the city to accentuate our regret that we could not devote more time to the most interesting place we saw in South America. There is an air of decayed greatness about the public buildings and the houses eminently respectable, if not satisfactory from a commercial or industrial point of view. There are many reminiscences of old Spain, tokens of the days when the Viceroy of Peru was the potential representative of one of the greatest empires in the world. The creation of great vice-royalties in Mexico, Grenada, Venezuela, &c., and the organized disorder in the Central American States, greatly diminished the prestige and power of the Court of Spain. As England was unable to overcome the revolutionary outburst of the American colonies, Spain was totally impotent, in the early part of the present century, to master the insurrection which destroyed her control of the vast regions which extend from Panama to Patagonia.

There is a considerable difference as regards appearance, dress, and bearing, between the population of Santiago and of Lima. There are more Indian-looking people in the latter than in the former city. They are smaller, less robust in body, but, I will not add, less prepossessing in aspect and manners; and the Peruvian ladies we saw in the capital were possessed of personal attractions which were by no means common in the south.

The Library of the University and Museo contains a series of portraits of the viceroys and Presidents of Peru, as well as some good specimens of Merino, the only South American artist who acquired a reputation in Europe, or rather in France, where he lived and died. I had the good fortune, at the Museum, to make the acquaintance of Professor Palma, whom I found in a waste of books. There were thousands on the floor awaiting arrangement, and destined apparently to give considerable trouble before they could be put in order. Many of these belonged to the suppressed religious houses. They lay in rank and file, and column, monuments of forgotten learning, cased in their sheepskin clothing—dissertations upon the Fathers, controversial works in Latin and Spanish—representing the aggregate work of hundreds of years of wasted labour. Prof. Palma is well known in Europe as a writer of the advanced liberal school. I gathered from his remarks that he did not take the least interest in the heaps of learned rubbish that lay around him, and that he had no veneration for purely academic learning.

A drive to the Public Gardens, which are filled with charming exotics, brought our excursion to a close. On our way back we drew up to look at a battalion of infantry at exercise in the square outside the gardens. I protest that no one could detect any difference in size, uniform, or drill between the Peruvian and French infantry. They were dressed, turned out, and armed exactly like a French battalion of the line, and as the Chilian soldiery affect the same approximation to the military attire of our lively neighbours it would be difficult to prevent mistakes, if there were another war between Chile and Peru. A detachment of a regiment coming out of the courtyard of the President's palace had the same uniform as the battalion at drill near the gardens, so I presume the Peruvian army is quite Galhezed. The President, General Caceres, owes his election to the gallantry he displayed at the ill-fated battle of Chorrillos, and sits firmly in his chair it is said because he has the support of the army. He is gifted with personal intrepidity, common sense, and moderation. The personal purity in nominations to office and in the distribution of the patronage of the State which is ascribed to him does not, it is said, belong to those whose influence is very considerable, very near his person.

Sir Charles Mansfield entertained us and some friends at dinner. I learned a great deal of interesting facts, which a far longer stay under less favourable auspices could not have afforded me.

Next day we started by special train to take a run along the railway, but the destruction of the great Oroya bridge and viaduct prevented our ascent to the commanding altitude which previous travellers generally attained, and we did not go beyond San Bartolomé. The railway, following upwards the course of the valley through which the sacred Rimac descends to the sea, passes by the battle-field of Chorrillos. But the scenery is not grand, and the snow peaks are generally hidden from view. On the low grounds Indian villages, or the remains of them, tropical vegetation, troops of llamas plodding along the tracks; sugar plantations, some few good country houses standing in fields, hills crowned with forts—then a dejeuner at Chosiça, a favourite station on the line, and so on to San Bartolomé—that was all we saw and did. It had been arranged that there was to be a bull-fight next day, and a famous bullfighter—brother, indeed, of the great Frascuelo, one of the master swordsmen of Spain—was engaged; the plaza was ready, the band was hired for a ball to follow. But these plans were suddenly abandoned because the captain of the steamer received orders to leave that night, and from San Bartolomé we proceeded straight to Callao, without stopping at Lima, and started at sunset that evening in the *Cachapoal* for Panama.

June 15th.—The mercury is rising rapidly in the thermometer. 85° to-day, so the awnings afford a grateful shelter from the sun. At noon a grand snow-clad peak was visible towering above the Andes, which recede from the coast as we approach Salaverry, and by calculation the cone was made out to be ninety or one hundred miles distant. Passing the Guano Islands at 1 P.M., sea smooth as glass, anchored for a few hours off the decayed little port of Salaverry, its former importance indicated by a fine pier and great resources for loading and unloading in the form of an array of lighters of unusual dimensions. All hands fishing. Miss North excited the envy of the anglers by capturing a fine Corbino, which could only be got on deck by the adroit use of a big basket as a landing-net. As the *Cachapoal* was leaving her anchorage she disconcerted an enormous turtle that seemed to have been asleep in alderman fashion on its back, and which was very nearly run down.

June 16th—Very like the day before; looked in at another port—Paita, where Lynch operated—and found the United States steamer *Mohican*, a very venerable craft, flying the stars and stripes, "forgotten by the navy department," it was said. One of the ships at anchor had a very curious colour. It was the result of the gas called the "Painter" or "Callao Barber," which turns white paint quite black in a night. It turns into dust when dry, and the black coating is then easily removed. The gas comes from the bed of the sea, some sulphurous emanation from subterranean fires. Had an interesting talk now and then with one of the passengers, an English sea captain named Whateley, an old Isle of Wight yachtsman who commanded a transport during the war. Grau, whose real name was Magrath, could have wrought tremendous mischief if he had acted with energy when the *Huascar* was mistress of the seas. He could have gone to Antofagasta, destroyed the transports there with 5,000 Chilians on board, and then left the troops (10,000) to capitulate or die for want of water by breaking the condensers. The heat is tropical, and mosquitoes are coming off the land to visit us. "Yes, sir, it's a fixed fact that at Guayaquil and places like that the donkeys and horses wear trousers! The skeeters would drive 'em mad if they didn't." I doubted, but it was true. The *Cuchapoal* entered the Guayaquil River at dawn on June 17, and threaded the muddy stream for eight hours till she reached her moorings off the city. The banks of the river are most picturesque. They are bordered with hills clothed in the most luxuriant vegetation, or by forests of noble trees. Here and there, there are vistas of cultivated lands and fields, with herds of cattle and droves of horses. The stream is in places six or eight miles broad. Took in pilot at Puna at 8 30. The river needs knowledge, and our courses were narrow and devious—now to the right and now to the left bank, now mid-stream, and now zigzag. And down the turbid current came a procession of floating weed islands, rich with water lilies and flowering shrubs, floating down to die in the salt sea—some but a few yards round, others almost as large as Thames eyots—and troubling vessels at anchor and small craft with their attentions, but the boatmen are expert in getting rid of these interminable assailants, and when their craft are quite enveloped they work their way out to one side or the other of the island as they float down with it, and then resume their course. The river is rich also in alligators, and sanguine expectations of sport animated the breasts of the owners of rifles and youthful spirits till the *Cachapoal* anchored off the town, and the native boatmen gave expression to their views on the tariff for the hire of a four-oar up the creek, where alligators are plentiful as swans at Chiswick, when it became evident that an expedition of the kind demanded the resources of Crœsus. The city looked very well from the river, the long quay was lined by steamers and sailing vessels — Norwegian, Danish, French, American — a long way from home, and between it and the street of lofty houses, with many-coloured fronts and gay Venetians, tram-cars plied busily. The Ecuador tricolour — yellow, black, and red — floated from the public buildings on shore and from a small man-of-war and a torpedo boat in the stream, and church spires rose above the house-tops, and on the quays there was incessant movement of carts and waggons. Large barges filled with cargo lay alongside the vessels in the stream, and an infinite variety of boats, all with canopies or awnings, dug-outs, canoes, &c, were busy on the water. The houses near the banks below the city are built on piles or framework, the dwelling-rooms being on the first floor and the second story. The women are as dark as Egyptians, and resemble them closely in dress. We lay in the stream till six o'clock taking in and discharging cargo. A Swedish engineer, who has a scheme for supplying the city with water by laying pipes in the bed of the river to it from a small island where there is a marvellous series of wells, is enthusiastic about the wealth and greatness of Ecuador in the near future. The State is larger than France. Chimborazo and Cotopaxi belong to it, and the Amazon waters its valleys for many hundreds of miles. Rivers which would laugh the Danube or the Rhine to scorn flow from the Andes through its plains to the coasts. It is rich in gold, silver, copper, iron, quicksilver, lead, sulphur, and precious stones; and it abounds in cattle and in precious barks, gums, and coffee. But there are not half as many people in the Republic as there are in Paris, and there is a respectable public debt, and there are—earthquakes. When they happen there can be no mistake about them, but it is nearly fifty years ago since Quito was simply shaken to pieces, and the people await the next visitation with perfect tranquillity. A column of skirmishing mosquitoes came off as the sun declined, and soon made us aware that they meant business. At the same time it was hot and stuffy under the awnings, and the thermometer marked 90°, when the sun took a header, and darkness at once set in The pilot took the ship down the river in the dark, but there were men in the chains heaving the lead all the way, and sometimes they made startling announcements, but the pilot never minded them. "By the mark thr-r-r-ree!" sung out Jack. Now three fathoms means eighteen feet, and the *Cachapoal* was drawing twenty-three feet! What did that mean? Well, that the bottom of the river is of the softest and deepest mud, and that the keel scooped through it, as the pilot expected it would! Passed Puna and out to sea at night.

June 18th.—At 7.30 A.M. passed an island with a cairn on the top. Land very indistinct. Two little birds like English linnets came on board, and snow-white birds, like small Soland geese, are skimming the sea and soaring with immense power of pinion. The island of La Plata on port bow—tradition says there is much treasure buried there—

practical explorers have failed to find any. The story on the coast is, that the buccaneers were wont to divide their plunder on the island, and that Drake buried the gold and silver he could not safely stow on board his ships, after he had made partition of the spoils of cities and galleons, in caves, hoping to return and carry them off. At 10 A.M. Cotopaxi showed its snowy front high up in the heavens, but all the range below was invisible. There is a Yankee whaler, with two boats out in pursuit of a whale spouting far ahead. The *Pizarro*, a steamer of the rival (P.S.N.C) Company, which left Guayaquil some time before we did, is seven miles ahead. It is the object in life of Capt. Chase, and of every man on board at this moment, to pass that *Pizarro* ere midnight. The engineer is admonished, encouraged, entreated. The Colonel visits the stokers. There is an impression that they have liberal bounty in hand, and, probably, largesse of beer. Any way the *Cachapoal* quivers with excitement, and bets are made freely on the race. The "judicious Hooker," Captain of *Pizarro*, tries various nautical devices—pretends to break down—then starts off with provoking liveliness. I made a *pari* that we would not pass our rival before 10 30. A stern chase is a long chase, but at 10.10 P.M. the *Cachapoal*, burning blue lights and flares, with a great noise of cheering, whistling, yelling from the deck passengers, passed the *Pizarro*, which sheered off into the darkened sea, beyond the glare of triumphant fires.

June 19*th*.—The heat prevented sleep. At daybreak I was on deck—could I believe my eyes? Yes! There is the hated *Pizarro* a good six miles ahead of us on the port bow. The contest becomes acute. It is not companies only—it is captains—it is passengers—it is the Chilian flag *v*. the British. As to the ships, there is rivalry too—the

Pizarro was built by Napier, of Glasgow; the *Cachapoal*, by Laird, of Birkenhead. What stoking there was!—what visits "down below"! How the burly engineer became a centre of attraction as he "came up to blow" on deck, and said evil things of one of his boilers! But he had the air of a conqueror—a modest one—and he was justified, for at 5 p.m. we passed the *Pizarro*, which gave us a berth three miles wide. Next morning the Britisher was some miles astern, but at 8.50 a "biler tube" gave way! Then we had but three boilers, and as Panama was approached *Pizarro* came creeping up, but *Cachapoal* made a supreme effort, and got away once more. We were now getting near to our destination, and "all hands" (passengers) came up from "poker," chess, backgammon, smoke, or sleep, to take a look at the lovely wooded isles which guard the bay in which the city is sheltered—Taboga, the Cemetery, the Hospital, &c. Suddenly a storm, which had been some time gathering on deck, burst forth! Frascuelo, our bullfighter, a very pleasant fellow with a delightful swagger, was a man of decided political and religious opinions, which he aired in such a way as to challenge the criticism and arguments of a friar, who was in every way the antithesis of the airy swordsman—small, bullet-headed, with high cheek bones, square skinny face illuminated by eyes that blazed with fire. What the point was I know not, but my attention was attracted by the altercation, and looking I saw the friar hopping around the bullfighter like a monkey, snapping his fingers, poking his digit into his opponent's face, gesticulating, and shouting with such vehemence that Frascuelo, after repeated but vain attempts to get in a word, slapped his cap down on his head, turned, and walked off, leaving the field to the ecclesiastic, who hurled anathemata after his retreating opponent.

The *Cachapoal* anchored in the beautiful bay outside Panama at 2 P M. on Thursday, 20th of June, and as the steamer for New York did not leave till the following Monday, Capt. Chase, to reduce the risk of catching the fever to a minimum, kindly allowed us to remain on board till his return passengers came off. There was a magnificent thunderstorm raging on shore. An ink-black pall from the heavens covered one-half of the hills which rise steeply behind the picturesque old city, whence incessant flashes of lightning seemed to strike the summits, and the roar and echo of thunder claps and peals were incessant. On the other half of the city the sun shone brightly, lighting up in its own way the sheets of rain which fell in veritable waterspouts. The venerable Cathedral, the churches, the ancient bastioned walls, were set in sheets of flame with an ebony background Near at hand the sea was smooth as glass, and the green of the vegetation and trees on the island close at hand was so fresh and bright that it was not easy to believe the air around us was infected. The harbour had a desolate air. There were *pour tout potage* the steamer for 'Frisco and another American, two P S N. steamers, and our friend *Pizarro* and a few small craft—a great change since I last saw it. The report of those who went on shore, rather a tedious matter at low water, as the channel is very long and narrow and there is very little to spare between the bottom and the keel of an ordinary cutter, made us very well pleased that we had not to leave our cabins and very thankful to the Captain for his indulgence. Next morning the tender came alongside at the top of the tide to take off the heavy baggage and those passengers who wished to leave for Colon, &c A negro "curio" dealer tripped on board intent on trade. The American near at hand had hauled his ensign down half-mast "What is that for?"

"The purser he pison his self, sah! He bad man, sah! Kill himself! He go to hell for sure, sah! Bad man! He cheat me, sah!" And he told us how "the Queen of England! God bless her! Amen! She send of de men-of-war and de steamers to take away de poor black chaps —twenty-five tousand dere was!—to their own country when de canal stop." And then he said evil things of the canal. The tender brought also some of the passengers who were to go south in the *Cachapoal*, among whom was Mr. Patrick Egan, United States Minister to Chile, who became my "next door neighbour," that is, he occupied the cabin beside mine on the saloon deck; but I was not aware of the fact till I saw a pile of luggage, very fresh and new, on the deck, with the name and designation of the owner upon them, outside his door, and I certainly could not have supposed that the pale, thoughtful, student-like looking little man, with sloping narrow shoulders and feeble frame, who was seated near me, was the pitiless conspirator to whose door is laid one of the most terrible crimes of modern times. He had been some time on shore, awaiting the arrival of a vessel under the Chilian flag, and he had paid the penalty of his national scruples, for he came on board very much worn in consequence of an attack of one of the Panama endemics. "Perhaps he would rather be ill on board a Chilian steamer than in good health on board a vessel flying the British ensign?" I do not think so. I became acquainted with Mr. Egan by accident— curious enough in its way—and had a long and to me interesting conversation in virtue of it, in which the Minister spoke of my old friend (and his) Isaac Butt, of the Greville election, of King-Harman, who was carried, he averred, on Carey's back down Sackville Street at the time, and of Pigott (the news of whose death had not long been known here), and of matters relating to the accusations against him. When I came back to my party after that conversation I perceived that I was regarded with the same feelings as little Florentine children had for Dante—only deeper, perhaps. *He* had only *seen* Hell—*I* had been *there* and talked *en ami* with the Evil One! Mr. Egan did not appear at meals. Had he done so Captain Chase would have had to put him in the seat of honour next himself.

We left the *Cachapoal* on Saturday forenoon, June 22nd, and drove to the Grand Central Hotel facing the Cathedral, and the rest of the day and the Sunday following were spent quietly on shore in the quaint old Spanish town which played such an important part in the days of the buccaneers.

Our windows looked out on the square. Early on Sunday there was a function at the Cathedral which attracted the feminine rank and fashion of the place. A constant stream of well-dressed ladies, well-bonneted, gloved, and booted, with fine fans and elaborate sunshades, trooped into the sacred edifice. Now and then a dandy, old or young, ascended the steps, but the mass of the worshippers were very dark indeed, and many were altogether African. Presently, to the strains of the organ pealing through the open doors, was joined the blare of brazen instruments, and a military band came down the street, heading a couple of companies of very smart and showily-dressed infantry of the garrison, marching *au pas* with fixed bayonets, to mass. They entered the Cathedral with their arms, in order, and soon the organ and the band united in a fine *Jubilate Deo*, which was hushed as the tinkle of a bell was heard, and the people in the square were silent, knelt, and crossed themselves.

It was a curious sight. It seems that as regards the

soldiers, it is not considered safe to let them go to church without their arms and store of ball cartridge, for the conspirators, patriots, professors of barricades, *et hoc genus omne*, of whom there is good store ever hereabouts, generally select the Sabbath for a pronunciamiento—the better the day the better the deed I paid a visit to Mr. Leay, the acting Consul, for whom every one who needs help or advice has only one word of praise, and I looked out from his window on the church (another) and buildings of a square, which had been the scene of serious fighting in the last rising, the British Consulate having its full share of bullet marks. The new order of things will, it is hoped and believed, be more peaceful, as a confederation is not so much given to eruption, as a separate state, in Central America. I was very anxious to look at the Canal works near at hand, but I did not find any eager offers to go with me. It is certainly very hot in the day time just now, and it is not safe to be out after dark, at this time of the year, near the water. And here was I much vexed that an inebriated and enthusiastic sporting skipper, who promised us a launch to take us to good alligator coverts in the early morning, had not kept or had forgotten his word!

The American landlord of the Grand Central Hotel, where we lodged, laughed to scorn the idea that Panama was an unhealthy place. "Look at me!" he said, "and look at my family!" And they were indeed most creditable testimonials! I confess, that but for a speedy and sharp experience I should not have believed the stories we were told of the mortal unhealthiness of the Isthmus. True, that in an excursion we made to the mouth of the Panama Canal, we saw on either side of us, a long road lined with magnificent trees, many vast cemeteries—with legions of crosses and stone and wooden pillars—but the air was pure and there seemed no taint of fever in it.

My wife and I got out of the carriage and walked down to the shore, when we were near the sea, through one of the small navy yards, as they might be termed, where some of the launches and boats of the Canal Company were drawn up on the beach. We had not been there above a few moments when one of the French *employés* in the yard called out to us to "come back from the edge of the water as the sun was getting low and it was dangerous." So we drove back to our hotel and thought no more about it. I shall not repeat any of the tales of woe and the complaints anent the Panama Canal and its management, but I may summarize the substance of them in the remark that if they were true the work might have been and should have been completed for the money actually expended up to that time upon it. I had seen the early days of the Suez Canal when it was derided as a ridiculous impossible project, and I had passed through it on the day of the inauguration, when it was hailed as the accomplishment of one of the grandest ideas that had ever entered the mind of man, and when I said so, my friend replied, "Yes! But then de Lesseps was in his prime! He is no longer able to inspire, direct, and order, and his lieutenants were corrupt or incompetent."

Next day, June 24th, Colonel North, to save an early start and long journey, engaged for £50 a special train which ran over the rail from Panama to Colon in less than two hours. What I saw on the way even from the windows of a special train filled me with regret that so many lives and so much money should be sacrificed in vain, should the work be abandoned. Nor could I, nor can I, understand why it should be. It is evident that every year will add to the cost of reclearance and reconstruction of the work that has been executed. The châlets, cottages, and workmen's villages at the stations, so well-designed and constructed, are in the occupation of negro squatters, who chatter like monkeys from their vegetable gardens at the passing train. The hotels are closed or occupied as drinking dens, and the masterpieces of mechanical science left by the sides of the cuttings are covered over with creepers and tropical vegetation, so that the *elevateurs* look like gigantic orchids. Nevertheless, having heard so much of the smallness of the results of a prodigious outlay, I confess I was astonished to find that so much had been done. But that was from the window of a special train!

We embarked in the *Newport* at once, and left Colon or Aspinwall at 5 o'clock in the evening, arriving off the Quarantine Station in New York on the night of July 1st, too late to land. The master of our steamer (one of the Jay Gould line in connection with the Panama Railway Co.) was "a remarkable man" from the point of view which took him in as a sailor. He wore a white neckcloth like a parson, and affected the staid deportment of an ecclesiastic, but his real forte lay in dealing with states and statesmen, for he was by inclination what he called a "die-plomatist," and he certainly made himself universally disliked on board his ship. He seemed quite glad to arrive late, and to let us know he could have got in much earlier had he pleased. *Cucullus non facit monachum*—the white tie did not make the Captain amiable. Two days after we left Colon my wife became unwell. Dr Stubbert, the surgeon of the ship, well-accustomed to read the symptoms of the malady, announced that she was suffering from Panama fever. So it was that walk of a few minutes by the Canal that had done the work. The fever increased rapidly, pulse 116, temperature 104° It was a great disappointment to her to learn, and indeed to feel, that on arriving, instead of being able to continue our journey with those friends in whose society we had travelled so many thousands of miles so pleasantly, we should have to part company under circumstances of great anxiety and distress. The party, which was joined in New York by the wife, brother, and son of Colonel North, and several friends from England, broke up to our great regret. Mr. and Mrs. E. Spencer and Mr. Prior went home direct, while Colonel North and his friends proceeded to Niagara, Canada, &c, before their return to take ship for England We were obliged to remain behind in our comfortable quarters at the Victoria Hotel, nor was it till the 13th of July that my wife was allowed to leave her bed. In a few days more, she was able to accompany me on a visit to some dear friends at Highland Falls on the Hudson. There care, quiet, comfort, and pure air did their work, and on the 20th of July we left in the *Etruria* for Queenstown.

I have now only to ask those who, having come with me so far, are inclined to follow me a little way further, to read the succeeding chapters in which I give some account of the genesis of the Nitrate Fields, of the policy and mining laws of Chile, and of the uses of nitrate of soda.

CHAPTER XXI

THE GENESIS OF THE SALINAS

The Rainless Region—Darwin's Theory—Inland Arm of the Sea—Captain Castle—Inland Seas—Mr David Forbes—The "Salinas" of Marine Origin—Recent Elevation of Coast—Salinas slowly formed—The Lagoon Hypothesis—Tropical Swamps—Vegetable Decomposition—Volcanic Exhalations not necessary—Herr Noller—Doubts and Difficulties—The Chilian Commission—The Local Experts—Camanchaca—General Conclusions.

THERE seems to be a general consensus of opinion, if not of knowledge, as regards the genesis of the nitrate fields in Tarapacá, and in Taltal, where there are also Salitres. The authorities are agreed that these vast beds of salts were formed on the Pampas by the evaporation of seawater in basins, the area of which was uplifted by some upheaval of the ocean bed, so as to cut off their communication with the sea, and thus to form lakes or lagoons. Darwin says he has convincing proof that this part of the Continent has been elevated from 400 feet to 1,200 feet since the epoch of existing shells.

The sun did its work in the course of years, and as there was no rainfall on the Pampas between 19° S. and 27° S. in South America to maintain the level of the water, or to liquefy the salt as it formed on the banks of the lagoons, the Salities were the result. If M. de Lesseps had not converted the great salt-pan—which is now the expanse of the Bitter Lake—into an inland sea, there would no doubt have been a nitrate field at Ismailia;

not very unlike those on the Pampas of Tamarugal. But then comes a difficulty. The geologists assert that there has been a change of climate in Northern Chile, and that there must have been more rain there "formerly"—that geologically means, much, or any, time—than there is at present. Traces of human habitations are found high up in the Cordilleras to-day. Cobs of Indian corn, axes, and knives of copper tempered to exceeding sharpness, arrowheads of agate, even pieces of cloth, are dug up, in arid plains, now without any trace of water for many leagues in or around them.

Now, if there was a change of climate, as Darwin seems disposed to infer, and if rain fell in this region, how is it that these nitrate beds were not liquefied and that the basins were not then converted into salt lakes like those existing in Patagonia?

The ways of this Continent of South America in the days when the world was young may be discussed scholastically or hypothetically. But they cannot be reduced to dogmatic certainty. Therefore, if those who contend that the Nitrate fields are the beds of salt-water lakes which were cut off from the sea by volcanic eruptions, so that the sea-water simmered down in the course of ages, evolving Carbonic Acid Gas which converted the salt (Chloride of Sodium) into Carbonate of Sodium, which ammoniated by the action of guano became Nitrate of Soda, are asked for proofs of their contention, they may reply by the question, "Why not? our doctrine is as good as any other."

Captain Castle says:—"Raw nitrate of soda, spoken of as *caliche*, is only found on the south-west coast of America, between the parallels of 20° and 27° south latitude; it is invariably situated in beds of not less than 2,000 feet above the sea level, and from fifty to ninety miles from the coast. It is met with in the thickest layers and of the best quality upon the sides of the basins, which in prehistoric times formed, undoubtedly, inland seas, or were caused by the subsidence of the ocean. It is a mineral deposit, formed chiefly, it is believed, by decayed animal vegetation, seaweed matter, mingled with sea salts. This theory is borne out in some measure by the fact that skins, also skeletons of animals, birds, shells, sea-birds' eggs, fish, feathers, and guano, are found constantly under the *caliche*, some fifteen feet below the surface. Mr. Watters, of the 'Aurora' oficina, has some most interesting specimens; the presence of iodine, as iodate of soda, also points to this theory. The best deposits are found on the border of Tamarugal Pampa in the province of Tarapacá, and contain some forty to fifty per cent. of raw nitrate, while those on the Atacama desert are more extensive, but less rich, containing only about thirty-three per cent. of the same material."

Mr David Forbes, in his elaborate disquisition on the geology of Bolivia and Peru, which appears in the "Quarterly Journal," of the Geological Society, vol. xvii., February, 1861, gives a more detailed account:—"Later in age than the Tertiary deposits, the saline formations so characteristic of this part of South America are not, as frequently supposed, more confined to the country surrounding the port of Iquique, but appear at intervals scattered over the whole of that portion of the western coast on which no rain falls; whilst to the south they run entirely through the desert of Atacama, and even show signs of their existence further south than Copiapo, in Chile, thus stretching more than 550 miles north and south; their greatest development appears, however, between latitudes 19° and 25° south. They are generally superficial, but occasionally reach to some small depth below the surface, and then may be entirely covered over by diluvial detritus; they always, however, show signs of their existence by the saline efflorescence seen on the surface of the ground, which often covers vast plains as a white crystalline incrustation, the dust from which, entering the nostrils and mouth of the traveller, causes much annoyance, whilst at the same time the eyes are equally suffering from the intensely brilliant reflection of the rays of a tropical sun."

"The salts forming these 'salinas,' as they are generally termed, are combinations of the alkaline and earthy bases, soda, lime, magnesia, and alumina, with hydrochloric, sulphuric, nitric, and carbonic acids, and occasionally with boracic, hydriodic, and hydrobromic acids, and in combination present themselves as the following minerals in a more or less pure state: common salt, epsom salt, glauber salt, thenordite, glauberite, soda alum, magnesia alum, gypsum, anhydrite, along with chloride of calcium, iodide and bromide of sodium, carbonate and nitrate of soda, and, in some places, borate of lime and borax.

"With the exception of the boracic acid compounds, the presence of which is due to volcanic causes, all the mineral substances found in these 'salinas' are such as would be left on evaporating sea-water, or by the mutual reactions of the saline matter thus left on evaporation on the lime, alumina, and organic matter found on the adjacent rocks, soil and shell-beds; and as we have indisputable evidence of the recent elevation of the whole of this coast, and bearing in mind likewise that no rain falls in these regions, it appears very reasonable to suppose that all these saline deposits owe their origin to lagoons of salt water, the communication of which with the sea has been cut off by the rising of the land. When studying the structure of the mountain ranges near the coast, it was observed that, at all the large saline deposits, the chain of hills to the westward or sea side of the 'salinas' is of such a formation as might on elevation be expected to enclose a series of lagoons, which, by means of the breaks or lateral openings in the chain itself, could for a longer or shorter period keep up a tidal or occasional communication with the sea when high, which thus would pour in a fresh supply of salt water to make up for the loss sustained in the lagoons from the evaporation produced by the heat of a tropical sun. It is therefore not necessary to suppose that the great amount of saline matter generally present in these deposits is due to the salts contained in an amount of sea-water merely equal to the quantity originally contained in the lagoon, or, in other words, to the cubical contents of the lagoons themselves.

"The occurrence of salt at different places along the coast at very small elevations above the sea, previously noticed, is no doubt due merely to the tidal infiltration of sea-water into the porous shingle and other beds, and its subsequent evaporation, and must not be confounded with the much greater and more elevated saline deposits further inland, which are met with at three very different altitudes above the sea, and which appear to indicate three distinct and important changes in level in this part of South America. The deposits, situated at about 2,500 to 3,500 feet above the present sea-level, include the important beds of nitrate of soda so extensively worked along this coast, and appear to run from latitude 19° southward into the northern part of the desert of Atacama, showing themselves, according to the configuration of the country, at distances varying from ten to forty miles inland.

"All the data that I could obtain appeared fully to confirm

the 'lagoon hypothesis' previously mentioned, and to prove that the original constituents of these beds had merely been such salts as would result from the evaporation of sea-water. The nitrate of soda and some other associated compounds are due to subsequent reactions and consequent decomposition of the salt of the original deposit, mainly produced by the agency of carbonate of lime and decomposing vegetable matter

"The first step in the formation of nitrate of soda appears to be the decomposition of the chloride of sodium, or salt, by carbonate of lime (in the form of shell-sand, &c.) with the production of chloride of calcium and carbonate of soda. both of which salts have been shown to be present in quantity in the soil of these nitrate grounds.

"The carbonate of soda thus eliminated, when in contact with the mixture of shell-sand and decomposing vegetable matter which may be expected to result from the luxuriant vegetation around such a tropical swamp, and from the abundant marine plants in the lagoon itself, would realise the conditions of the French artificial nitre-beds, substituting only carbonate of soda for the carbonate of potash there used. We may consequently, with all fairness, expect a similar result in the production of nitrate of soda on a still larger scale.

"This view appears much strengthened by the occurrence of wood, reeds, or rushes, and other vegetable matter in the nitre-grounds at but little below the surface, as well as from the general position of the nitrate of soda in the saline deposit, as it invariably occurs in the margin or outer edge of these, representing the shelving sides of the hollow or lagoon-basin, the central part of which is composed of layers of sea-salt only, frequently several feet in thickness.

"In seeking for nitrate of soda the searchers always look to the rising edge of such salt-basins, and further judge of the probability of finding the nitrate from a peculiar moist or clammy state of the ground, which is due to the presence of the chloride of calcium produced by the decomposition above explained.

"The quantity of sulphates, and more especially of sulphate of lime, included invariably in these deposits might at first sight appear to the observer too great to suppose it due only to the evaporation of the sea-water; but I believe that this impression will be dissipated when he sees the enormous amount of gypsum removed in the form of hard white cakes, or sedimentary crust, from the boilers of the large distilling machines in use along this arid coast for producing from the water of the sea a supply of fresh water for the maintenance of the inhabitants, beasts of burden, and even the locomotive engines of the railways along this coast. It appears not necessary to suppose, as has been put forth, that the sulphates present have been formed by volcanic exhalations acting upon the beds of salt. The boracic acid compounds met with appear, however, to be due to this cause; and the borate of lime met with in such large quantities appears to be indirectly produced by the condensed vapours of volcanic fumeroles, many of which are still in full activity in this district. The saline deposits of this series do not rest directly on the rock itself, but on a beach more or less level or hollowed out into lagoon-basins, and composed, as the present and the raised sea-beach previously described, of the *débris* of the adjacent porphyritic, dioritic, and volcanic rocks."

Now, having set forth at length and *ipsimis verbis*, the theories of such scientists as Darwin, Forbes, *et cæteri*, which have a fair share of support in the opinions and theories of local experts like Mr. Whitelegg, it must be admitted, I think, that there are objections of considerable gravity to the easy acceptance of some of them. Take the lagoon theory and then explain how it is that the Nitrate has settled on the western slopes only? A commission directed by the Chilian Government to inquire into and report on the origin of Nitrate fields some time ago expressed the opinion that the lagoon theory would not hold water, and that the idea of the salitreras being due to volcanically-formed fiords was fanciful. The Commission came to the conclusion that the nitrate of soda deposits were simply the result of the decomposition of feldspathic rocks by the action of dry air, their soda was carbonized and thus became Carbonate of Soda, which then, from contact with the nitrogen of the air, produced Nitric Acid, and in conjunction with the oxides in its surroundings, finally formed Nitrate of Soda.

Herr Noller, more than twenty years ago, announced it as "indisputable that the Nitrate of Soda owed its origin to seaweed, the nitrogenous collector of Iodine. By the volcanic elevation of the ground, either gradual or sudden, immense salt-water lakes were formed in which prodigious beds of seaweed, such as are found to-day in the Sargasso Sea, were isolated, and decayed as the sea-water evaporated. Nitric Acid, which is the final product of the decay of nitrogenous or organic matter, became Nitrate of Calcium by uniting with the chalk supplied by the shells and limestone in the beds of the lakes. This reacting on Sodium Sulphates yielded Nitrate of Soda and Calcium Sulphate."

There is a theory which finds acceptance among some writers that it is our misty and chilly friend, "Camanchaca," which has provided Tarapacá with such ample compensation for its presence. This vaporous Camanchaca is, they say, gifted with an infusion of Ammonia. Near at hand you see the tremendous workshop of the Andes, for ever pouring, in solution in the melting snow, the salts which are contained within their rocky entrails on the Pampas, where the Ammonia of the Camanchaca, aided by electric influences which prevail in the district of Tarapacá, &c., converts the Chloride, into Nitrate, of Sodium!

The intelligent gentlemen who are at the head of the *oficinas* concur generally, I think, in the theory which Darwin favoured. Some of them are very precise indeed in their theories, and demonstrate the *modus operandi* with as much positiveness as if they had assisted at it. I was not able, however, to obtain a satisfactory explanation of one matter. If the *caliche* was formed by the evaporation of sea water, how is it that the components of *caliche* are not identical with those of the precipitate obtained by the evaporation of sea water? The proportion of Nitrate of Soda to Sulphate and Chloride of Soda is considerably larger in *caliche* than it is in the result of a simple evaporation of sea water. The answer given by the experts to the difficulty was that when the lagoons were gradually drying up a chemical change took place in consequence of the decay of vegetable, as well as of animal, substances, the presence of which cannot be readily explained, and that the result was the formation of Nitrate of Soda. An expert will be able to determine the site of *caliche* by a mere inspection of the ground. He will look for it not on the level plain, but in the upheaved hills on the western slopes of the cavities, where the sea, in the course of many centuries, fretting against a margin of weeds, rushes, and marine vegetation, gradually evaporated by the heat of the sun, deposited its solid treasures in this rainless region. Large deposits of shells, eggs, guano, feathers, bones of birds, beasts, and fish are often found many feet down, with beds of *caliche* resting upon them, and I saw in the collection of Mrs. Jones at Primitiva several specimens of fossilized reeds or grasses, which had been found on the *Cova*.

CHAPTER XXII.

CHILE AND HER NEIGHBOURS.

The Pacific Coast—The South American Republics—Peru and Chile—Bolivia—Santa Cruz—The Confederation of Peru and Bolivia—The Liberating Army—Invasion of Peru by Chile—General Manuel Bulnes—Battle of Yungai—The Frontier Question—Bolivia and Chile—Melgarejo—The Desert of Atacama—The Secret Treaty—Mr Hicks—*Causa belli*—Antofagasta—The Corruption of Riches—Mr Rumbold's Warnings—Temptations—Crime and Violence—The Feudal System—Law and Order in Chile—The Republic—An Oligarchy with a Chief—The Constitution—The Suffrage—The Council of State—The President's Messages

VERY few people in England, except those who have relations—personal, commercial, or family—with South America, have any idea whatever of the nature of the political passions which have so frequently left the records of their outbursts in disorder and bloodshed on the page of contemporary history, since the yoke of Spain was broken by the people of Mexico, Venezuela, New Grenada, Equador, the Argentine provinces, Chile, Peru and Bolivia, &c., very much as the rule of England was repudiated by the North American colonies some forty years before. It is almost pardonable for a European, considering the nature of the news which has come from them for many years, to regard the South American republics as uncivilised—almost wild—countries, where governments are continually subjected to the shocks of revolution, just as the land itself is shaken by earthquakes. Allowances have not been made for the difficulties created by the extraordinary conditions under which the several Republics constructed themselves, on the vast continent from which they had shaken off the grasp of Spain.

In very old days, almost at the outset of Spanish domination, there were jealousies and contentions between the Viceroys of Peru and the other lieutenants of the King, who ruled over tracts far more extensive than the Peninsula at home, but the hand of the King, for the time being, held the swords of his lieutenants in the sheath. Frontier questions especially occasioned acrimonious disputes. Between Peru and Chile there was a very early manifestation of traditional dislike when each was free to act for itself. An opportunity for active aggression was given to Chile in 1835, by the interference of the President of Bolivia, General Santa Cruz, in the internal affairs of Peru. He was a man of great ability and of enlightened views. Accused by his enemies of aspiring to a dictatorship or to a throne, he would very probably, had his policy been allowed to run its course in Bolivia, have saved that rich and interesting region from the insecure isolation in which it is at present situated, distrustful of its neighbours, without a port for its commerce, its voice almost unheard on the American Continent and altogether silent in Europe. Santa Cruz invaded Peru, defeated Gamarra, the President, and founded a confederation based on the offensive and defensive alliance of Peru and Bolivia. The Chilian Government of the day resolved to attack the menacing alliance which they saw rising up on their borders. General Manuel Bulnes, whose conduct of the operations was marked by ability and sagacity, anticipating the operations of the late war, marched into Peru, and, using with success the superior maritime resources of Chile, obtained possession of Callao and Lima, and finally defeated Santa Cruz with great slaughter at Yungai in January, 1839. He was thus successful in breaking up the confederation, and—more than that—in creating a conflict between Peru and Bolivia which led to the despatch of an army under Gamarra, now installed as President of Peru, into Bolivia, where it was completely defeated by General Ballivian, the President. Santa Cruz was not restored to power, and from 1848, when Ballivian's term of office expired, till the war which established the supremacy of Chile in 1879-81, Bolivia was ruled by savage despots, the heroes of insurrections and conspiracies, who were fortunate in the indifference of the neighbouring states to their excesses.

A frontier dispute is generally bitter, and in 1861 there arose a question between the republics respecting their respective boundaries in the desert of Atacama, which very nearly led to a declaration of war by Bolivia. Chile drew her northern frontier at lat. 23° south. Bolivia insisted on lat. 24° south as the demarcation of her territory from Chile. There is a line now drawn on the map between the States, but it certainly would not be impassable if those on either side of it had strength to risk the consequences of a step beyond. The dispute, which was a constant cause of apprehension and anxiety for nearly ten years, was settled for the time without bloodshed in 1872. Six years previously Melgarejo,[*] who provoked Lord Palmerston to decree that Bolivia should be wiped off the diplomatic and political map of the world, made a treaty with Chile for the adjustment of the frontier quarrel, which was annulled by his successor Morales. The Chilians, claiming the land as their own, flocked into the desert of Atacama, just as the Americans flocked into Texas before the war with Mexico, which

[*] It is only when they are on the western coast that Englishmen hear of incidents like the treatment of their Minister by Malgarejo, which the great fighting Premier and Foreign Secretary, ready at any time to do battle for his *civis Romanus*, was unable to avenge or to punish.

resulted from their immigration. Active and comparatively industrious, as well as adventurous, they were actuated in their dealings with Bolivia by a natural desire to obtain possession of the land.

Mutual apprehensions that Chile might attack each of them, were probably at work all the while, fostering the tendency of Peru and Bolivia to confederate, and while the fears and the interests of the northern republics induced them to bind their fortunes together, Chile was resolute to prevent such a consummation at all hazards. The Government at Santiago came to know of a sudden that Peru and Bolivia had made an offensive and defensive treaty which was in effect intended to combine the powers of both the republics, in case of war, against Chile. It was one of those diplomatic jokes called a "Secret Treaty," which is known to everybody, although it might be difficult for a Government which had not the power of laying its hands on the actual document to verify its existence.

There can be no doubt, I think, in the mind of any one who consults the records, that the bad faith of the Government at La Paz was the main cause of the irritation between the republics which culminated in the war of 1879. But it is possible that the Chilian Government was ready, if not eager, to enter upon a war in which, notwithstanding the maritime superiority which Peru would give the confederate cause, they had confidence in their own strength and believed in their ultimate triumph. It was the old story—if Chile was not "*sui profusus,*" she was certainly "*alieni appetens.*" The nitrate fields furnished inflammable material for an explosion.

The trifling cause of the great events which agitated the Pacific seaboard for two years, and of a war which gave Chile supremacy on its shores, was found in the vigorous defence against the demands of the Bolivian custom-house officers for the payment of increased export duties on certain cargoes of nitrate of soda, at the port of Antofagasta, by our friend Mr. Hicks, who was manager of a Chilian Company there. The Government of Chile resolved to protect the Chilians against imposts which they declared were violations of treaty rights, and when the Bolivian authorities seized on the property of the Nitrate Company and decreed the sale of it by public auction, they were disagreeably convinced of their inability to execute their decree by the appearance of 500 Chilian soldiers from Caldera, who landed at Antofagasta and took possession of it.

If the desert of Atacama, which had a traditional reputation for mineral wealth, had not blossomed into cuprates and nitrates, Chile, perhaps, would not have found any particular charm in the region, nor would she have sought, under any compulsion, to remove her neighbour's landmarks. Why should it have been otherwise? The wealth poured into the treasury of Peru from the barren rocks which were the haunts of pelicans and their congeners for countless ages, might well have aroused the cupidity and inflamed the jealousy of a neighbouring state, which was, it is said, struggling hard at the time to keep its head above the rising tide of bankruptcy, and the conduct of the Government of Peru, and of General Daza, gave Chile an excellent opportunity of making a bold stroke for fortune with some show of reason and excuse.

"No one," says the proverb, "becomes very wicked all at once." I say people may do so, if they become all of a sudden immensely rich, for then they at once seek to become richer. Now Peru was, according to all observers, almost instantly demoralized by the prodigious prosperity of her citizens, arising from the products of the rich mines and the wealth from the deposits of guano, and the State itself launched out into every extravagance.

A very charming, intelligent, and well-informed journalist at Iquique, well acquainted with both countries, attributed the corruption which tainted the body politic of Peru to the riches which, in a few years, deluged the Republic and destroyed the morality of the people, and he argued that Chile, following the same evil courses, was in danger of becoming like Peru. "She is borrowing money and building forts, and ordering ships and arms and guns. She is puffed up with military pride, and if any great shake were given to her financial position, from the failure of exports on which her revenue depends, she would look beyond her frontiers for some profitable appropriation. Neither Peru nor Bolivia would be able to make head against her. Who, then, are likely to do so? The Argentine Republic might find it convenient to have an ally instead of an enemy at the other side of the Andes who could be of substantial assistance in the direction of Uruguay in case of need, and Brazil is now not at all likely to step across her western and southern frontiers, so Chile would have nothing to fear if the Great Powers did not interfere. Here there is obvious danger for the future peace of the Pacific States."

Mr., now Sir Horace Rumbold—whose flattering Report is regarded by Chilians as a just description of the country of which he recognised the rising prosperity—found it necessary, when he was Minister at Santiago in 1875, to utter what might be taken as friendly notes of warning to the Government of the day, respecting the alacrity with which successive Presidents and Ministers plunged Chile into debt. "In the last ten years, she had contracted fresh obligations, and had borrowed twice as much again as she did in the first fifty years of her national existence. Admitting that her extraordinary expenditure was destined to be productive, since it was incurred mainly on account of public works," he still thought that a little more had been attempted than was warranted by the financial position of the country. "The pace has been somewhat forced, and it would be well," Mr. Rumbold suggested, "if Chile devoted the next few years to the reform of her fiscal system."

The words in which Mr. Rumbold resumed his general review of the conditions of the country is quoted with pride by the friends of Chile. "A sober-minded, practical, laborious, well-ordered and respectably governed community, standing out in great contrast to the other states of similar origin and kindred institutions spread over the South American Continent. The blessings which Chile enjoys are due," he wrote, "to the pure traditions implanted in her administration, to the preponderating share taken in public affairs by the higher and wealthier classes, to the happy eradication of militarism, to the nearly entire absence of gold, guano, and nitrate so lavishly bestowed by Providence on some of her neighbours, to the consequent necessity of strenuous labour repaid by a bountiful soil, to the patient endurance and capacity for toil of her hardy population, above all, perhaps, to the neglect of her former master, which when she had cast off the yoke drove her to create everything for herself and called forth exceptional energies in the nation."

And then he reminds the Chilians of what they owe—and urges that they should not forget what they owe—to foreign and especially English assistance, to the strangers who fought for her, taught her children, built her railways, and made her ports. "They have," he remarks, "attained a remarkable degree of prosperity, but if friendly criticism may be permitted to one who sincerely wishes them well, he thinks they have lately shown some signs of the intoxicating effects of good fortune. The debt, which was £6,397,400 in 1875, was, at the date of the latest returns accessible to me, £18,413,000 and odd; and it is by no means clear that an addition to the national debt will not be necessary to carry out the programme which was announced by the President."

Since that time, what the English minister described as "accidental sources of wealth," which were denied to Chile and which were lavished on her neighbours, have become altogether her own. The Desert of Atacama has become the possession of Chile, and the rich mines which extend for 240 miles between Caldera and Mejillones are open to Chilian enterprise. The failing supplies of guano have been replaced, as sources of national revenue, by nitrates. In addition to the nitrate, rock salt, borax, and iodine, which the pampas of Tarapacá yield, every conceivable mineral product—silver in abundance, copper in great quantities, gold, iron, lead, nickel, and cobalt—are found there and in Taltal.

The districts which contain these great reserves of mineral wealth stretch away over the frontiers of Chile into Bolivia. It is easy to conceive that the inhabitants of that distracted republic—which has, however, been lately enjoying an unwonted repose from revolution and civil war—would hail with satisfaction the introduction of a firm government which accorded security for life and property to those living under its protection. It is true that crimes of violence are still too frequent throughout the Republic of Chile and that brigandage has not been put down within its borders; but many allowances must be made for the difficulty of establishing respect for the law and regard for human life amongst wild populations which have scarcely been brought within civilising influences The hot blood of the Indian and of the Spaniard, in combination not always felicitous, leads to the use of the knife amongst people who have a long way to go to find a policeman or a magistrate to settle their disputes, who are all armed, and who are not always members of temperance societies.

The old feudal system has left its traces in Chile; the *corvée* still exists in the form of forced service, which may, or may not, be severe, according to the disposition of the landlord or the traditions of the estates. The great Hacendados, like some landed proprietors nearer home, have not been very careful in improving the condition and attending to the comfort of their tenants, but they have not an excuse for their indifference by alleging that they were encountered by race hostility and by religious animosity. Perhaps their best plea for their neglect would be that they did not know how and where to begin their labours, and that till they had themselves learned some of the arts of civilised life, they could not teach them to others. The Hacendado, very like a Cork or Kerry squire not long ago—given to "sport," as he understood it, living coarsely and wastefully, flying to London or the Continent when his purse was full, and returning to his estates and his country to squeeze his people when his money was out—was not likely to do much for the improvement of the peasantry. He left their education to the priests, but he led his voters to the poll without any fear of opposition from the local *padre*. By degrees, as his estancias, yielding crops of increased value, and the fields of *alfalfa*, pasturing myriads of cattle, gave him larger means, he sent his sons and daughters to France and Spain for their education, and set up a house at Santiago. He is, and was, an oligarch, living under a Republic, in which he and his class are supreme.

The resemblance which might have been traced between Chile and Ireland does not now exist, for legislation has greatly interfered with the relations of landlord and tenant in the distressful country. The peasant farmer in Chile is generally a tenant at will. He has his small patch of land, perhaps more than the three acres and the cow which have been set forth as the *summum bonum* of the English labourer, but he has very little capital. His wants are small, his idea of household comfort limited. Perhaps a Dorsetshire labourer would not think a pound loaf at breakfast, a pound of beans or maize cooked with lard for dinner, and a pound loaf and a dish of bruised corn at night very sumptuous fare. But it is at least ample in quantity. It is in quality wholesome and nutritious, and a Chilian will work on it for twelve hours a day under a broiling sun. The people who enjoy such abundance are, however, the fortunate *adscripti glebæ*. The peons, or day labourers, constituting so large a portion of the rural population as to cause considerable inconvenience and anxiety to the Government, are almost entirely nomads, travelling about from place to place in search of work. They have an innate restless spirit which is developed and maintained by the discovery of new fields of labour. Wherever mines are to be worked, cities to be built, railways to be constructed, and industries developed, the Chilian is to be found, strong in arm, independent in opinion, violent in his cups, but on the whole a valuable agent in the work of civilization in countries inhabited by races of less physical strength and powers of endurance. The Chilians are scattered all over the South American Continent, Central America, and the Pacific seaboard of the United States

It is calculated that at least sixty per cent. of the people of Chile are employed in agriculture. The mass of them have no interest in the land, and on the whole the state of society in the Republic is very like what may be supposed to have existed in the old days in Sparta or in Russia after 1856. But it is not to be supposed that this state of things will long endure. The schoolmaster is abroad, and Señor Balmaceda is driving him ahead and far afield. Whether the exclusively secular education which seems to be in favour will conduce to the happiness and morality of the people and the prosperity of the state, must be left to time to determine The rising generation are "liberal" enough, in all conscience.

At the Cauquenes Station, the day of our return, a band of urchins, employed as light porters, were playing at voluntary drill as soldiers, and to pass the time, whilst awaiting the train, one of the party began to chat with them. They were all at school, they said, but that was a "Saint's day." "What Saint?" "Oh, some of the padre's humbugs!" "Do you dislike Saint's days and padres?" "I would shoot all the priests if I could" "Why?" "Because they are scoundrels." "But they teach you religion?" "They teach stuff and nonsense; we don't believe them here! Do we, my boys?" he asked, turning to the others. They answered "No." And then the gamin continued, "We want the French revolution—where all the princes and priests had their heads chopped off!" So he was *educated*; he had learned *something*. But it is said that a better and a wiser policy is exerting its influence amongst the people. Let us hope it is true.

Chile has enjoyed an exemption from any serious disturbance for nearly forty years. The reason, perhaps, for that exemption from the curse of the States of South America is the aristocratic nature of the government, and the ready submission of the governing classes to the power of the President, who is virtually Cæsar for five years. The constitution which was reformed, or at all events reorganized, in 1833, while it did not interfere ostensibly with the rights guaranteed under the legal code of the South American Justinian, Señor Bello, conferred upon the President a power which is practically, when it is supported by the Senate and the Chamber, absolute. He governs, if he does not reign. With the concurrence of his Council of State he can apparently do in Chile all that the Parliament can do in England, and the exercise of his power is only limited by considerations of public policy. As the qualifications of the voter are based upon education and upon the payment of a considerable income-tax, a very high class of voters is secured. Based on that of the United States, the constitution of Chile has, however, some remarkable departures from the excessive liberality which characterizes the suffrage in some of the States further north. There is a property qualification required from senators and deputies, which under the old value of money would represent £100 and £400 per annum respectively. The elector must be able to read and write, and prove that he earns at least $150 a year. The members of the Council of State, appointed by the President, are necessarily his own, for they are appointed by him and are removable as he pleases. His ministers countersign decrees *pro formá*. It is only in the case of very strong men, indeed, that the resignation of ministers is regarded as of much consequence; but behind, if not above, the power of the President, is the national will, the public opinion of the nation, the intelligence and spirit of the great proprietors or hacendados—the broad-acred squires and landed gentry—and the sturdy resolute character of the people, who combine with an ardent patriotism a considerable amount of respect for their own individual liberties and of regard for the rights of others.

The Chilian giant stands on silver, copper, and nitrate of soda; but at times he seems disposed to pick away some of the ground on which he rests his feet. The respectable financial condition of Chile depends mainly for its maintenance on the export of silver, copper and on nitrate, the export duty on which furnishes more than one-third of the entire revenue of Chile.*

The President and his advisers are anxious to resume metallic currency and to abolish paper, but Señor Balmaceda was obliged to tell Congress last year that all efforts in that direction would be ineffective until the balance of trade in favour of Chilian exports was established. "It is necessary," said he, "to encourage by all reasonable means the copper trade, agricultural pursuits, and the manufacture of nitrate, and to obtain for Chile at least a part of the immense benefits of the nitrate business."

President Balmaceda, announcing a number of projects of law for the improvement of finance, declared that the most important was one regulating the sale of the nitrate grounds — that is, the nitrate grounds in the province of Tarapacá, now possessed by Chile, formerly belonging to the republic of Peru. The President pro-

* The value of the exported silver and copper in the four years from 1884 to 1888 was $613,436,214, being 68 per cent of the value of all the mineral produce sent out of the country. In the same period Chile exported $1,205,284 of gold.

posed a "solution," as he called it, "in a matter concerning an article which belongs to Chile, and can only be exported from its territory." He proposed that "the nitrate grounds should be divided into districts, to be sold at public auction, good, medium, and inferior caliche being included in one lot, and that 4,000 estacas, selected from best Government land, should be appropriated, to be worked by Chilian companies, all the shareholders to be Chilians, the shares not to be transferable for a time, and then to be transferred to Chilians only." Then would come another golden age. Once the redeemed salitres were sold, and the 4,000 estacas were distributed for the establishment of national works, every succeeding year one-half of one estaca should be sold at auction to the highest bidder, and the other half of the estaca to Chilian buyers, on the basis of shares not transferable to foreigners. In this manner the free production of nitrate would not be impeded, and the pursuit of this business would be confided to men with Chilian capital and the oficinas would be worked by Chilian manufacturers.

"The importance of nitrate in agriculture and commerce, and the gradual increase of its production," said the President, "warns the legislature and the authorities not to demur in solving this problem, and to protect effectively the legitimate interests of our countrymen. It is true that we should not exclude the free competition and manufacture of nitrate in Tarapacá; but we cannot consent that this rich and extensive region should become simply a foreign factory. It is a certain and important fact which cannot be disguised, that owing to the singularity of the business, the manner in which property has been acquired, the absorption of the small foreign capital, and the character of the different races that will contest the control of that vast and fertile business, a special legislation is necessary on the basis of the nature of things and the peculiar needs of our commercial and financial existence. This question is of great importance for the future, and on it depends to a great extent the development of our individual wealth, now held at a distance from this centre of labour and general prosperity."

The President did not attempt to explain why it was that Chilians, on ground which had been made their own by force of arms, needed special legislation to enable them to work nitrate fields, which were as open to them as they were to the strangers whose capital and enterprise were to be handicapped by restrictive legislation. He was not concerned to show how capital was to be provided to turn to account the properties which the State proposed to assign to them. There are very wealthy people in Chile, and there are many Chilians with capital. But, though there are many Chilian nitrate makers, there has not been a very marked tendency to turn the money possessed by merchants and landed proprietors to the extension of the nitrate industry. No bank would lend money on property over which it can exercise no legal rights. Chilians alone must advance the money which is necessary to turn the possession of them to account for the working of these Chilian nitrate-fields. No non-Chilian can enter on possession of these national nitrate properties, and there is apparently no means of securing money advanced upon them.

The result of the policy thus enunciated is to be seen hereafter, for as yet there has been, I believe, no general movement among the Chilians to take advantage of the privileges accorded to them. But the principle is announced and it meets with general approval. The year 1888 was exceedingly prosperous The effect of the copper "krach," and of the disturbances in nitrates, on the returns of 1889, will not be known until this year is well advanced, but it will be surprising if the great increase in the value of exports and imports, which marked 1888 as compared with 1887, will be sustained. Mr Kennedy, the British Minister at Santiago, in forwarding an extract from the "Extradista Comercial" of Chile to the Foreign Office, makes a significant summary of the opinions of Señor Torres, which probably represent those of his countrymen.

"It is admitted that Chile can no longer regulate the price of copper, but it is claimed that she can still retain her hold as an important factor in the copper industry of the world by the adoption of certain measures; such as, for instance, the expropriation of the mineral railways, the construction of roads, the introduction of improved systems of mining and smelting, and the employment of the necessary amount of capital in mining undertakings."

"Expropriation" is an ugly word, if it means that Chile is to place her own price on the property she seeks to acquire. Mr. Kennedy goes on to say—

"With respect to nitrate, Señor Torres does not share in the opinion, recently mooted here by a firm of brokers, of a crisis being imminent owing to over-production; but, on the contrary, he is of the opinion, and he bases his opinion on interesting facts and figures, that what with the probable depreciation of gold, the extension of the actual consuming markets, and the opening up of new ones, there is a brilliant future in store for the salt, which in 1888 figured in our exports for $33,866,196, and in eleven years, 1878—88, for a grand total of $231,451,444, and which contributed to the national revenue, in 1888, in the form of export duty, the large sum of $17,838,978."

At the interviews which the President had with Colonel

North at Viña del Mar and Santiago, he evinced an equitable appreciation of the true interests of the State, in respect for private rights, and of the policy to be pursued in a country which needs a continuance of the steady flow of the capital by which it has been floated into a condition of comparative ease, to place it in a position to mature its own resources, and at the same time to secure the advantages derived from the inventions, enterprise, industry, and wealth of foreigners.

His Excellency's speeches at Iquique, and at other places where he addressed audiences, foreign and Chilian, early in the year, excited uneasiness in the minds of those engaged in the mineral industries. It was natural that a President of Chile, speaking to Chilians, should point to the great extent of territory abounding in mineral riches which had as yet been untouched, and that he should encourage Chilians to enter into the race for wealth, in which foreigners had hitherto been permitted to run almost alone. His meaning was, it seems, imperfectly conveyed, and Señor Balmaceda disavowed the construction placed on some of his words. But it was inferred, especially from his speech at Iquique, that he intended, if he could, to close the course to any but native competitors, to handicap those who had been the winners, to refuse industrial concessions in the country to non-Chilian residents, and to reserve the State lands still unappropriated, exclusively and inalienably, to citizens of the Republic. Although there was no express intimation of any intention on the part of Government to lay hands upon, or, as the phrase in Chile goes, to "expropriate," the railways, it was well known that such a project was in favour with some politicians at Santiago, and some expressions in President Balmaceda's discourses were taken to indicate the likelihood of future action in that disagreeable direction ; but no one supposed the President would injure vested interests.

When a President of Chile with full ability to carry into effect the expression of his opinions delivers himself of any exposition of his policy in public, as much weight is naturally attached to it as men were wont to give to the New Year's Day announcements of Napoleon the Third. The messages of the President on the opening of Congress are State documents which announce the lines of his policy; they naturally attract the attention of the governments of America and Europe. There was very little uncertainty in the words of the speech which President Balmaceda, in very guarded terms, addressed to the Chilian Congress last year as a programme for legislation.

But in speeches of less responsibility and greater freedom, delivered by the President in various towns in the course of his progress through the country, there were other references to the same topics which created considerable agitation. It would be regretable indeed if events proved that the uneasiness was justified, but experience, short though it be, may open the eyes of the Government to the dangers with which Chile would be menaced by the possible loss of confidence in her good faith.

The most powerful despot in the world cannot be indifferent to the national feeling of the country he governs. Let it be admitted that it needs tact and resolution in Chile as elsewhere to manipulate political parties so as to promote the interests of the State without creating jealousy at home, or want of confidence abroad. Whether Señor Balmaceda, when he is again eligible, is re-elected or not, it must be his object to leave behind him a good record, that he may have a chance of succeeding Señor Santa Maria should that popular gentleman, who was his predecessor, be recalled to the presidential chair.

When you enter a great house of business in a town on the coast, you generally see a map of Chile, or a map of Peru, spotted all over with red, or blue, or yellow circlets. These indicate mines formerly worked and abandoned, and mines still in the course of exploitation. The State owns all precious ores, stones, and fossil substances, but it gives power to private persons to search for mines, and to work them. The working of coal and of other fossil mines is ceded to the owner of the soil. The State reserves to itself deposits of guano, nitrate and ammoniacal salts, in land in which mining rights had not been acquired by private persons.

The mining laws of Chile constitute a *corpus juridicum* of great extent and complexity. To encourage explorers such liberal protection is accorded to prospectors that it seems inconsistent with the rights of property. No owner can veto the operations of a mineseeker upon his land; the compensation awarded by law, in relation to results, is, however, strictly defined.

Darwin says that the Chilian Government, or rather the old Spanish law, encourages by every method, the searching for mines. " The discoverer may work a mine on any ground by paying 5s., and before paying this he may try even in the garden of another man for twenty days."

Miers, who lived in Chile for some years before Darwin's visit, says in his excellent work :—

" I should lament to hear that any British capitalist, however flattering the offers made to him, should invest his capital in any enterprise upon the soil of Chile; having myself failed in such an attempt from impediments that naturally exist in the country, together with the absurd obstacles opposed by the general and local authorities, as well as by the obstinate jealousies of the natives, notwithstanding all the flattering inducements that were held out and the outward show of protection afforded in an especial manner to me individually."

Apparently his experience of mining was not favourable, and his warning was no doubt well founded when it was written. Under the most liberal conditions mining is precarious, and in Chile the risks were much increased in the case of foreigners. The mining laws of Chile were described to me "as the plague of owners of property, the dread of capitalists, and the delight of lawyers." It was said in the old days, "a man will make money out of a copper mine; he may make money out of a silver mine; he is sure to lose in a gold mine." I met men who had lost large sums of money, and I met some who had attained to great wealth in mining enterprise. I am bound to say the former far exceeded the latter in number. But whatever may have been the defects of the old law, the code which came into force quite recently has, undoubtedly, done much to facilitate the acquisition of mining property, and the working of mines in Chile. Mr. J. H. Thomas, British Vice-Consul at Santiago, lately forwarded through Mr. Kennedy, the Minister, a translation of the Code, which has been laid before Parliament. The Minister, who had only recently arrived, in sending the Report to the Foreign Office, although agreeing with Mr. Thomas in the opinion that the new laws would confer great benefit on the mining industries, influenced perhaps by his want of knowledge, thought it right to add that "he was not prepared to support the recommendations of the Vice-Consul as to the advantages offered to investors by the gold mines of Chile.' According to Mr. Thomas, "the facilities offered by the new law over the old lies in the establishment of perfect titles to the properties without the risk of their being disputed, which was constantly the case under the former order of things. To maintain the legal possession of a mine under the old law, four men had to be constantly employed in it, whether there was work to do or not; and without regard to the owner's ability to support them, either out of his own funds or the produce of the mine. The result was that the poorer miners were obliged to seek aid to carry out the preliminary works of the mine, and to maintain the four workmen therein by ceding a part of their discovery or property, or run the risk of having the property denounced any day by unscrupulous parties only too vigilant in surprising him in the non fulfilment of that very onerous condition, either to blackmail him, or actually obtain possession of the mine, if it was thought to be a good one; the whole affair generally ended in one or more law suits, each more complicated and interminable than the last, and not in the profitable working or development of the mine.

"The present law obviates all those difficulties in the most effective way, by constituting a perfect title to the property in virtue of the payment to the Government of an annual license, in accordance with the nature of each property. Under this title, which, when properly established by law, is immutable and perpetual, the owner may work his property or not, as he pleases, and with the number of workmen and in the conditions he may think fit; and he may freely transfer his property to anybody, and the latter may receive it without any fear of his title being impugned, until he voluntarily relinquishes it.

"There are other and important improvements in the new law, which will doubtless produce their fruits before very long, and especially in opening up the gold-mining industry of the country, an industry which has been almost dormant since the time of the Spanish Colony in Chile, but which was an inexhaustible source of wealth to the Spaniards during the entire period of their occupation of Chile and Peru; and I would here call the attention of the British investor to the fact, that the reopening of the old and the discoveries of the new gold mines in this country is soon going to be the principal mining industry of the Republic; copper mining here having become a precarious business after the collapse of the syndicate, and the creation of a keener competition than ever between European and North American producers."

It was with reference to these statements, as regards the great future of gold mining in Chile, that Mr. Kennedy, the Minister, addressed a *caveat*, but it was more specifically directed to the proposal that European capitalists should form syndicates to send out mining engineers to the country and examine the mining grounds for themselves. According to Don Marzial Martinez, formerly Envoy Extraordinary of Chile in England, whose memorandum Mr. Thomas refers to, the working of gold mines in Chile was only abandoned when the country became the principal producer of copper for the whole world. All the gold mines ran at a certain depth into iron pyrites, and as the chlorination processes were then unknown fully 60 per cent. of the gold was lost in washing the pyrites. But Chile still, according to Señor Martinez, possesses the largest number of gold mines and deposits in the world. When I was at Santiago I heard of many gold mines in the ravines near the sources of the Mapocho River, of the Colmo, &c., but there was little or no work, and therefore little produce from them. There are said to be many gold mines in the province of Rancagua, especially at Elque. Mr. Thomas believes, if his plan were adopted, that Chilian gold would in a year become more famous as a source of wealth than nitrate of soda. For my own part I would prefer making an investment in an oficina to sinking money in a mine.

The Spanish jurists bequeathed to the South American Republics a very intricate and perplexing legal system. In disputes between Chilians and natives, the theoretical equality existing in the eye of the law between them is occasionally subjected, it is said, to "dislocation." But, as far as I could learn, the bench is above corruption, being very different in that respect from the magistrature in an adjoining state, where the judges can be and are bought at a price. The same high official character is maintained in the political life of Chile. The statesmen and chief politicians in and out of Government are above suspicion. It would be more correct to say, perhaps, that any accusations of corruption levelled at them by opponents were incapable of proof. Lobbying has not attained to the status of a profession in Congress, but it is scarcely to be expected that private influence should be altogether ignored in legislation dealing with concessions, contracts, public works, and so forth.

The Chilians call themselves, I was told, "the English of South America." I am bound to say that I never heard any Chilian make use of the expression, or of the phrase "on the word of an Englishman," attributed to them as the strongest affirmation that they can make of a fact. Nevertheless, they affect a high standard of public and personal integrity, and there is nothing any official of the Republic would fear so much as the insinuation that he had been "got at." Even the highest personage in the State feels that he is not above the shaft of malicious suggestion, and that he is obliged to take heed to his ways lest he should be subjected to the odium which would be incurred by any Chilian supposed to have been influenced in public life, even in the best cause, by what may be, euphemistically, styled "a consideration."

The efforts made from time to time to abate the inconveniences arising out of differences in the codes of the various republics have not, notwithstanding the labours of Andrés Bello, altogether succeeded. The English press, which only seems to be aware of the existence of the States of South America when there is a revolution affecting bonds and shares, a great convulsion of nature, or a war there, scarcely noticed the International Congress held at Monte Video, at which, as President Balmaceda announced, the Chilian representatives signed treaties with their neighbours concerning artistic and literary rights, trade-marks, patents, international commercial rights, partnerships, insurances on land and sea, life-insurance freights, maritime loans, averages, lawsuits, judgments, and decisions of arbitrators, &c. The delegates of Chile, however, would not sign the treaties proposed by the Argentines concerning criminal and civil international codes, because they were not in harmony with the law of Chile. With similar caution, and perhaps more reasonably suspicious, Chile, in accepting the invitation of the United States to the great conference at Washington this year, declared that she would attend it solely to discuss social and economical problems. It remains to be seen what will be the actual outcome of her attendance at the Pan-American Congress.

CHAPTER XXIII.

NITRATE OF SODA LEGISLATION.

The Government of Peru—Attempts to Expropriate the Salinas—Compulsory Sales—Peruvian Certificates—The Export Duties—The War—Chilian Occupation—The Reaction—The Classification of Oficinas and Certificates, 1882—Foreigners and Natives—Iquique—Initial Difficulties—Overproduction—Restrictive Combinations—The Comité Salitrero—Comision de Peritos—Their Duties and Attributions—Their measures—Their General Character—The Comité Salitrero Expires—Attempts to Combine to Regulate Production—The Government and the Nitrate Makers—Expediency of a Policy of Give and Take.

THE province of Tarapacá belonged to Peru when the old Spanish viceroyalty was overthrown and disrupted. Its limits southwards were conterminous with the northern frontier of Chile.

I have not been able to ascertain when the native manufacture of nitrate of soda began on the Pampas, or when the value of it was recognised. Bolivian agriculturists have the credit of being the first to import the salt from Peru. The early native manufactories (*paradas*), of which there are abundant ruins and traces all over the Pampas, were built of *adobe*. The raw material or *caliche* was boiled down in copper boilers (*fonda*) placed over open fireplaces, the salt being doubtless subjected to some refining process to fit it for the market.

When attention was first directed to the mineral wealth of Tarapacá the Government of Peru divided the Pampas into small holdings, about four acres in extent, and gave them to residents there. It may be inferred that there were at the time disputes about the mines, or that the uses of nitrate of soda as a fertiliser were already recognised. According to Captain Castle, the Government of Peru became aware that there was a great future for nitrate industry for the first time in 1832, but what they did to facilitate its advent I do not know. When the exports from Iquique began to mount up to millions of quintals per annum, the Peruvian Government thought that they would derive some benefit from the business. In 1873 accordingly they promulgated an ordinance that the *oficinas* on the nitrate fields should be sold to the State, and that, in the event of the owners refusing the terms offered, a duty of 1·50 dollars per quintal should be levied on the export of the salt. The owners selected the first of the alternatives, but the State was not ready with the money for the purchase, and nothing was done. In 1875 the Peruvian Government made another attempt, passed a compulsory Act for the sale of all nitrate properties to the State, and arranged that the value of these should be assessed by Peruvian officials. Captain Castle says:—

"Arbitrators were appointed to fix a reasonable price for sale. However, the amount assessed by the arbitrators reached to such an enormous sum that the Government were unwilling to pay the money down, and had recourse to issuing certificates, each representing the amount of $1,000 at 44d., bearing 8% interest and 5% amortization. On these terms the Salitreros still continued manufacturing, the Government contracting to pay them $1·70 per quintal, at 40d f o. b. (that is, "placed in lighters outside the surf") The Government also claimed all nitrate beds not actually working as State property. Thus the State came possessed of all the nitrate manufactured, which was sent by them to their agents in Europe, who sold it at great profit. The

THE STATE AND THE OFICINAS.

monopoly was afterwards rented by the Cia Salitreros of Peru to pay advances made by the Government, and afterwards to the Bancos Asociados for a similar service. The Banks thus became Government agents. In 1878, during the war, the nitrate district came under the rule of Chile. The manufacturers feared their new masters, and sold, as best they could, their interest in it. Really there was nothing to fear, for when the Chilians took possession of Tarapacá they allowed the owners of the Peruvian nitrate certificates or bonds to take and hold the various oficinas, the face of the bond being cancelled on their being handed to the Government, thus relieving the Chilian Government of all responsibility. Next came the reaction after the war. On the 2nd September, 1880, the President of Chile addressed a memorandum to Antonio Alfonso, Military and Civil Governor of the province of Tarapacá, ordering him to permit and encourage the manufacture of nitrate of soda, and stating that further instructions would be sent to him. A survey was made of the nitrate district; the certificates which had been issued to the former Government were for the time recognised; and finally, in 1882, the certificates were classed as follows:—Oficinas redeemed in virtue of the Supreme Decree of 28th of March, 1882; oficinas sold by public auction in virtue of Supreme Decree of 31st of July, 1882; oficinas restored to their original owners by the Intendente of the State; oficinas occupied on leases of elaboration in accordance with the order of the Supreme Government of 21st September, 1881; oficinas held by the State, and in keeping by the Inspector-General of Nitrate.

"The value of nitrate property was as follows:—

Appraised value of the 166 oficinas of nitrate of soda property on Tarapacá . . . $21,375,203 (a)
Value of nitrate grounds which do not pay rent $1,617,600 (b)

Total value of the obligations by the Government of Peru in payment to Salitreros	$a - b =$	$19,757,603
Value of certificates and bonds corresponding to the oficinas redeemed	$6,941,400 (c)	
Value of certificates and corresponding bonds sold by auction	$1,845,755 (d)	
	$c + d =$	$8,787,155
Value of certificates and corresponding bonds of the nitrate works belonging to the State also in 1879	$10,970,488	

Oficinas held by the State were	103
Let out	63
Total	166

"Since that date sales by auction have been made, oficinas have been returned to their original owners, the properties have been improved, and facilities for the economic elaborations much increased. Thus—

In 1883.

Oficinas redeemed by virtue of Supreme Decree 28th March, 1882	39
Oficinas sold by public auction	18
„ rented at 25c. per quintal	14
Oficinas held by the State	96
Total	166

"Out of these 166 oficinas 39 are working; they are capable of elaborating 26,000,000 quintals annually, now increased (1886) to 35,000,000. We will next pass to the work that has been accomplished by enterprising foreigners and natives. It was no small venture for a foreigner or even a native to lay out capital on acquired property on the desert of Tarapacá, for desert it was. Nothing but space, no tree on which the eye could rest; no communication with the outside world except on foot or horseback; self-abnegation, so predominant in the pioneers of commerce, was soon rewarded. The fame of nitrate of soda reached the agriculturists of Europe; demands came from Germany, the Netherlands, and France, and

THE RISE OF IQUIQUE.

as fast as it could be produced it found a ready market at remunerative prices. Greater and greater became the demand for this wonderful fertilizer; it eclipsed guano, and the Peruvian Government saw before it a source of revenue that would facilitate its financial operations for many years to come. In those days business between the Peruvians and foreigners was easy; concessions were made freely, machinery was imported, and the desert of Tarapacá was teeming with industry. The anchorage of Iquique became the resort of shipping varying from 500 to 1,200 tons. Ship freights were high; business brisk; and labour expensive. Skilled labour rose to an immense value; machinery for want of transport often remained in the port of Iquique, there being no skilled labour to erect it. There was no railroad to the Pampa; every article of food had to be carried on mule back to an elevation of 3,000 feet, and then across a desert; water, however, was procurable in certain places; wells were sunk to water cattle, and to assist in the elaboration of nitrate of soda. In the port of Iquique great difficulty was experienced in landing heavy plant, and embarking and disembarking goods of every description. The anchorage, although exposed to the sea, is well protected. An island off the port breaks the long rolling swell of the Pacific, and the wind never blows home. Ships lay at anchor, moored head and stern in long tiers; as many as 100 ships have been at anchor off the port, flying the flags of Great Britain, Germany, France, Italy, Norway, and America, besides smaller craft of Peru and Chili. During the war, the blockade of the coast adjacent to the nitrate districts had materially altered the basis of this industry, having reduced the exportation from 7,122,266 quintals in 1878, to 3,307,000 quintals in 1879. Further, the Chilian Government had imposed a tax of 1 60 cents. per metrique quintal, against 4 cents only imposed by Peru on a Spanish quintal. The supply of nitrate in the home market had become short and large quantities had been demanded, so when the blockade ceased, and elaboration could be re-continued, oficinas were erected in haste, and the work was conducted on a more economical and improved principle. By the year 1884 the following was the total capable of production:—In Tarapacá and Tocopilla, 23,245,000 quintals; Antofagasta, Caleta Oliva, Taltal, and Agua Blancas, 3,059,200 quintals; total, 26,304,200 quintals. Thus more nitrate was made than could be consumed by the home markets. Far-seeing men recognised that if this state of things continued, not only the large elaborators, but the small would suffer. At this time some 30 to 40 oficinas were at full work. With a view to control the supply to the demand, a suggestion was made that the nitrate manufacturers should combine and fix the amount that should be elaborated at each oficina, and how much should be exported; the latter, of course, would govern the quantity of the former. Early in 1884 this movement was on foot. On the 21st of April, 1884, Herm. G. Schmidt issued a circular to the principal nitrate houses, asking them—(1) If they would entertain the idea of reducing the elaboration, and for what time? (2) How much their oficina actually could produce? (3) If they were disposed to accept the quota assigned to them by the committee on elaboration and general export, which had been arranged in consequence of the demand for this article? On the 16th May, Herm. G. Schmidt issued another circular, calling a general meeting for the 10th June, 1 P.M., at the Salon Filarmonico. On the day named the meeting was held and was largely attended. The articles, as revised, which had been before the Salitreros during the early part of the year, were agreed to unanimously. At the termination of the meeting the representatives of many of the principal nitrate houses engaged to subscribe their names to a public deed, binding themselves to support faithfully the Articles of the Association A 'Comité Salitrero' was next formed. The 'Juncta Directiva' consisted of nine gentlemen, representing the districts of Tarapacá, Tocopilla, Antofagasta, Aguas Blanca, Taltal, and Valparaiso. Nine other gentlemen, practically acquainted with the elaboration of nitrate, were selected to form the Commission of Experts (La Comision de Peritos); and four gentlemen, skilled in accounts, to form the Comision de Contabidad, or Inspectores de Cuentas. Next followed the election of President and Vice-President, and the order in which, in either of their absence, the vacancy should be filled H G Schmidt was nominated to the important post of President, J. M Inglis as Vice-President · both these gentlemen representing very considerable interests, the former German, the latter English. Both had taken part in the formation of this Association. Next followed the election of the President and Vice-President of the 'Comision de Peritos.' On the 16th June, Señores L. G. Pochet and P. G. Pascal were elected to fill these offices. July 14th, 1884, the President issued a circular to the effect that, in order to start fair, and render equivocation impossible, it would be desirable to ascertain on the 1st of August the total quantity of nitrate of the 'Asociados' in canchas, bodegas, or in trans-shipment, as without this knowledge it was impossible to regulate the amount to be elaborated. With this object in view, the Salitreros of Tarapacá were to transmit to him by the 31st July a statement as exact as possible, showing the amount of nitrate of soda on their inventories, books, and other accounts; also the quantity on that day on the cancha at their oficinas or *en route* for embarkation, or embarked as cargo. And in order to give a true statement of the amount existing on the cancha, it would be necessary to appraise what was actually in the boiling tanks, bateas, by a scale which would be common to every oficina; and that at dawn on the 1st August the oficinas in Tarapacá were to cease charging the cachuchos, and stop altogether the elaboration of nitrate of soda until the dawn of the 16th morning of the same month. Also, if from any unpreventable cause the canchas at any of the oficinas on this date were out of repair, or being cleaned, and the effect of carrying out these directions would entail a greater loss than gain to the Salitrero; on his representing this, the 'Comité Salitrero' would permit him to make his quota up to the evening of the 15th August, and the 'Comité Salitrero' would inform by circular the other members of the 'Combination' their reason for so doing. The Comision de Peritos were ordered to visit all the oficinas on Tarapacá during the first fortnight of the month of August; to compare the Salitreros' statements with regard to the power of elaboration with their own observation; and to settle definitely the amount of saltpetre on the cancha, each amount to be vouched for on duplicate documents by the members of the Comision, the owners' legal representatives, or the administrador of the oficina. A copy of this document was to be sent to the President of the Comité by the 'Comision de Peritos.' If a Perito appointed to inspect an oficina had any interest connected with it, he was to absent himself from it during the inspection. The President, Vice-President, and other members of the committee might also visit any bodega or nitrate ready for trans-shipment to ascertain if the amounts corresponded with the statement forwarded to them on the 31st of July. With respect to ascertaining the existence of saltpetre at the oficinas at Tocopilla, Antofagasta, Aguas Blancas, and Taltal, the Committee did this duty as was most convenient. The President, in addressing the members of the Association, said.—' It is necessary for one and all to strictly comply with the rules issued for the inspection of the various oficinas, as they had been formed for the benefit of all the Salitreros.' He further placed implicit trust, that every person concerned would show perfect faith during the coming proceedings, and that individuals would not only study their own interests, but also those of others Accompanying these circulars were printed forms, to be used for furnishing the information required. The President next informed the Salitreros of the names of the Peritos who were selected to visit their oficinas. They were told off into sections of three, the district of Tarapacá was also divided into three districts—north, central, and southern; three Peritos were to visit each oficina in their respective districts; they were each supplied with a statement showing the greatest capable make of the oficina they were to visit. The Comision del Norte were to verify the stock-in-hand of the oficinas in their district, the Comision del Sur were to audit the accounts of the stock-in-hand of the oficinas of their district; the Comision del Centro were to revise the stock-in-hand of the oficina in their district. The names also were promulgated of the gentlemen who were to inspect the stock-in-hand at the ports. On the 6th August, the President informed the 'Salitreros' that the Committee approved of the statements presented by the Comision de Peritos on the capability of the various oficinas that they had visited. These statements would, therefore, serve as a basis for a time without prejudice to pending claims, further, that all the reclaims were to be presented in writing, also the capable production of the oficina, and that these claims should be presented before the 15th August, 1885, to the Comité de Peritos as new matter; also that during the year, commencing 1st September, only 45 per cent. of a 'full make' should be elaborated, taking as a basis the amount reported as the greatest capable make by the 'Comision de Peritos.' On the 21st of August, the President informed the Salitreros that the demands made by oficinas claiming additional productive capacity had been considered, but disallowed, he also forwarded a new form (Contrato de Compra-Venta) between buyer and seller, setting forth further particulars as to the standard of the nitrate, the fines the producers were liable to, the rules for embarking, and every particular concerning the shipment. On the 29th of August the Salitreros were informed that during September 'the make' would be reduced from 45 to 40 per cent. On the 9th of October a circular was issued decreeing that no nitrate was to be manufactured during the month of November, with an alternative, that if an oficina worked during that time, it would be only allowed to work 30 per cent. between 1st November and 1st April, 1885, inclusive, and any oficina that stopped work during November would be allowed to make 40 per cent. during the months of January, February, March, 1885. Many of the oficinas in the combination stopped work during November During the early part of 1885, it was decreed that only 7,000,000 quintals should be elaborated by the Salitreros of the Association. Early in January, 1885, special authority was given to the President of the Saltpetre Committee; his position was recognised by the Supreme Government of Chili. The Association was officially recognised as a corporate body, and registered by the name of 'Comité Salitrero.' In March following it was settled and promulgated that for the remainder of the year—viz., from the 1st April to 31st December—only 25 per cent. of the full capable production should be elaborated, reserving the right for the Committee to alter this quota if desirable in the interests of the Combination, by giving thirty days' notice. The oficinas which elaborated nitrate during the month of November were allowed to elaborate 30 per cent from the 1st April to 31st December. During May, 1885, the 'Juncta Directiva' were increased in number from 9 to 11; the Vice-President retired. Also the number of Comision de Peritos were increased in a similar manner, and delegates from Valparaiso were accredited to the 'Comité Salitrero' of Iquique. About the same time the sum of £2,000 was appropriated to be spent in the United States of America, advertising the innumerable benefits that nitrate would bestow on the agriculture of that Republic. The proceedings of the 'Comité Salitrero' have been carried out with dignity and judgment. To a person not resident in Iquique it is difficult to realise the power which the 'Comité Salitreros' possess. Firstly, they have the support and are recognised as a corporate body by the Republic. Secondly, the object of the combination, the banking interest, and of all trade depending on the manufacture of nitrate, are so closely bound together, that a fiat issued with regard to any firm or individual who has persistently offended against the Articles of Association means to them immediate ruin. The firm or individual is treated as one whose signature is not worth the paper it is written upon; he or they are in every form of the word boycotted. One individual, after fair warning by the 'Comité Salitrero,' was placed in the condition I have described. Quite lately, another very strong firm informed the Committee that they should not conform with the

Articles of the Association after the end of 1885. This rather staggered them, but it was shown to this firm that the 'Comité Salitrero' were a unanimous body, and the firm afterwards recanted. Thirdly, they have in a great measure checked the erection of new plant, as since 1884 oficinas of a capable capacity of only 3,830,000 quintals have been established Just at present the world does not consume more than 17,000,000 quintals yearly It may require more when the £2,000 has fixed definitely in the minds of the intelligent American farmer the wonderful effect of nitrate of soda. Perhaps some day India, China, Japan, and Australia may seek its salutary properties; * then there will be room for many more elaborating establishments."

It is much to be regretted that the unanimity and cohesion which characterised the action of the nitrate makers assembling to maintain a fair average of price to the consumer, moderate profits for the producer, and an equable revenue to the Government, were not preserved.

The Comité Salitrero ceased to exist some years ago, and the nitrate manufacturers in Chile are now engaged in trying to form a committee in Iquique, which will co-operate with the permanent Nitrate Committee which sits in London, but there have been differences between the great houses which prevent as yet the desired agreement and co-operation. But if the manufacturers regard their common interests they must come to terms. It is obvious that the interest of the Government in collecting as much revenue as possible from the exportation of nitrate does not accord with that of the manufacturers. When the manufacturers restrain the output and the shipments they touch the treasury of the State, which does not pay much regard to the profits of the oficinas. The latter naturally seek to keep the prices of

* But England must set the example

nitrate of soda at a fair remunerative rate; the Government looks only to revenue. It is equally obvious that a policy of give and take should be followed on both sides.* If the small oficinas are crushed out of existence by low prices the supply of nitrate of soda will be, *pro tanto,* diminished; and if they insisted on the manufacturers sending down their nitrate to the coast and shipping it irrespective of consequences, the Government of Chile would deliver a heavy blow, and cause great discouragement to capitalists. The Chilian Government has at present no "peritos," but there is an Inspector-General of Nitrate Works, with extensive powers. There is a feeling—or there was when I was in Chile—that the Government of the day were exerting undue pressure on the Nitrate Railway Company to force it to lower its tariff, and thus to stimulate the produce of the oficinas. It is plain that, though in one sense they are apparently antagonistic, the interests of the Railway Company and the nitrate manufacturers are really indissoluble. They are one and indivisible. Whatever affects the prosperity of one will injure that of the other; and having regard to the conditions of the nitrate trade itself, and of the traffic of the Railway, it is manifest that great care should be taken not to disturb the just equilibrium between production and demand on the Pampas by external agency.

The Nitrate Railway Company have established a scale of charges for goods and passenger traffic under State supervision which I, as an outsider, consider reasonable. But the constant change in the value of the dollar renders a just estimate of the rates by no means easy. Originally, the cost of carriage of nitrate of soda was fixed at 1½ cents.

---

* As an instance of the value of the Nitrate trade to Chile I may mention that Colonel North was paying export duty on nitrate of soda from his oficina to the amount of £1,000 a day—in round numbers, £350,000 per annum.

in silver per quintal a mile by the Peruvian Government. The Chilians on entering Iquique in the war time reduced the tariff to 1 cent. per mile, fixing the exchange at 37d. to the dollar. This rate, after a wrangle with the Peruvian Government, was altered into 1 cent a mile, the exchange being calculated at 36d. to the dollar, with a maximum charge of that rate for forty-five miles, that is, no excess over that distance could be charged for. If the Railway Company find it difficult, under present circumstances and conditions, to complete the whole of the Tarapacá system and to pay a fair dividend to the shareholders, they would certainly collapse if the Chilian Government, for the sake of a temporary increase of the revenue derived from the duty, allowed rail or tramways to be laid to all the oficinas over the Pampas to carry their Nitrate, and the Republic of Chile itself would feel, sooner or later, the impolicy of controlling the action of the manufacturers in the production of Nitrate of Soda and of dealing a deadly blow at the railway by which it has secured such great advantages.

The English companies make more than one-half of all the nitrate in Tarapacá. It is certain that a combination or agreement to limit the production of the works on the Pampas is the one thing needful in order to secure a certain revenue to the Chilian Government, and to give fair working dividends to the companies, and it is estimated that if an equation between supply and paying demand could be established, the oficinas ought not, at the present rate of price and the market demand, to manufacture more than 40 per cent. of the nitrate which they could turn out if they developed their full manufacturing power.

It is very difficult to determine a fair mode of establishing the ratio of the contributions of the oficinas to the whole stock. No means can be suggested so satisfactory as the action of a board or commission like that of the old Comité Salitrero. The Comité was recognised by the supreme Government. It was dissolved in 1887, but it is felt, in the face of the general distrust and of the great depreciation which menaces the business, that some substitute must be selected; or that over-production, competition, and dissension will work serious injury to the great nitrate interest, and with it to agricultural progress in large districts in Europe and America. The Comision de Peritos is dead, but from the time the Chilian Government assumed the administration of the province of Tarapacá up to the present moment there has been no cessation of the active superintendence and close control exercised by the Government over the nitrate manufacturers

It is not easy to determine how much nitrate of soda Europe requires. A few years ago the authorities were of the opinion that 450,000 or 460,000 tons were as much as could be placed upon the market, but the oficinas have exported in some years more than 100,000 tons of nitrate in excess of that maximum. Improvements in machinery and in the process of manufacture effect changes from time to time in the productive power of oficinas, and the poorer makers are easily tempted to sell at any price.

I did not attempt to differentiate in regard to the oficinas of Tarapacá—there are sixty or more of them. And I would remark that any account of the extent or produce of an oficina which may be found in these pages must be taken to apply to it at the time of my visit to the Pampas. Companies are continually acquiring fresh tracts, altering their combinations, amalgamating or dividing, as the proprietors sell, or buy, or retire.

CHAPTER XXIV.

THE USES OF NITRATE OF SODA.

Guano—The Buccaneers—Known to Indians—Old Nitrate Works—Paradas—Fossilized Forests—The British Farmer—The Comité Salitrero—Prize Essays—Dr. Stutzer—Professor Damseaux—Professor Wagner—Lawes and Gilbert—Experiments—Results—The imports of Nitrate of Soda to Europe—Statistics

The valuable properties of the Nitrate of Soda as a fertilizer, either in combination with ammonia, phosphates, or *per se*, have probably been known to the Indians and Spaniards since they began to cultivate the land of South America. It would appear, from occasional notices in the accounts of voyages, that the use of guano as a fertilizer was known along the coast three centuries ago. The buccaneers were offended by the smell which came from it "between the wind and their nobility" when cruising off the rocky shores of Peru, and it is stated in one of the earliest accounts of travel in those parts that the deposit of the sea-birds (to which the name of "guano" appears to have been given from the islands chiefly affected by them) was used by the Indians to enrich the soil. The Nitrate of Soda on the high plateaux of the Andes was not known so early, and did not come till recently into competition with guano, as an article of commerce of immense utility to the agriculturist, to be sought for in the rainless region of Tarapacá and exported thence to all parts of the world. But it is very probable indeed that hundreds of years before Nitrate of Soda became an article of commerce largely imported into Europe, the people living in the valleys of the Andes were acquainted with its value, and that it was worked on the Pampas in a rude kind of way and transported to Bolivia and the adjacent cultivated districts for the purpose of increasing the native crops.

The pampas of Tamarugal are covered in places with the ruins of the works erected in the early days before foreign capital and science were brought to bear upon the operations of the manufacture, and speedily put an end to the paradas system which died out after a few short years of struggling and suffering. The old pots of iron and copper, the brick piers and fireplaces, and the walls of the cabins where the people carried on these nitrate works, are still to be seen. The fondas or pots, each of which contained 100 gallons of water and *caliche*, were suspended between piers of *adobe* over fires, the material for which was furnished by partly fossilized wood found in the pampas,* and when the contents were boiled they were tilted over into pans to precipitate the nitrate of soda. The extraction of the nitrate from the *caliche* was imperfect; and the refuse round these old oficinas sometimes yields nitrate in sufficient quantity to pay for the cost of extracting it.

Modern chemists have determined with accuracy the general results to be obtained by the use of artificial manures, and the manner in which manure increases the produce of the soil. The land is so exceedingly fertile that artificial manures have not been much sought after in the valleys and the watered plains of Chile, but where they have been employed it has been shown that the richest ground was improved. Recent researches by scientific

* There are still patches of forest left, and it is believed that there was a period when the pampas were covered with timber.

chemists and agriculturists have proved that Nitrate of Soda is generally of extraordinary value, but it does not follow that its beneficial effects are uniform, or that great results can be obtained from the use of the salt in all cases. Much discredit has attached to Nitrate of Soda because it did not answer the extravagant expectations of those who employed it without reference to the conditions of the ground or the nature of the crop. Few English agriculturists are willing to enter on experimental courses which cost money, but the application of Nitrate of Soda to land for certain crops cannot be included in the category of experiment at all—the result is certain. Some farmers who tried Nitrate upon clover, peas, &c., and discovered that their pains and their money were wasted, denounced the use of it, and laid the blame due to their own ignorance at the door of the salt. But others, having found that turnips, potatoes, corn, &c., responded to the touch of Nitrate in exact proportion to the quantity of the manure, became alarmed when they were assured that they were exhausting the land, without taking the trouble to ascertain whether the statement was true or not.

The British farmer, conservative to the core, was with difficulty induced to resort to guano at first, but when he had once taken to it his faith was steadfast. Phosphates and nitrates scarcely shook his belief in the virtue of his old friend when they came into the field, and it was only when he saw what those farmers who were bold enough to invest in the new fertilizer, Nitrate of Soda, got for their money, that he could be induced to look at it. And then it was only askant. "The price was," he said, "a formidable obstacle to any lavish purchase of the new manure, no matter what results the use of it gave!" Manufacturers in Chile say the English farmer dislikes

Nitrate because it is a pure odourless mineral manure, and because he is accustomed to strong-smelling guano and similar highly-scented preparations; but whatever may be the cause of disfavour with which the Nitrate of Soda is regarded in England, it is certain that for one ton used here thirty tons are used abroad and in the United States. There is, as I have said, an idea in England, for which there is no solid foundation whatever, that Nitrate of Soda exhausts the soil I have heard the statement made by gentlemen who never used an ounce of it. One of my friends said he had tried it in Lincolnshire, and that it had produced a good crop, but that he "did not think it did so well the next time, therefore he had given it up altogether!"

It is one of the most curious of the problems connected with the study of our agricultural system to understand why the English farmer, who is always struggling, he says, with adverse circumstances, domestic and foreign, scarcely deigns to use Nitrate of Soda, whilst the agricultural classes on the Continent, where the farmers certainly are not rich, use it in hundreds and thousands of tons. The retail dealers ought to sell Nitrate of Soda and make a fair profit, at £11 a ton,* and 1 cwt. of Nitrate is found to be a stimulating and sufficient dressing for one acre of land!

Before it was dissolved the Comité Salitrero issued an invitation to scientific agriculturists, chemists and others to compete for very handsome prizes to be given for the best essays of a popular character upon the importance and value of Nitrate of Soda as a manure; the essays to consist of two parts, one theoretical, dealing with the chemical

* At the close of 1889 the price of nitrate "off coast" was £8 7s 6d per ton, but it has been falling gradually all the early part of this year, and is now nearly 20s lower

action of Nitrate of Soda on vegetation as distinguished from other nitrogenous manures, the other giving instructions for the best means of adapting Nitrate of Soda to the various crops and plants used for food.

A further prize of £500 was offered for an account of actual experiments conducted by the essayist, and a committee of judges of the most eminent agricultural chemists of Belgium, France, Germany, England, Holland, Russia, and the United States was appointed to award the prizes. The first prize was awarded to Dr. Stutzer, president of the Agricultural Experiment Station at Bonn. The second prize was given to the essay of Professor Damseaux, of Gembloux. Dr. Stutzer's pamphlet is entitled "Nitrate of Soda: Its Importance and Use as a Manure." The judges who awarded the second prize to Professor Damseaux seem to have called in the assistance of another expert, Dr. Wagner, professor and president of the agricultural experiment station, Darmstadt, who rewrote and edited the prize essay of Dr. Stutzer.

Professor Wagner, agreeing with the chemists and naturalists who have conducted experiments on a large scale, divides plants into "nitrogen collectors" and "increasers," and "nitrogen eaters." He shows how a grain of wheat and a pea differ in their early lives—how the first lives on the nitrogenous salts which it takes from the soil around it; how the pea, on the other hand, does not find sufficient nitrogen in the soil, but must take it from the air. If the professor be right, peas, vetches, &c., largely increase the circulating nitrogen capital of a farm; whilst cereals, potatoes, turnips, carrots, tobacco, maize, grass, &c., take the nitrogen they find in the soil, and incorporate it in the crops. Those who are interested in agricultural chemistry can easily test the value of Dr. Wagner's experiments. It is for the practical farmer to judge, by the colour of the leaves and the appearance of the plant, when his crops are suffering from the want of nitrogen Crops which draw nitrogen from the air do not acquire the property of doing so till they have attained a certain degree of maturity. If there be enough of nitrogenous matter in the ground it is waste to apply more. If, when a plant is sickly, nitrogen, in the form of Nitrate of Soda, be added to the soil which wants it, the leaves soon become green and assume the appearance of health. Vetches and peas and the like will languish to the point of death in sand, till they are able to absorb the nitrogen of the air. A top-dressing of Nitrate of Soda, says Dr. Wagner, strengthens seed sown in autumn, and assists badly-developed seed, &c., not only in soil which contains inconsiderable quantities of, but in one which is rich in nitrogen. Increased crops are produced by the use of nitrogen hastening the first development by supplying its food to the plant.

The tables, based upon the results of careful experiment, given in the work of the Darmstadt Professor, show that 18 lbs. of Nitrate to the acre gave an increase of 61 per cent of barley, that 45 lbs. of nitrate gave an increase of 172 per cent., and that wheat and flax were largely developed, whilst peas and lucerne were not affected to any appreciable extent. The inference, he says, is that peas, vetches, lucerne obtain nitrogen where barley, rye, turnips, carrots, potatoes, flax, oats, &c., are unable to take nitrogen from the air, and being dependent for it on the soil in which they grow, cannot do so unless the latter be supplied with it. Potatoes, turnips, flax, rape possess the same power of abstraction. In the pamphlet there is an account of an interesting little experiment with barren sand — " The sand was put into pots, and provided with all the materials necessary for the growth of plants, nitrogen alone excepted, and barley, rape, vetches, lucerne and peas were planted. Barley and rape developed so scantily in this soil, which was almost free from nitrogen, that they yielded only from 20 to 35 grains of vegetable matter, while, under the same conditions, vetches, lucerne and peas vegetated very luxuriously, the last-named producing no less than 1,390 grains of crop Taking the nitrogen contained in the yield of barley and rape as 100, then, under the very same conditions, the enormous quantity of 8700 of nitrogen was contained in the crop of peas."

Here there can be no doubt. Experiment and experience have proved that the theories of chemists are correct. Professor Wagner puts the matter in a clear light in the little pamphlet translated by Mr. Henderson, of the University of Glasgow. He says.—" According to E. Lierke's* new calculations 68 lbs. of nitrogen are contained in an average crop of about 2,400 lbs. of oats and 4,000 lbs. of oat-straw. The question now is: Will a crop of 2,400 lbs. of oats and 4,000 lbs. of oat-straw be obtained if the soil contains 68 lbs. of readily soluble nitrogen (apart from other nourishment, which of course must be present in sufficient quantity)? The answer is, No. The soil must contain a considerably *larger* amount of nitrogen, because the roots of the oats, which were not included in the above-mentioned crop, also require nitrogen, and besides, we cannot reckon on the plant taking up the whole of the easily-soluble nitrogen which is contained in the soil or added to it by manuring with nitrate of soda. In order to produce this

* E Lierke's praktische Düngertafel

crop, the soil must not contain 68 lbs but about 100 lbs. of nitrogen in an easily soluble form. We may count that on the average only two-thirds of the nitrogen supplied will be recovered in the crop. Thus, if 100 lbs of nitrate of soda are put into the ground, it may be assumed that in round numbers 10 lbs. of the 15—16 lbs of nitrogen contained in the nitrate are employed in producing the crop. The next question is, What yield of the different cultivated plants can be produced from the 10 lbs. of nitrogen? It is easy to calculate this. If 68 lbs. of nitrogen are contained in 2,400 lbs. of oats and 4,000 lbs. of oat-straw, 10 lbs. of nitrogen—as a simple calculation shows—produce 355 lbs. of oats and 585 lbs. of straw, whence it follows that *manuring with 100 lbs of nitrate of soda must cause an increase of 355 lbs. in the crop of oats, and 585 lbs. in the crop of straw.* As the average quantity of nitrogen contained in the produce of all cultivated plants is known, it is possible to extend the calculation just made for oats to all other field produce, and to find in this way the average increase in the yield which 100 lbs. of nitrate of soda can produce."*

But something more conclusive than the "theories of philosophers," as I heard one country gentleman denominate the hard and exact practical experiments of the experienced gentlemen who have been recognised as authorities in the department of scientific agriculture, must be put under the farmer's eyes before he will yield to a "new fad"—and the only conclusive argument for him is a profitable return for the use of it. But then this Nitrate "exhausts the soil," he says "You must go on giving more Nitrate to your land year after year; the toper must have larger glasses of stimulant. If Nitrate has been used

* See Appendix

once and a good crop has been raised, the land will give a poor crop next year"! There is no truth whatever in the assertion—it is a theory without fact or philosophy to support it. The alleged exhaustion can only arise from the Nitrate causing the plant or crop to take more potash and phosphoric acid out of the soil, in such a way as to prevent their being restored, than would have been the case had Nitrate not been used. Most careful experiments in Saxony with Nitrate on oats have shown that the increased consumption of plant food taken by the use of Nitrate from the land is in exact proportion to the increase of the crop itself. There is no mystery here. Any farmer can try if it is so for himself. He has before him the experiments, long continued and careful, of Lawes and Gilbert to determine whether Nitrate diminishes the fertility of the soil in a greater degree than Ammonia, and he can very readily test the truth of the statement that the soil is not actually deteriorated by the Nitrate taking out of the ground the nutritive property, and that any exhaustion in that sense is in proportion to the increase of the crop, which represents, of course, an increased supply of food.

Dr. Stutzer arrived at the conclusion that the soil is not in the least degree deteriorated by Nitrate; that an increase is obtained from its use not only in the amount of straw, but in the weight of grain; that if attention be paid to the nature of the soil and the quantity of nitrogen in it, there is always a good return to be had in all cereals, potatoes, beetroot, turnips, &c., from Nitrate; that on light sandy soil it has as good an effect as Sulphate of Ammonia; that it can be used in autumn as well as in the spring, but that it should not be employed in meadows, and that peas, vetches, clover, &c., carrots, parsnips, *kohlrabbi*, do not yield a profitable return from the use of it.

If the farmer takes a bag of Nitrate powdered, or as it is imported, and, without regard to the nature of the soil or the crop, spreads it indiscriminately over his land, he may be disappointed. But it is surely worth while for him to try, on the authority of such men as Lawes and Gilbert, whether by the use of 1½cwt. of Nitrate he can obtain an increase of 369lbs of corn, and of 462lbs. of straw per acre. They state that they obtained by the use of that quantity of Nitrate an increase of 5,888lbs. in roots, and all through the long series of their experiments they noted most beneficial results from the use of Nitrate of Soda. It may be true that we have no sufficient data to enable us to determine with certainty what results may be always expected from Nitrate, but the experiments referred to show that it gives an increase of 3⅓cwt in rye, of 7cwt. in oats, and of 16½cwt. in oat straw in comparison with Ammonia. With wheat and barley the results were equally definite. When the Nitrate is worked into the ground the quality of potatoes is much improved. Sulphate of Ammonia is inferior, as a fertilizer, to Nitrate of Soda, especially in the case of beetroots, potatoes, cereals, and grapes.

Nitrate of Soda was exported for the first time in 1830, when 18,700 quintals of it—the quintal being roughly 101 lbs.—were shipped at Iquique, and the export trade had been going on there for five years when Darwin visited the port. It was at first, as we see, a very insignificant trade—less than 150 tons a year. Still the demand was stimulating supply, and the Pampas was becoming an object of interest to travellers and of wealth to the people. In his "Journal of Researches," new edition, p. 363, Darwin, describing his visit to the Salinas from Iquique, says:—

"We did not reach the saltpetre works till after sunset.

having ridden all day across an undulating country, a complete and utter desert. The road was strewed with the bones and dried skins of the many beasts of burden which had perished on it from fatigue. Excepting the *vultur aura* which preys on the carcasses, I saw neither bird, quadruped, nor insect.

"The nitrate of soda was now selling at the ship's side at fourteen shillings per hundred lbs.; the chief expense is its transport to the seacoast. The mine consists of a hard stratum — between two and three feet thick—of the nitrate, mingled with a little of the sulphate of soda and a good deal of common salt. It lies close beneath the surface, and follows for a length of one hundred and fifty miles the margin of a grand basin or plain; this, from its outline, manifestly must once have been a lake, or more probably, an inland arm of the sea, as may be inferred from the presence of iodic salts in the saline stratum. The surface of the plain is 3,300 feet above the Pacific."

It will be readily understood that the difficulties in the conveyance of the Nitrate from the factories on the Pampas to the port of Iquique were very great, and that the cost of the Nitrate was handicapping the export. But in 1840 it increased from the insignificant total first quoted to 1,095,572 quintals. That quantity was tripled between 1840 and 1850. The decade 1850—1860 witnessed an increase in like proportion. In the ten years from 1860 to 1869, the export was 17,572,486 quintals. In 1867, 13,000 tons were landed in Hamburg, in 1881, 96,700 tons, and a corresponding increase took place generally at the other European ports.*

The exports from Peru increased by leaps and bounds

* See Appendix, Returns

till they reached in the decade 1870—1880 44,656,941 quintals. The summary of imports from the last year of that decade up to 1889 is :—United Kingdom, 1880, 48,270 tons; Continent, 90,900; total, 139,170. 1881, United Kingdom, 58,190; Continent, 173,250; total, 231,440. 1882, United Kingdom, 96,550; Continent, 240,710; total, 337,260. 1883, United Kingdom, 105,870; Continent, 355,870; total, 461,740. 1884, United Kingdom, 104,040; Continent, 415,590; total, 519,630. 1885, United Kingdom, 110,110; Continent, 288,210; total, 398,320. 1886, United Kingdom, 74,200; Continent, 266,265; total, 340,465. 1887, United Kingdom, 81,690; Continent, 369,370; total, 451,060. 1888, United Kingdom, 100,650; Continent, 540,350; total, 641,000. 1889, United Kingdom, 117,930; Continent, 657,730; total, 775,660.

It will be observed that the amount of direct shipment and exports to the Continent increased rapidly every year from 1880 to 1884, the quantity of Nitrate imported in 1884 being nearly five times as great as that taken in Europe in 1880—that the importation in 1885 and 1886 and 1887 fell below that of 1884, but that in 1888 and 1889 there was a considerable increase on the high figure of the latter year. The imports of Nitrate by the United Kingdom increased, however, between 1880 and 1890 very slowly, and the ratio shown in the figures between foreign and home use of Nitrate is very significant. It must be remembered that much of the Nitrate entered for United Kingdom ports is sent to await instructions, and that a large proportion of the cargoes is sent abroad on order.

The exchange at the close of last year was $25\frac{1}{2}$ (2s. $1\frac{1}{2}$d). There were 100,000 tons to be shipped in December, leaving only 24,000 tons of shipping in the Nitrate ports of Chile; but the price was still quoted at $2·50, and the equivalent price remained at 8s. 7½d. without commission. For the whole of the year the figures stood thus—

		Tons
Total European imports		770,000
,, ,, deliveries		670,000
,, ,, stocks, 31st December		180,000
,, visible supply	.	580,000

But when the distribution of the cargoes is investigated, it is found that, whereas four-fifths of the tonnage of the shipping employed in the carriage of Nitrate of Soda to Europe is British, the quantity of Nitrate actually landed at British ports for home consumption is scarcely one-fourth of the cargoes exported from Chile. Antwerp, Ostend, Hamburg, Dunkirk, Brest, Havre, Bordeaux take far more than London, Liverpool, Newcastle-on-Tyne, or Glasgow. In July, 1889, 22,087 quintals were exported to England, 223,894 quintals to Germany, 57,262 quintals to the Mediterranean, and 769,741 quintals were shipped on order for England or the Continent. In August of the same year England took 11,044 quintals; France, 144,310 quintals; Germany, 414,435 quintals; Holland, 67,243 quintals; on orders, 687,487 quintals *

It seems that whilst the farmers of Great Britain remain comparatively indifferent to the advantages to be derived from the use of Nitrate of Soda, the quantities of it imported by the agriculturists of the United States and Europe are on the increase every year.

The most conclusive deductions of the value of Nitrate from the English farmer's point of view were drawn in 1889, when a series of experiments, of which a summary appeared in the *Times* of Feb. 24, 1890, was made with various manures. After alluding to the Norfolk experiments in 1885-6, and the opposite results in the ex-

* See Appendix

periments of the Bath and West of England Society, the account proceeds. "The tests were multiplied in 19 cases and on farms in the counties of Cornwall, Devon, Somerset, Hereford, Gloucester, Berks, Hants, Wilts, Kent, and Oxford. In order to secure as much uniformity as possible the experiments were confined to land in which barley was grown after wheat, while in the history of the experiments (of which an early proof has been issued) the history of each of the 19 fields on which the experiments were made is given for the four previous years. Both in the method of conducting the experiments and in the manner in which they are related the faults in the 1887 experiments have thus been avoided

"In each case the plots were manured as follows:— H.—$1\frac{1}{4}$cwt. nitrate of soda, 2cwt. mineral superphosphate, $\frac{3}{4}$cwt. muriate of potash I.—1cwt. sulphate of ammonia, 2cwt. mineral superphosphate, $\frac{3}{4}$cwt. muriate of potash. K.—No manure. L.—$1\frac{1}{4}$cwt. nitrate of soda, 2cwt. mineral superphosphate, 3cwt. common salt. M —$1\frac{1}{4}$cwt. nitrate of soda, 2cwt of mineral superphosphate. N.—No manure.

"These thus give the following very interesting comparisons.—1. Between the addition of potash in plots H and I and its omission in plot M. 2. Between the relative efficiency of nitrate of soda and sulphate of ammonia in plots H and I. 3. Between the effect of nitrogenous manure with and without salt, as shown by plots L and M. 4. A test of the advantage or otherwise of any or all of these manurings by comparison of their produce with the average of the two unmanured plots, K and N.

"The results obtained were very uniform. In one case there was a failure, or rather results that cannot be depended upon, but in the other eighteen the results were as follows:—

	Average Produce per Acre		Increase per Acre		Cost of Manure in 1889
	Corn	Straw	Corn	Straw	
	Bus lb.	Lb	Bus lb.	Lb.	£ s d
Unmanured	29 32	2,002	—	—	—
H Nitrate of Soda, super-phos., and potash	36 47	2,673	7 15	671	1 8 5
I. Sulph ammonia, super-phos., and potash	36 35	2,616	7 3	614	1 6 3
L. Nitrate of soda, super-phos., and salt	39 34	2,862	10 2	860	1 3 11
M Nitrate of soda and superphos.	36 5	2,537	6 29	535	1 0 2

"These figures are very interesting, and point to several very interesting practical results. These are given by the society as follows :—1 That the addition of potash in plots H and I has produced larger crops than in M, where it was omitted, but not sufficiently large to pay its cost (about 8s. an acre). 2. That nitrate of soda has produced rather more corn and straw than sulphate of ammonia, but that its cost this year has been 2s. 2d an acre greater than sulphate of ammonia 3. That the addition of 3cwt. of salt to nitrate of soda and mineral superphosphate has been decidedly beneficial, and bearing in mind the small cost of the salt, 3s. 9d., has proved a very profitable addition. 4. That the nitrogenous manures combined with superphosphate alone have given an increase of marketable barley above the cost of the manures, without taking into account the increase of straw, and that with the addition of 3cwt of common salt they have shown a very profitable increase."

It is probable that in time the importation of Nitrate of Soda to be used in Great Britain will increase, as the advantages to be derived from the employment of it as a fertiliser are more clearly demonstrated by the results, and the considerable reduction in price which has followed on over-production of the salt certainly removes one objection to the use of it which needy farmers resorted to, not without reason, as an excuse for their neglect. Those who can afford to lay in good store of Nitrate of Soda will assuredly find their account in it—if not now, by and by. It is an article used in many ways, and it is always saleable for chemical purposes, &c., over and above the demand for it as a fertiliser.

FINIS.

APPENDIX.

THE NITRATE RAILWAYS—THEIR HISTORY.

November 1, 1860 —The first Nitrate Railway concession was granted by the Peruvian Government on this date to Messrs. José María Costas and Frederico Pezet, for the construction of a line from *Iquique* to the *Nitrate Grounds* of *La Noria*, &c.

May 27, 1864 —The above concession was declared to *be forfeited*, because the works were not begun within the specified time, or the further time which had been granted by a decree of July, 1862.

November 8, 1864 —The Peruvian Government granted a concession to Messrs. José Pickering and Manuel Avelino Orihuela for the construction of a railway from *Iquique* to the nitrate grounds of *La Noria*.

December 21, 1864 —A concession was granted by the Peruvian Government to Messrs Pickering and Orihuela for a railway from *Pisagua* to the *Nitrate Grounds* of *Sal de Opisbo*, &c. This concession was granted in accordance with a proviso to that effect contained in the concession of November 8, 1864, for the Iquique and La Noria Railway.

June 10, 1868 —The concession of November 8, 1864, to Pickering and Orihuela was *declared forfeited* for abandonment of the works and other irregularities, and this declaration of forfeiture included the Pisagua Concession of December, 1864, the latter being merely an outcome of the Iquique Concession.

July 11, 1868.—The *existing concession* for the construction of the IQUIQUE RAILWAY was granted by the Peruvian Government to Messrs Montero Brothers Exclusive privilege was granted for twenty-five years from the date of opening the railways for traffic, and the right of ownership for forty years more, it being declared that after the lapse of sixty-five years the railway should become the property of the State.

By this concession the right to construct a pier in the port of Iquique was also granted. The railway was declared exempt from all taxes during the term of the privilege, and also free during that term from all import duties.

The maximum freight allowed to be charged was $1\frac{1}{2}$ cents per Spanish quintal per mile.

A preferential right of constructing all other railways in Tarapacá was also granted, to be extensive with the duration of the privilege.

May 18, 1869.—The *existing concession* for the construction of the *Pisagua Railway* was granted by the Peruvian Government to Messrs. Montero Brothers.

Exclusive privilege was granted for twenty-five years, and the right of ownership for sixty years more, at the expiration of which term (85 years) the railway is to pass to the State.

By this concession the right to construct a pier in Pisagua was also granted.

The railway was declared exempt from the payment of taxes during the term of the privilege, and during that term also free from the payment of import duties.

The maximum freight was fixed at $1\frac{1}{2}$ cents per Spanish quintal per mile.

October 26, 1871.—The Peruvian Government granted to Messrs. Montero Brothers the *existing concession* for the construction of branch lines from the district of *La Noria* to the other nitrate grounds of Tarapacá, and for the *prolongation of the main line to the frontier of Bolivia*.

Exclusive privilege was granted for twenty-five years, and right of ownership for ninety-nine years from the date of opening the railway for traffic.

The exclusive privilege granted by this concession is very extensive, being to the effect that during the term of twenty-five years no other railway, whatever may be its motive power or the character of its permanent way, shall be constructed from the coast to any nitrate ground to which the branch lines contemplated by this concession shall be made, or between the coast-line of Tarapacá and the frontier of Bolivia.

The works of the branch lines were to be begun within one

month from the date of the concession, and to be finished within one year

The line to Bolivia was to be begun within two years, and to be finished within four years. This line to Bolivia has never been made.

Import duties were remitted during the time of construction, and the railway was exempted from the payment of taxes during the term of the privilege.

The concessionnaires were authorised to form their bye-laws and tariff of freights, to be submitted to the Government for approval (which was subsequently done).

April 26, 1872.—The time for completing the branch lines was extended to a further term of thirty months and the right to take water whereon found near the railway lines on public property was granted to Messrs. Montero.

June 28, 1872.—The first mortgage of the railways was made and was for £1,000,000. The issue of this loan was conducted by Messrs. J. Thompson, T. Bonor, and Company, of London, and the mortgage deed was made in favour of Messrs. C. Weguelin and A. de Gessler, as trustees for the bondholders. The interest payable on this loan was 7 per cent per annum, and the principal was redeemable half-yearly by drawings, according to a table annexed to the deed of mortgage.

1873.—In 1873 another loan (of £450,000) was raised on the security of the railways through the agency of the Anglo-Peruvian Bank, it being part of the arrangement that a company should be formed to acquire and work the railways, and several agreements were entered into in London about this time between Messrs. Montero Brothers, the Anglo-Peruvian Bank, and other parties, relating to the advance of £450,000 to the projected company.

1874.—In 1874 a company was formed to which the railways were transferred, this was *The National Nitrate Railways Company of Peru*, with a capital of £1,200,000.

The Company was never registered as an English company, but was a Peruvian company with directors in London, and a working committee in Lima.

Shortly after the formation of the company default was made in providing for the service of the loan of £1,000,000, and in accordance with the terms of the mortgage deed the trustees demanded and obtained from the London directors of the company an order to place their representative in possession of the railways. This order was carried out by the Lima Committee, and the railways were delivered to the representative of Messrs. Weguelin and de Gessler on behalf of the bondholders

About the same time disagreements arose between the Messrs. Montero and the Lima Committee, and the former began legal proceedings for the dissolution of the company and the restoration of the railways to themselves. In these proceedings Messrs Montero succeeded in obtaining the appointment of a receiver by the Court After considerable litigation the law suit was settled out of court, and the terms of the settlement were embodied in two agreements made in London on July 22 and August 28, 1878.

July 22, 1878 —The agreement of this date provided for the issue of what is known as the *Second Mortgage Loan*, the foundation of which was the advance of £450,000, arranged by the Anglo-Peruvian Bank, as before mentioned

By the agreement of July, 1878, the terms of that advance were defined, and the amount for which the loan was agreed to be issued was fixed at £850,000, bonds for £600,000 being delivered to the parties who subscribed the advance of £450,000 in 1873, and bonds for £250,000 being delivered to Messrs. Montero Bros. The interest on the loan of £850,000 was declared to be 7 per cent per annum, and a table of half-yearly redemption was inserted in the agreement, and the whole debt was secured as the second mortgage on the railways

August 28, 1878 —The agreement of this date modified and defined the terms of the first loan of *One Million Pounds*, and provided additional securities for the punctual service of the interest and sinking fund

By the two last agreements it was provided that the railways should be returned to the Company by the bondholders' trustees, and accordingly in *February*, 1879, the railways were restored to the National Nitrate Railways Company of Peru.

April, 1879 —War was declared by Chile against Peru and Bolivia. The port of Iquique was immediately blockaded by a Chilian squadron, and Pisagua was shelled and burned, and, as a consequence, the work of the railways was paralysed, and this state of things continued until

November, 1879, when the Chilian forces took possession of

APPENDIX.

Pisagua and Iquique, and finally of the entire province of Tarapacá The railway work was then resumed.

Soon after entering Iquique, the Chilian military authorities took possession of the railways, and retained such possession until the year 1881, when on the 22nd of June the railways were restored to the National Nitrate Railway Company

August 24, 1882 —*The Nitrate Railways Company Limited* was incorporated as an English joint stock company, with offices in London, for the purpose of taking over and working the railways belonging to the National Nitrate Railways Company of Peru

The capital of the Company was fixed at £1,200,000, and a new loan of £1,100,000 was issued under the auspices of Messrs Fred. Huth & Co, of London, bearing interest at 6 per cent per annum, and redeemable as mentioned in the mortgage deed which was dated *August* 30, 1882

August 30, 1882 —By this mortgage deed provision was made for paying off the capital remaining unredeemed of the original first mortgage of 1872, and for substituting the new mortgage as a first charge on the railways, the mortgage for £850,000 remaining a *second* charge, but with some variations as to redemption and other particulars

1888 —In the year 1888 arrangements were carried out by which the amounts remaining unredeemed of the loans of £1,100,000 and £850,000 were paid off and a new loan of £2,000,000, bearing interest at 5 per cent per annum, was issued This new loan was secured by a mortgage deed, dated *January* 23, 1888, and is the only remaining charge upon the railways.

In the same year (1888) deferred shares to the value of £180,000 were issued by the Nitrate Railways Company, Limited.

The questions which arose out of the presidential decrees abrogating the privileges of the Company on the ground of *non feasance* of conditions in their concession, the conflict between the Courts of Law and the Executive, and the results of it which led to an appeal to the friendly interference of the Foreign Office, are alluded to in the body of the work.

THE NITRATE RAILWAYS—THEIR STATIONS, &c.

The Nitrate Railways are connected with two ports of the South Pacific—Iquique and Pisagua. Iquique is situated in lat 20° 12' 15" south and in long. 70° 13', Pisagua in lat 19° 36' 33" and in about the same long as Iquique

Beginning with Iquique, at a distance of 2½ miles from Iquique is a reversing station, and 8 miles from the latter is the first station on the line called *Molle*

Molle is 1,578 feet above the sea. The gradients between Iquique and Molle vary from 2 50 to 3 85 per cent, and some of the curves are of 450 feet radius Leaving Molle, we pass the stations of *Santa Rosa* (close to the well-known silver-mining district of that name, and within sight of the even better known Huantajaya—also silver mines), *Las Carpas*, and *San Juan*, arriving at the *Central Station*.

From the Central Station the railway divides—one line running north and the other south

The Central Station is important in the working of the traffic; it is the junction of the La Noria and Solidad line with the Pozo Almonte and Pisagua line. It is used as a depôt for trains going from Iquique to the two divisions of the railway just mentioned, and for trains meeting there on their way from the different branches to Iquique

The Central Station is provided with a small workshop for minor repairs, and engines are stationed there for work on the pampas

The Central Station is about 29 miles from Iquique, and is about 3,220 feet above the sea

Taking the southerly line of railway first, the first station reached is *La Noria*, which is 34 miles from Iquique and is more or less 3,300 feet above the sea

Passing La Noria, the line continues in a southerly direction until reaching the *Altode, San Antonio*, when it divides; one branch running in an easterly direction until the oficina of "Santa Elena" is reached, when it stops 52½ miles from Iquique The other branch goes westward into what is called the "Solidad" district, and stops at an oficina called "San Lorenzo," 47 miles from Iquique

The oficinas served by the branch which runs in a southerly

direction from the Central Station, and which has just been detailed are those of *Sebastopol* (not yet complete), *Paposo, Pernana, Sacramento, San Pedro, San Fernando;* then, on the Santa Elena branch, *Solferino, Argentina, San Pablo, Virginia,* and *Santa Elena ,* and on the Solidad District branch, *San Juan de Gildemeister, Esmeralda,* and *San Lorenzo.*

It may be mentioned here that it is from or near Virginia (48 miles from Iquique) that it is proposed to extend the railway to Lagunas.

Returning to the Central Station and taking the northerly line of the railway, the first station reached is *Monte Video,* which is 36½ miles from Iquique, and is the highest point on the railways, being 3,811 feet above the sea

The only nitrate oficina between the Central Station and Monte Video is that called *Yungay Bajo*

After leaving Monte Video the line descends, and seven miles beyond that place is the important station of *Pozo de Almonte* (3,371 feet above the sea), near which are grouped the oficinas *Buen Retiro, Calacala, La Palma,* of Gibbs & Co., *Peña Chica,* and *San José,* and from Pozo de Almonte there is also a branch or siding to the other oficinas called *Serena, Normandia, Tegethoff*.

At Pozo de Almonte there is a workshop for minor repairs, and it is also a station for engines—besides being the depôt for the traffic to and from the oficinas just named, and others more remote along the line to Pisagua.

At Pozo de Almonte there are wells which supply the railway with water; the quality of this water is inferior, and before being used for steaming purposes is subjected to a purifying process; the purifier used is unrefined carbonate of soda, which being mixed with the well water and the latter treated, causes a partial precipitation of the carbonate of lime and other substances in solution, thus leaving the water in a state in which it can be used for locomotives, though the precipitation not being complete the water still remains of a most unsatisfactory quality, and after being used a short time leaves a hard shell-like deposit or scale in the boilers of the engines

The purified water is also pumped from Pozo de Almonte through a line of pipes to tanks at Monte Video, and from thence it runs down to the Central Station, the pipes being continued thus far

From the Central Station the same water is run in car tanks down the line as far as Las Carpas, whence a line of pipes conducts it to Santa Rosa, so that at present it will be seen the inferior water from Pozo de Almonte is supplied to a considerable section of the Iquique line.

The Tarapacá Water Company is laying a line of pipes from Pica, some 30 miles distant in the interior from La Noria, and 60 miles from Iquique, where there is an abundant supply of excellent water. The line of pipes will feed the Iquique railway, as the water will run through La Noria and along or near the railway line to Iquique; besides which, a branch pipe will carry the water to Pozo de Almonte, and thus do away with the use of the existing wells. The branch pipe line to Pozo is already laid, and in a short time a regular supply of Pica water may be expected there.

The quantity of Pozo de Almonte well water now used is about 50,000 gallons a day.

After leaving Pozo de Almonte the railway gradually rises, until it attains a height of 3,752 feet above the sea at *Primitiva*, 71 miles from Iquique, whence the descent begins, until at the "*Nivel*" (or "*Level*") Station, 105 miles from Iquique, the height of the railway is 3,610 feet above the sea; the drop is then more rapid, and at the *Cuesta del Arenal*, 114 miles from Iquique, the height above the sea is 2,067 feet, at the *Hospicio*, or first cliff above Pisagua, 119 miles from Iquique, it is 1,200 feet, and thence in 6 miles the railway descends to the sea at Pisagua. The length of the railway from Iquique to Pisagua is 125 miles. The total length of the railways, including sidings and branches is (May, 1889) 230 46 *miles*.

After leaving Pozo de Almonte, the railway runs past several oficinas already enumerated, and at a distance of 55 *miles* from Iquique reaches the station of *San Donato*, near which is the oficina called *Ramirez*, belonging to the Liverpool Nitrate Company, and that of Mr J Devesconi, called *Constancia*.

The next station is *Huara*, 64 miles from Iquique, near which are the establishments called *Santa Rosa de Huara*, *Rosario de Huara*, *San Jorje*, and *Tres Marias*.

At a distance of 71 miles from Iquique are the station and oficina of *Primitiva*, and from *that point the Pisagua Section may be said to begin*, for though "Tres Marias" is the official dividing point, some traffic for Primitiva is brought to Iquique, and beyond that place it is carried (it may be said) exclusively to Pisagua

After Primitiva comes the station of *Negreiros*, 76½ miles from Iquique, and this is the focus for the oficinas *Progress*, *Mercedes*, *Amelia*, and *Aurora*, as well as for those lying on the branch line, which here juts out and connects the station of Negreiros and the main line with *Salvadora*, *Democracia*, *Puntun chara* (London Nitrate Company), *Rosario de Negreiros*, and *Agua Santa*

Although Agua Santa is connected by a branch with the Nitrate Railways, the traffic to and from that establishment is carried in carts to Caléta Buena, where is an inclined plane and steam lift for lowering and hoisting to and from the sea shore. At Caléta Buena is an anchorage for ships, so that the Agua Santa business is carried on independently of Iquique and Pisagua

After leaving Negreiros, the first station is *Santa Catalina*, 87 miles, with the oficinas *Reducto, Concepcion, Aguada, Bearnes,* and *Camina*, as also on a branch line those of *Angela*, of Messrs. Loayza & Pascal, and of *La Patria*, of Messrs. Gibbs and Company (now Tamarugal Nitrate Company)

The next station to Santa Catalina is *Dolores*, 91 miles from Iquique. From Dolores there is a branch line to the oficinas *La Union* and *Santa Rita*, and adjacent to the station are also the establishments called *San Francisco* and *San Patricio*, and at a little distance *Carolina*, which last is not connected as yet with the railway, and the traffic of which is worked to and from the small port of Junin by carts

At Dolores are wells of good fresh water, which is used as well for drinking as for the locomotives Water is here pumped into an elevated tank, from which it runs in pipes to the stations of Zapiga and Nivel, and, indeed, as far down towards the port as the Cuesta del Arenal The quantity of Dolores water used on the railway is about 24,000 *gallons* a day

The station following Dolores is *Zapiga*, 94 miles from Iquique, near which are the oficinas *Sacramento de Zapiga, San José del Rosario, Cruz de Zapiga, Compania, Matamungi* (not working), and *San Antonio* (not working).

There are an engine-house and workshop at Zapiga, which is a very important station on the Pisagua side, and serves as a depôt for up and down traffic

After Zapiga station comes that of *Jaz Pampa*, 101 miles from Iquique, which name is also given to the adjoining oficina of Messrs North and Company. Close to Jaz Pampa a branch lately constructed runs to the new oficina, called *Paccha*, also belonging to Messrs. North and Company.

After Paccha there are no oficinas, the next station towards Pisagua is called the *Nivel* (*Level*), 105 miles from Iquique and 20 from Pisagua. It is an important station in the working of the line, serving as a depôt, watering place, &c., &c.

From the Nivel station the railway rapidly descends to Pisagua, passing the station of *San Roberto*, and the stopping places of *Cuesta del Arenal* and *Hospicio*. At the Cuesta del Arenal are some large rock cuttings worthy of notice, and the gradients to Pisagua vary between 2.70 and 4.73 *per cent*.

From the Hospicio the railway zigzags down to the sea shore at Pisagua, there being three reversing points between the two places.

Note, page 59

According to recent scientific travellers, it is in the latitude of Coquimbo that the distinctive members of the flora of Chile present themselves. Between the desert—where rain in a measurable quantity is unknown—and the southern forest-belt extending from Magellan to Valdivia, Central Chile has a long, dry, and rainless summer, followed by an autumn and spring in which rain falls scantily; but there are exceptions every four or five years, particularly after severe earthquakes, and then the consequences are by no means beneficial. The rainfall here and at Copiapo is 4 or 5 inches a year. In the central section of Chile about 30 inches fall, in the lake region from 60 to 80. In the island of Chiloe and in Valdivia the rain may be said to be perennial, "thirteen months in the year," as one writer has it. We arrived in Chile in the autumn—that is, in the month of March—and were there for the rest of that season. The winter begins in June and lasts till the end of August, and in the first of these months we were at Iquique and on the Pampas, therefore we escaped the summer; but after all the mean temperature is 70° F in summer and 52° in winter, being 5° hotter than the average in Paris or London, and 9 warmer in winter.

Note, page 66

Dr. C—— says that the hills around Valparaiso, which are exceedingly uninteresting in form, consist of sienitic granite stratified, with sienite nodules or round lumps embedded in it, and that there are similar formations along the coast. The authorities differ. D'Orbigny, Pissis, Darwin, Forbes, Ball, &c., do not agree with each other in their diagnoses of the structural geology of the Cordillera.

Note, page 92.

There is great diversity of spelling of proper names according to the nationality of the spellers, and I am not at all sure of my orthography. According to some, Santiago stands on the "Mapoche," according to others, on the "Mapocho." One writer spells Maipo "Maipu," and so forth. I have great doubts about San Dominic as I find it in my diary.

Note, page 104

According to Dr Espejo's book, the predominating salt is chlorure of calcium, nearly 22 per cent chlorure of sodium, sulphate of calcium, silicic acid, chlorure of potass, ammonia, magnesia, occur in small quantities, the proportions varying according to the different springs. The waters are used both for bathing and drinking. Indications are not wanting that the Baths will be rendered attractive by musical entertainments, as there was the foundation laid down for an open-air orchestra in the pretty park or garden by the side of the river, in which ample shade is provided from the summer sun by thickly-growing oak-trees and eucalyptus.

Note, page 106

In a detached building standing in a pleasant grove outside the hotel there is an interesting museum of Natural History, mainly due, I believe, to the labours of Mr Edwards, formerly Professor of Natural History at the Naval School, Valparaiso. The butterflies, moths, and beetles are fast crumbling to dust. The birds form a large and well-preserved collection, and the animals are for the most part in good condition.

Although we had some keen sportsmen (not always successful, by-the-bye), in our party, we had no botanist, but a Chilian gentleman, a member of Congress, whom I met at the Baths, told me that the tall cactus which grew upon all the rocky hills around was the *Cereus quisco,* and that the red or scarlet outbursts upon the stem and arms were a parasite like the mistletoe, belonging to the genus *Loranthus.* The grounds around the hotel were thickly planted with an oak very similar to the English, furze grew on the higher slopes, and in the valleys were dense natural shrubberies of evergreens (*colletia*), among which rose the *peumo* and the *quillaja* or soap-tree. There were also bushes with very sharp and lacerating thorns

Note, page 109.

The operation of collecting the cattle and of marking and branding them in the corral is generally the occasion of a convivial gathering on the estancia. It is called a *rodeo,* and occurs at stated times in the year. If the haciendado is present, as is usually the case, a dance and music wind up the evening

Note, page 111

I perceive I omitted the page of my diary in which I mentioned the humming-bird alluded to in the text. There were several of them constantly twittering and flitting about on the verandah, much engaged in warfare, perhaps in love, but I am inclined to think the latter One of these evinced either confidence or indifference, which was in contrast to the general habits of his fellows, who flew away when we came close This pretty little fellow, however, when tired of hunting about amongst the flowers, would perch on a branch within a few feet of the place where we sat on the verandah I am sorry to say that I instructed one of our sportsmen in the art of humming-bird shooting, as he was anxious to get specimens, and I showed him how to load a light cartridge with fine dust, but that was later on, and my little friend at Cauquenes remained unscathed

Note, page 115

I have already mentioned amongst the ornaments of the city the outrageous equestrian extravagance of the O'Higgins statue, but I should have stated that the sculptor intended it to be understood that the general was leaping his horse over a breastwork The statue of a man, at least as eminent, San Martin, is also to be seen in the Alameda, as well as those of the three Carreras. These and the Bello monument are, as well as I recollect, the principal, if not the only, illustrations of the great men of Chile to be seen in the capital Government House, the Post Office, the Congressional buildings are very well designed, imposing, and commodious ; some of the private houses are of palatial proportions and elegance Amongst these, however, none is comparable to the sumptuous house—I cannot call it residence—of Madame Cousiño, where we were received by her son a day or two before our departure The apartments are filled with furniture from the finest establishments of Paris, Vienna, and London, and decorated throughout with a perfect indifference to cost, which is generally combined, in this instance, with good taste and refinement Bronzes, statuary, vases, fill the salons and corridors. The walls of the grand staircase are decorated by the artist who painted the Italian opera-house in Paris, who came over expressly to Santiago for this work ; the curtains in one of the salons cost £4,000 There is a gallery well furnished with specimens of the best masters of modern France The house stands in a charming garden, with conservatories, greenhouses, and the apparatus of a *maison de campagne*.

Note, page 179

The illustrations give a better idea of the "plant" at and of Primitiva than words can convey, and attempts to describe machinery without the help of wood-cuts are not generally interesting The works and all the accessories of the *Maquina* are on the largest scale, and of the best design The massive steam engines, the three towering chimneys, the electric lighthouse, the array of boilers, twelve in number, each 30 feet long ; the broad line of boiling tanks, twelve in number, each 32 feet long and 9 feet broad , the bateas, of which there are no less than one hundred and sixty, each 18 feet square and 3 feet deep (with inclined floors to assist precipitation) , the irresistible crushers grinding night and day ; the laboratory and test houses ; the busy locomotives, dragging the long trains of trucks, full or empty, on the labyrinth of rails , the powder factory, the workmen's mess-house, the town of galvanized iron huts and its swarming life, must be seen in their busy work-day dress before the impression made by the oficina and its surroundings on a visitor can be understood.

The capital of the Company was not a fifth part of that of the new Rosario and the aggregated oficinas, and as I have stated in the body of the work, Primitiva was turning out 10,000 quintals a day last May

Note, page 201.

I remember hearing, in the Crimea, of a remonstrance being sent from home out to the Director-General, because of the extravagant expenditure of iodine in the hospitals It was then about ten times the present price, but it is now so very cheap —5d an ounce, I believe—though the nitrate manufacturers some time ago formed a combination to restrict the output, that the profits have been reduced In some nitrate grounds the amount of iodine in the caliche is so small that it is scarcely worth extracting, but that circumstance is not necessarily indicative of a serious deterioration in the quantity or quality of the *caliche*

The "Iodine house" is a *huit clos,* and each oficina has its little secret in some detail or another, but the principle of the manufacture is common to all. The iodine is contained in *caliche* as iodate of soda, varying very greatly in quantity, the maximum reaching 50 per cent. It is taken up in the mother-water, or *agua vieja,* which plays such an important part in nitrate oficinas *Caliche* has, as a normal rate, 50 per cent of nitrate of soda, 26 per cent of chloride of soda, 6 per cent of sulphate of soda, 3 per cent of sulphate of magnesia, 15 per cent. of insoluble matter, but iodine in the form mentioned enters largely into the ingredients of it at some places

At the Peruana oficina the mother-liquor contains 28 per cent of nitrate of soda, 11 per cent. of chloride, 3 per cent of sulphate, 3 per cent. of sulphate of magnesia, 22 per cent. of iodate of soda, 33 per cent of water

When iodate of soda is contained in sufficient quantities in the *agua vieja* of the caliche to make it profitable to extract the iodine, the latter is precipitated from the solution by an acid sulphite of soda made on the spot Nitrate of soda and powdered charcoal or coal dust are mixed in proportions—85 of nitrate to 15 parts of carbon—moulded into enormous "devils," five or six feet high, which, after they have been saturated with water, are set on fire. Liquid carbonate of soda is formed by the combustion, and is run into a pit at the base of the devil, where it cools and hardens into the substance called *sal natron*. This carbonate of soda is then dissolved in water, and is exposed in closed vessels to the fumes of sulphur, in combination with which it forms acid sulphite of soda.

A certain amount of practical knowledge is necessary to ascertain the proportion in which the sulphite should be put into the *agua vieja* to precipitate the iodine.

The acid sulphite of soda and *agua vieja* are mixed together by paddles driven by steam or by manual labour in the precipitating tanks. The liquid turns from its original orange to blue, and gradually deposits iodine at the bottom of the tank. This deposit of crude iodine, with the result of a filtration of the liquor in the tank (which is now called *agua malo*), through sieves, is put into an iron vessel and pressed into cakes, which are finally put into a retort and sublimed. The iodine of commerce appears in the form of crystals. They are collected and packed in barrels, containing about 33 lbs., which are made airtight by coatings of tar and raw hide. When the *agua vieja* has given up all its iodine, it is drawn off to the tanks, where it becomes again charged with *caliche*.

Note, page 252.

A traveller is always received in the house of a Chilian, and is welcome to food and shelter, but their hospitality is not gratuitous. Every stranger who has been in the country recognises very speedily the *guaso* and the *guacho*. The latter is a sporting, idle, gentleman equestrian, who eats and drinks the best he can get, while the *guaso* will work for hire as an agricultural labourer and is content with his beans, as the Irish peasant was with his potatoes, and the Scotchman with his oatmeal. All classes on the plain or on the Pampas wear the *poncho*.

Note, page 263.

According to the census of 1885 the population of Arica consisted of 4,220 people, of whom 3,600 were Peruvians

There was a strange collection of scraps offered by the remaining 622, to wit—120 Bolivians, 237 Chilians (troops), 120 civilians, 62 Chinese, 12 Germans, 13 Greeks, 6 Frenchmen, 40 Italians, 2 Argentines, 2 Equadorians, and 6 English   Arica existed as an Indian town many years before the discovery of America   It received the title of city from the Spaniards in 1537   The Chilian Government may prefer to have a claim against Peru and let Arica "slide," but if they desire to retain the department of Arica and the province of Tacna, of which Arica is the port, it is thought that they may effect their object, notwithstanding the numerical ascendency of the Peruvians. There are ways of doing these things, and all the Peruvians here are not devoted to the distracted Republic north of the Chilian frontier   The comparison of Tacna-Arica to Alsace-Lorraine does not hold good, because there is no virtue in a plebiscite to deliver the French provinces from the grip of Germany, and no equity of redemption in the case

Note, page 337

Mr. Markham states that the nitrate fields defined up to 1882 covered 50 square leagues, which, allowing one cwt of nitrate for every square yard, would give 63 million tons Since that time the area has been much extended   Scientific travellers who have visited the Pampas are satisfied that the lagoons or salitreras were the beds of inlets and bays, such as those which intersect every part of Tierra del Fuego, which Chile, they think, must have closely resembled.

Note, page 343

"With the help of Lierke's tables I have made this calculation for a number of the most important plants, and now give the results

"Manurings with 100 lbs of nitrate of soda produce, according to calculation, the following increases in the yield :—

Wheat	350 lbs	of grain and	500 lbs	of straw	
Rye	330	,	,,	850	,,
Barley	420	,,	,,	600	,,
Oats	350	,	,,	580	,,
Maize	420	,,	,,	580	,,
Rice	1000	,,	,,	1200	,
Buckwheat	420	.	,	640	.

Potatoes	2600 lbs	of tubers and	300 lbs	of straw
Beet-roots	4500	,, roots	900 lbs	of leaves
Cattle-turnips	3900	,, ,,	1000	,,
Carrots .	3700	,, ,,	560	,,
Chicory	3400	,, ,,	410	,,
Meadow-hay .	645	,, hay		
Green Maize	5300	,, green plant-substance		
Rape .	210	,, grain and 600 lbs of straw		
Poppy	170	,, seed ,, 500	,,	,,
Cotton	270	,, ,, ,, 100	,,	fibres
Hops	70	,, flowers ,, 320	,,	leaves and tendrils
Tobacco	180	,, leaves ,, 150	,,	stalks
Sugar-cane	2000	,, sugar-cane		
White Cabbage	4200	,, heads		
Cauliflower	1500	,, ,, and 1500 lbs. of leaves		
Kohl-rabi	1400	,, bulbs ,, 1200	,,	,,
Cucumbers .	6000	,, cucumbers		
Onions .	3700	,, onions.		

"This table shows in a surprising manner how very different the increases in the produce are, according as the crop is rich or poor in nitrogen. The less nitrogen contained in 100 lbs. of produce, the greater must be the crop obtained by the application of 10 lbs. of nitrogen, i e, of 100 lbs of nitrate of soda, and *vice versa*; the more nitrogen necessary to produce 100 lbs of crop, the less must be the increased yield which can be obtained by applying 100 lbs of nitrate of soda

"As a matter of course the profit obtained from manuring with nitrate of soda does not always stand in proportion to the increase in quantity of the crop A greater increase in the crop of one fruit may often yield a considerably smaller profit from manuring with nitrate than a smaller increase in the crop of another It depends upon the *market value* of the produce

"If we assume the following to be the prices of 100 lbs. of each of the substances named, viz, hay, 1s 6d, rape-seed, 9s, cattle turnips, 6d; corn, 5s 6d; straw, 1s 2d, beet-roots, 9d, and poppy-seed, 27s., we can calculate from the weight of produce given in the table above, which could be produced by 100 lbs of nitrate of soda, the following values:—

Hay .	=	15 shillings	
Rape-seed	=	19 ,,	
Cattle-turnips	=	21 ,,	and sixpence
Corn + Straw	=	27 ,,	
Beet-roots	=	32 ,	and nine pence
Poppy-seed	=	46 .	,, three pence

"This shows how great the differences are in the profits obtained by manuring with nitrogen, and how remunerative it is to manure freely with nitrogen and so force on to the greatest possible productiveness those plants in particular which yield market produce of high value

"But from the figures given a very considerable profit from manuring with nitrogen can be estimated even for the produce which is at present low in price, corn, straw, and beet-roots, for, from manurings with 100 lbs of nitrate, sums of from 27s to 32s can be obtained, while that amount of nitrate can be bought for from 9s to 11s. 6d"

Note, page 350

EXPORTS OF NITRATE FOR SEPTEMBER, 1889

EUROPE—
England	18,368	
France	282,456	
Germany	378,852	
Belgium	40,110	
Orders U K or Continent	1,199,052	
		1,918,838
UNITED STATES		79,060
Quintals		1,997,898

EXPORTS FOR OCTOBER, 1889

EUROPE—
France	261,474	
Germany	844,851	
Belgium	27,176	
Mediterranean	35,286	
Orders U K or Continent	1,250,976	
		2,419,763
UNITED STATES		188,822
S A COAST		2,500
Quintals		2,611,085

COMPARISON OF EXPORTS

	1884	1885	1886	1887	1888	1889
Exported up to date, Oct 31st	10,082,122	7,535,386	7,060,585	10,694,950	11,767,987	15,461,779
Loading on ditto	1,024,100	955,000	1,039,200	3,211,700	2,539,200	2,494,500
Charters up to ditto	495,900	770,600	1,225,500	1,001,300	3,031,100	1,215,900
	11,602,122	9,260,986	9,325,285	14,907,950	17,338,287	19,172,179
Increase in 1889	7,570,057	9,911,193	9,746,894	4,264,229	1,833,892	—
	19,172,179	19,172,179	19,172,179	19,172,179	19,172,179	19,172,179

EXPORTS DURING NOVEMBER, 1889

Europe—
France	298,962
Germany	562,690
Belgium	42,725
Mediterranean	62,000
Orders U K or Continent	1,709,224
	2,675,601
United States	281,237
California	18,108
S A Coast	3,067
Quintals	2,978,013

TOTAL LOADING ON NOVEMBER 30th, 1889

Quintals	1,521,600
On same date —1888	2,659,200 quintals
,, ,, 1887	2,191,700 ,,
,, ,, 1886	734,400 ,,

VESSELS LOADING NITRATE ON NOVEMBER 30th, 1889

Europe—Orders U K or Continent	1,375,500
United States	95,500
California	50,600
Quintals	1,521,600

The tonnage to foreign ports in 1889 was thus distributed

Imports—
	1889
Germany	302,800
France	187,510
Holland	52,310
Belgium	105,150
Italy	9,960
	657,730

AVERAGE PRICES

1880	1881	1882	1883	1884	1885	1886	1887	1888	1889
15/6	11 9	12 10½	11	9 9	10 1½	9 9	9 3	10/	9 3 per cwt

Price 31st December, 1889 — 8 1½ per cwt

Nitrate produced by the principal oficinas during January, 1890 —

		Quintals
Primitiva { Iquique		171,135
{ Pisagua		101,839
Liverpool	.	66,822
Donato	.	18,722

		Quintals.
S. Pablo		35,734
S. Jorge and Solferino		199,100
Colorado		33,601
S. Elena		4,367
Jaz-Pampa		15,864
Paccha		23,362
S. Rita		26,821
Tamarugal	{ La Patria, 44,493 / La Palma, 65,299 }	108,792
London N. Co.		55,941
Rosario	{ Iquique / Pisagua }	263,155 / 24,415
Aqua Santa		38,613